Brave New Teachers

Brave New Teachers
Doing Social Justice Work in Neo-liberal Times

R. PATRICK SOLOMON, JORDAN SINGER,
ARLENE CAMPBELL, & ANDREW ALLEN

with the assistance of
JOHN P. PORTELLI

Canadian Scholars' Press, Inc
Toronto

Brave New Teachers
by R. Patrick Solomon, Jordan Singer, Arlene Campbell, and Andrew Allen
With the assistance of John P. Portelli

First published in 2011 by
Canadian Scholars' Press Inc.
180 Bloor Street West, Suite 801
Toronto, Ontario
M5S 2V6

www.cspi.org

Canadian Scholars' Press Inc. gratefully acknowledges financial support for our publishing activities from the Government of Canada through the Canada Book Fund (CBF).

Library and Archives Canada Cataloguing in Publication

Brave new teachers : doing social justice work in neoliberal times / R.
atrick Solomon ... [et al.].

Includes index.
ISBN 978-1-55130-397-0

1. Educational equalization—Canada. 2. Multicultural education— Canada. 3. Teaching—Social aspects—Canada. 4. Educational change— Canada. I. Solomon, R. Patrick (Rovell Patrick)

LC213.3.C3B73 2011   379.2'60971   C2011-905560-0

Text design by Colleen Wormald
Cover by EmDash designs

Printed and bound in Canada

Canada

Contents

PREFACE

JOHN P. PORTELLI

In the last 20 years or so the rhetoric in educational discourse has focused primarily on common standards, accountability, value for money, preparing students for global competition, economic considerations and profit, and the basics (understood as numeracy and literacy in a narrow sense). This discourse is a reflection of the impact of neo-liberalism in education both at the policy and practice levels.

Neo-liberalism is a new form of liberalism. Liberalism is based on the rights of individuals, equality of opportunity for all, and the freedom of action and speech. Unfortunately, in the neo-liberal context, these principles have been taken to extremes such that they have become unrecognizable from their original meaning. Individualism has been interpreted in an excessively individualistic manner to the extent that actions that do not lead to personal gain have been deemed not worthwhile. Equality of opportunity has been translated into a one-size-fits-all mentality where the standard norm has, by definition, excluded any deviations from the norm as abnormal—a move which is contrary to the liberal support for diversity. And freedom has been interpreted as complete free choice in an open market without regulation—a position that assumes that all are financially able to make all the choices they desire. The misinterpretation of liberal principles has led to the present context which is dominated by excessive competition, a rugged individualism, a narrow utilitarianism, and reductionist accountability.

The neo-liberal beliefs and practices contrast sharply with a critical-democratic perspective that builds on the liberal beliefs but also goes beyond these beliefs. A critical-democratic perspective is based on John Dewey's notion of democracy as a way of life, Paulo Freire's concern for oppressive contexts and the importance of the community, Maxine Greene's notion of creativity and imagination, bell hooks's understanding of engagement and empowerment, George Dei's notion of integrative anti-racism, and Chantal Mouffe's notion of agonism (rather than antagonism). A critical-democratic perspective values and honours equity (rather than simply equality of opportunity), community participation that does not disregard individual needs and contexts, cooperation (rather than excessive competition), open discussion and dialogue as well as activism, and an acknowledgment, respect, and support for difference both in theory and practice.

There are several responses to the claim that a critical-democratic perspective is inconsistent with neo-liberal values. Some argue that neo-liberal values are in fact democratic since they value choice. Others claim that the emphasis on equity will hinder excellence. And yet others believe that equity and social justice have nothing to do with education and leadership. Finally, there is the claim that the critical-democratic position is new and untested. There are many problems with these claims. First, there is much more to democracy than choice. The neo-liberal conceptualization of democracy is a very minimalist one and does not resemble at all the major democratic beliefs. Second, equity and excellence go hand in hand. If a category of the population is marginalized simply by definition as a result of standardization, then the excellence that emerges is a very limited one. To have full excellence we need to consider seriously the needs of all. Third, those who exclude equity and social justice from education would be working with a very narrow notion of education that resembles more training and drilling. Equity and social justice in education are similar to good health in medicine. Finally, it is just not the case that the critical-democratic perspective is new. Since the inception of public schooling in North America, there has been a conscious and explicit struggle for democracy in education. Moreover, there have been educators who have shown that a critical-democratic perspective can be realized in practice. But to do so, our policies and political decisions have to be based on a different set of values and beliefs other than the neo-liberal ones.

Given the contradictions that arise between neo-liberal policies and critical democratic beliefs and practices, it is very common for teachers and administrators to ask how one can navigate such contradictions and what are the possibilities. The significance of Brave New Teachers is that it offers examples of such possibilities. The book, which is based on a study that the late Professor Patrick Solomon and his associates carried out, focuses on the impact of the Urban Diversity Program at the Faculty of Education, York University, Toronto. This is a program which Solomon developed and enacted since the early 1990s. In his last study, he documented the nature of the program and the impact the program has had on graduates of the program. The participants in this study openly talk about the contradictions they faced. But they also clearly highlight the embodiment of equity principles in practices, as well as ways to challenge the deficit mentality that the fatalism of neo-liberalism engenders.

The program and the practices that are the focus of this book reflect the professionalism, genuine love, and hope that Professor Solomon exhibited throughout his career in teaching, research, and meetings. I have noticed such beliefs and dispositions in Professor Solomon since I first met him in 1991. Luckily for me, I had the pleasure and honour to work with him on several research and writing projects. He has taught me a lot. He was a true friend and a first class mentor.

In our last conversation, two weeks before he passed away, I delivered the letter from the publisher which included the very supportive comments of the reviewers. Although he was weak, he gained energy and smiled, and gave me the honour and responsibility to see this book published. I am very glad that this book is now available to educators and the general public. It was Professor Solomon's wish that the book be discussed so that the practice of equity and social justice in education will continue to remain alive and refined. Contrary to popular beliefs that programs such as the Urban Diversity Program at York University are no longer needed since now all teacher education programs focus on equity and social justice, Professor Solomon firmly believed, based on his research and experience, that such programs are still very much in need since not all those who claim to do equity and social justice work in fact fully understand what this work conceptually means and entails for the practice. Unfortunately, many believe that equity and social justice are consistent with neo-liberal values. He also firmly believed that robust equity and social justice are inconsistent with the belief that there are no foundational principles in education or that such beliefs are not needed. Professor Solomon was always open to critically question his beliefs and practices. But he also warned that such openness does not entail that anything goes, or that some principles and practices are not better than others. The "anything goes" mentality and non-foundational positions ultimately privilege those that are already privileged!

This project would not have come to fruition without the help and support of many people. First, I would like to thank the participants who shared their practices and views with us. I also thank the Social Sciences and Humanities Research Council of Canada for their financial support for this project. I should also thank York University, which supported this project in a variety of ways. Any project of this nature requires the assistance of very competent and hard-working assistants and associates. Hence I thank the following: Karen Pashby for organizing the data, assisting in the literature review and the data analysis, and for her valuable conceptual contribution in the early stages of the project; Dr. Christine Chow for her preliminary work on earlier drafts of Chapters 2 and 3; Arlene Campbell for assistance in data collection, for authoring Chapter 6, and for contributing to Chapter 7; Dr. Andrew Allen who contributed to the conceptual development of the book as well as the data collection, and who wrote Chapter 4; and finally, but definitely not least, Jordan Singer. Jordan co-taught with Professor Solomon during the last five years before he came ill, and he also worked very closely with him on this project. Jordan acted as a very capable research manager of the project, he assisted in the collection and analysis of the data, he contributed to the design of the project and the conceptual development of the book, he co-authored and authored several chapters, and he assisted greatly with the editing. I also thank Canadian Scholars Press for their continued support and enthusiasm about the book. Thanks also to Natasha Jamal who carefully and meticulously developed the index for the book. And finally, I thank Sylvia Solomon and Christopher Solomon for the support they gave Patrick and all of us at several stages of the development of this project and book.

I end with my salute to Professor Patrick Solomon:

You have left us
like an autumn leaf
growing warped and yellow
blowing in the wind
thoughtlessly.

You have left us
like birds of the seasons
passing away quietly
without any greetings
without any tensions.

You have left us
like a stroke of lightning
illuminating the skies
without warning

and swallowed up in eternity.
You have left us
with all the memories
of your thoughts and deeds
all humility
and with hope in the courage
of the ceaseless struggle.

You have left us
with power
in peace ...

Toronto, 12 June 2011

Distinguishing Our Present Context: The Meaning of Diversity and Education for Social Justice

R. PATRICK SOLOMON AND JORDAN SINGER

The recent wave of educational reform and restructuring that has been sweeping across Western democracies has dramatically impacted the pedagogical, social, and political conditions of teachers' work. State-mandated curriculum standards, the design and implementation of standardized testing, and the "marketization" of education and other forms of state and business intervention into schooling have created an ethical dilemma for those committed to the principles and practices of social justice, curriculum diversity, anti-oppressive education, and democratic schooling. Ultimately, school environments have increasingly become arenas of conflict as equity-based curricula that integrate issues of diversity and social justice are forced into a contradictory and tumultuous relationship with standards-based, test-driven, and pre-packaged curricula. In such an incongruous environment, it is not surprising that teachers, principals, policy-makers, teacher educators, and parents, despite their disparate views, can find both support for and opposition against what they believe educators and the public schooling system *should* be doing.

Concurrent to these developments is a marked emergent interest in research concerning the impact of education grounded in issues of equity, diversity, and social justice. The central aspect upon which many progressively minded academics, teachers, and a variety of other professionals concerned with education, culture, and socialization agree upon is that teacher education programs must prepare teachers for the global demands of the 21st century, and that this preparation must be grounded in an anti-oppressive framework; however, only a few teacher education programs have seriously attempted to achieve this most necessary task (Zeichner & Flessner, 2009). This study focuses on the enduring experiences of teachers who have graduated from a program that has met these challenges—the Urban Diversity Teacher Education Program at York University, Toronto, Canada.

Specifically, we trace the continuing impact on Urban Diversity graduates of a program that has taken seriously the implementation of anti-oppressive approaches within every aspect of its design and application. We also inquire into what can be understood about their commitments and practices in relation to the theoretical, practical, and experiential groundwork laid during their social justice–oriented Teacher Education Program. In addition to exploring the influence that this progressive program has had on its graduates and their practices, we explore and examine the dynamic ramifications of these practices on those communities and political landscapes within which these teachers are placed.

The present political context of this study is crucial as it occurs at a time when the work that teachers do, and the classrooms within which they teach, are being increasingly characterized by the language and ideas of business practice. Indeed, some educators, including the authors of this book, have argued that teacher education itself has done little to foster critical democracy and social justice, and instead often plays the role of another institution "retrofitting" individuals for corporate structures (Giroux & McLaren, 1986; McLaren, 1998; Simon, 1992; Apple, Au & Gandin (2009). Within this turbulent context, we dialogically engage with progressively prepared teachers in order to investigate how they have been able to sustain their commitments to a more equitable society, a seemingly daunting challenge in the light of the overwhelm-ing "market-based reforms" that have thoroughly infiltrated the educa-tional landscape within many Western states.

A Watershed Moment for Social Justice in a New Century

The trajectories and character of many Western democratic histories, while distinguished by many salient historical, cultural, social, and political differences, share a colonial-oriented past that continues to infect our social discourse, institutions, and individual consciousness with racism, ethnocentrism, classism, heterosexism, ableism, and a variety of other hostile and exclusionary thoughts and practices. Col-lectively, we can no longer deny that the intolerance that shaped our history continues to be embedded in our daily lives, imprinted in our texts, and embodied in our beings. We must also acknowledge that these deeply rooted inequities are transmitted, as well as reproduced, often beyond our everyday perceptions and, tragically, with little notice.

One notable example of this legacy of intolerance was the forced assimi-lation of Canada's First Nations, Inuit, and Métis population through resi-dential schools. More precisely, the goal of these church-run, government-funded schools was the "aggressive assimilation" of all Indigenous peoples (Aboriginal, Inuit, North American Indian, and Métis) (Royal Commis-sion on Aboriginal Peoples, 1996; Department of Indian and Northern Affairs, 2003). In many cases children were separated from their parents for 10 months of the year and taken to the schools, where they were sub-jected to various forms of physical, psychological, and spiritual abuse. The schools' federal mandate was to Christianize the students (officially described as "killing the Indian in the child"), which included telling the children that their people's heritage was uncivilized and evil. In addition, the children were harshly punished for attempting to speak their own lan-guage. Indeed, it is fair to describe life in these schools as one of abuse, coercion, and powerlessness (Haig-Brown, 1988). Thousands suffered sexual abuse and tens of thousands more died as a result of deplorable conditions, which resulted in chronic disease and malnutrition (Milloy, 1999; Annett, 2005). Today, unquestionably, the tragedy of subjecting over 130,000 Indigenous peoples to this heinous treatment continues to unfold. The intentional destruction of their language, culture, family, and traditional belief systems, which was almost successful, continues to reverberate today, as can be witnessed in endemic addiction problems, as well as commonly reported deep feelings of trauma and estrangement from themselves, the land, their culture, language, history, and heritage (Canadian Collaborative Mental Health Initiative, 2006).

Likewise, at this moment, similar atrocities and abusive individual and social practices *have and continue to occur* in many locations across the planet. As we reflect on our past, and consider the increasingly multicultural and multiracial nature of our cosmopolitan present, we are convinced that there has never been a more critical time for a renewed commitment to social justice and equity through the pursuit of non-assimilationist pedagogies. Recently, our hopes for our children and our world have been buoyed by a heightened interest in the value and significance of projects that aim to form a more just future.

In considering the scope of these injustices and what needs to be done to change this cycle of destructive repetition, it is becoming increasingly clear that nothing short of a transformation of the structurally embedded inequities of our societies and a contiguous paradigm shift in the perceptions of individuals will suffice. Of course, when one pushes against the grain of society, the grain often cuts deeply and does not wear away easily or give up space, position, or ground without resistance and anguish. Yet, regardless of the inevitable pain of change and transformation, we must ask: How can teachers, in the light of our collective pasts, make a significant contribution to changing our social structures? And how, given the colonization of education by the language and practices of business, can teachers sustain their commitments to social justice while continuing to transform their schools and communities?

4

THINKING BEFORE CHANGING: PRESENT CONTEXT

Educational initiatives forged on a grand scale, the goal of which is nothing less than to contribute to systemic transformation, is grounded in the logic of social reconstructionism. In education, this philosophical vision of a more equitable future must translate into pragmatic practice(s). To bring this about, educators need to have, at minimum, a working knowledge of the various social differences that make up particular communities in a society. In our experience, this familiarity often helps teachers become more sympathetic and empathetic to the needs and experiences of heterogeneous student populations. As a result of this increased sensitivity, teachers become increasingly attuned to alternative ways of empowering their students and, in due course, learn to engage in advocacy work aimed at helping to ameliorate the widening distributional disparities between the privileged and disenfranchised sectors of society.

Discouragingly, at present there are few progressive teacher preparation programs, and those that exist work in a climate of market-driven educational reform predicated on standardized measures intended to increase the quality, rigour, and accountability of education. However, the methods and goals of business and the methods and goals of education are often antithetical. While business representatives and politically based supporters of these reform initiatives claim that they will raise the standards of education, and in so doing help students succeed and become more competitive within the global economy, others from the fields of education and sociology, whose research attends to education as a place within which to develop human potential and democratic citizenship, have shown that these reforms may indeed have the opposite effect (Supovitz & Brennan, 1997; Apple, 2001b: 421; Au, 2008). What remains unclear and to date relatively unexamined is what impact these reforms are having on the emerging practices of teachers who are dedicated to the principles and practices of democratic education.

Undeniably, the work of teachers is central to school reform, although their power, social status, professional designation, and duties continue to be attacked. One illustration of this is how the new emphasis on accountability reduces their roles to operational and technical tasks due to a preoccupation with record keeping and "accounting duties." The reduction of teachers' work to that of mere technicians is not only a tragedy for the future of our children and our society, but fundamentally counteracts and contradicts the crucial educational, social, and political roles and duties ascribed to teachers in democratic societies. According to Hartnett and Carr (1995), democratic societies expect teachers to utilize their judgments, knowledge, and values and to act as intermediaries between the state, parents, and educationally based institutions. Fortunately, despite the draconian restrictions on their professional roles, research conducted in U.S. schools indicates that some teachers have demonstrated creativity and innovation in working with the tensions and contradictions of school reforms despite increasing restrictions on their teaching environments and a bureaucratization of their professional roles (Lipman, 1998; McNeil, 2000; McLaren & Baltodano, 2000; Meier, 2002).

A clear expression of the ideologically driven "marketization" of education can be seen in Ontario's recent history. In 1997, the Conservative Party–led government implemented Bill 160, which carried the Orwellian title "The Education Quality Improvement Act." This massive bill, along with Bill 74, legislated key tenets of the Conservative Party government's mandate in which they proclaimed a "Common Sense Revolution." For the field of education, this meant major reforms that included a "back to basics" approach to curriculum, increased business influence in schools (including being a part of the curriculum-building process), across-the-board high-stakes testing for both students and teachers, and tax incentives for parents to send their children to private schools. Some of the changes to the education sector, which *still persist today* despite a change of government that is "more sympathetic" to teachers and educational issues, will prove illustrative. Bill 160 included the following directives:

6

1. Centralization of decision making and power within the Ministry of Education

Local decision making about *local* educational programs was virtually eliminated and power was transferred from elected trustees in order to allow the government to have controlling influence over teacher contract negotiations, classroom sizes, and the right to strike.

2. Effective separation of principals and teachers

Principals were removed from the unions of their teacher colleagues, which created a schism in collegial relations. In the past, principals were viewed as curriculum leaders whereas now they are perceived as business managers. Since this change, the average time a principal has spent in the classroom (prior to becoming a principal) has diminished dramatically.

3. Implementation of an equalized funding system

All students in the province were given equal funding regardless of their school location or individual operational needs. In consequence, older schools (which needed extensive repair and new equipment), schools in areas with higher immigration levels, schools in impoverished locations (which lack the possibility of parents augmenting school operating costs), and schools with other unique challenges were allotted the same funding as those without such overheads and expenses. In this context, it seems clear that equal funding would be an inequitable and unfair practice as the needs of some dramatically differed from the needs of others.

4. Allocation and concentration of immense power within the office of the Minister of Education

The questioning of the minister of Education's authority and any decisions by other stakeholders was eliminated. In the name of safeguarding schools, the minister is now authorized not merely to order criminal background checks of all school personnel, but to compile exhaustive dossiers on teachers and board employees. This authority extends to students and potentially even parents.

In the same vein as Bill 160, Bill 74 was based on the premise that the education system was flawed and needed to be steered and reshaped. Bill 74 mandated new teachers to write a comprehensive exam, the Ontario Teacher Qualifying Test (OTQT), and required all other teachers to upgrade their credentials at their own expense and on their own time. Teachers found this particularly galling in the light of Bill 160, which had almost completely eliminated professional development days from the school calendar in addition to drastically reducing teacher preparation time.[1] The government claimed that the impetus for all these reforms was to bring "accountability" and "universal standards" to the education sector while forcing "fiscal responsibility" (i.e., cutting funding to education) on its "management." Many believed that the removal of $1 billion from the education sector was actually designed to help the Conservatives finance a promised tax cut. A quote from the "Common Sense Revolution" platform regarding education is illustrative: "With a core curriculum set province-wide, and with standardized testing at all levels, we know that we can spend more efficiently, while improving the quality of education we offer to students" (The Common Sense Revolution Official Platform, 1994).

One example of the detrimental effects of high-stakes testing can be seen in grades 3 and 6. Due to the funding formula's inequities and budget cutbacks, principals of schools with high-needs students, such as those with many English language learners and English as a foreign language students, were forced to redirect educational assistants to compensate rather than to hire specialist teachers and support staff. Educational assistants (who were not let go due to funding cuts) were also redirected to grades 3 and 6 classrooms in order to focus attention on improving test scores. Thus, educational assistants were transferred out of their elementary classrooms to other classes and, at times, to other schools, where the new Education Quality and Accountability Office testing was to take place. In effect, they were removed from classes where they greatly enhanced teachers' abilities to attend to students individually, an increasing necessity as more and more classrooms are being occupied with large numbers of new immigrants and EFL students. In addition to this loss of primary teacher attention, students' opportunity to engage with another knowledgeable educator in the classroom was also lost. Teaching assistants were placed in classrooms where their main function was to improve standardized test scores. Further to these hindrances is the very real loss of quality time and instruction; for instance, teachers reported that "teaching to the test" seriously reduced the time necessary to teach anything well, or to attend properly to students' diverse learning needs. As a result, instruction often reverted to the "drill and kill" methods of past inculcation, most cogently and derisively described by Paulo Freire as the "banking method" of education (Freire, 1970).

Many crucial aspects of the Ontario situation are not unique. In fact, similar reforms are occurring, or have already occurred, in the U.S., Britain, Australia, New Zealand, and a growing number of other countries (many of which still continue to reproduce the inequitable practices inherited from their colonial legacies). Common to these reforms is the alliance of neo-conservative and neo-liberal forces that share a common belief in the power of free markets to create greater wealth for all, although on closer inspection, it is fair to say that they believe free markets will create greater wealth for them. Counterintuitively, these forces continue to sustain their hold on power despite the economic collapse of 2008. Indeed, rather than electing more progressively based political parties that aim to reform the global monetary system and place restrictions on unfettered and unregulated capitalism, recent elections demonstrate how conservatives have managed to co-opt temporarily the language of assistance while maintaining a steadfast belief in the power of deregulation and trickle-down economics. The complex reasons behind their shared beliefs are, not surprisingly, often myopic, if not Darwinian, paradigm-blind, religiously intolerant, greed-based, and xenophobic. Michael Apple provides insights into the different interest groups that have found common ground in their beliefs concerning educational reform:

> This power bloc combines multiple fractions of capital who are committed to neo-liberal marketized solutions to educational problems, neo-conservative intellectuals who want a 'return to high standards' and a 'common culture' authoritarian populist religious conservatives who are deeply worried about secularity and the preservation of their own traditions and particular fractions of the professionally and managerially oriented new middle class who are committed to the ideology and techniques of accountability, measurement and 'management' (Apple, 2006: 246).

These seemingly disparate ideological, religious, political, and economic forces have manifested not only in regional policy-making, but through global economic agreements such as the World Trade Organization's (WTO) General Agreement on Trade in Services (GATS). The agreement is complex, although many public sector organizations and trade unions view GATS and its attempt to deal with economic "discrimination," which hinders international education providers' access to foreign markets (Snape, 1998), as imposing increased pressures to privatize education (Altbach, 2001; Education International and Public Services International, 2000, cited in Ziguras, 2005: 102). In fact, the Joint Declaration on Higher Education and the General Agreement on Trade in Services, signed by the Association of Universities and Colleges of Canada, the European University Association, the American Council on Education, and the U.S. Council for Higher Education Accreditation, argues that GATS could chip away at national prerogatives and jeopardize quality, integrity, accessibility, and equity (Association of Universities and Colleges Canada, 2001: 2–3).

International business agreements like GATS reinforce regional, provincial, and state economic policy reforms designed to economically harmonize educational funding and equalize standards. In order to accomplish this, local and regional autonomy over curriculum and finances (the collection of taxes) must be centralized in the hands of the government. As a result, the centralization of power for the purpose of harmonizing "standards" and equalizing funding often leads to the loss of local and community input into educational design and content. For those of us concerned with social justice, the detrimental effects of these mirror-like reforms among similarly positioned economies are deeply disturbing as the mutually reinforcing dynamics described above influence how governments frame and envision the entire field of education. This distorted vision does not view education as a site where society passes on its most prized values and talents in an effort to strengthen its democratic structures to build a more equitable future, but instead observes a place of profit generation, where schools are factories and students are widgets. Reforms in other Western democracies have followed similar trends.

In the U.K., the Education Reform Act of 1988 introduced a national curriculum that included major reforms in assessment procedures and processes. The introduction of benchmarks and descriptions of standards of student achievement, introduced in Toronto (Rutledge, 1993), "closely resemble these developments which occurred in England and Wales" (Elliott & Hughes, 1998: 1). Similarly, in the U.S. there has been an almost fetishistic implementation of "standards" and "outcomes-based education" often involving centralizing the governance of education. In Australia, as part of the government's economic reform, education was treated "overwhelmingly as a mechanism for economic development at the expense of something to be intrinsically valued for its own sake" (Carter, 1994: 6–7). In addition, the language used in Australia's educational reforms is almost identical to the language used in Ontario, including: improved efficiency, increasing the emphasis on skills training, centralizing curriculum and decision making, and "involving the private sector in educational reform" (Carter, 1994: 7).

In New Zealand one prominent study that examined whether similar reforms had improved educational standards among the working class and minorities found that the changes led to an overall decline in educational standards. Their findings indicated that the reforms "[p]aradoxically have a negative, not a positive, effect on the performance of schools with large working class minority populations" (Apple, 2001b: 421). Essentially, the opportunities of new immigrants, the poor, and the working class were being "traded off" to the children of the privileged. Similarly, studies in England and Wales have shown that the massive government-mandated Educational Act (1993), which "subjected education to increased regulation, centralization and consumerism" (Harris, 1994: 251), had no discernible impact when compared with traditional models of schools and schooling (Power et al., 1994). It is clear from the study that these reforms certainly didn't lead, as the government had claimed, to greater curriculum responsiveness and academic improvement. Rather, transforming the structures and culture of learning in schools with language and concepts transplanted from business led to the persistence of inequity. Often not only have the same inequities persisted, but they have been exacerbated and reinforced. A good example of this can be seen in the common discourse of "increased choice," a common refrain evident in all these reforms. Parents and/or other education stakeholders are given greater flexibility (and sometimes offered tax incentives) to choose schools often outside of the public sector; however, as Lauder and Hughes (1999) point out, "By changing the process of selection to schools, middle-class parents can raise the stakes in creating stronger mechanisms of exclusion for blue collar and post-colonial people in their struggle for equality of opportunity" (p. 49).

What Does This Book Accomplish and Why Is It Important?

The main purpose of the book is to document how Canadian teachers are responding to conservative, market-driven school reform by exploring how the graduates of a progressive teacher education program are being affected by and responding to these changes. An analysis of their perspectives and experiences provides insights into how teacher engagements in the field may foster transformative changes that create culturally relevant pedagogy and, in consequence, a more equitable social, political, and educational landscape. The teachers with whom we speak, and who share their experiences with us, are graduates of the Urban Diversity (UD) Teacher Education Program at a Canadian university. This is a progressive program designed to help pre-service teachers expand their pedagogical perspectives and envision a broader, more inclusive understanding of social justice within the framework of equity. In addition, the program helps teachers develop their critical thinking skills, as well as an educational philosophy and mission while conceptualizing and envisioning their future roles and responsibilities as political advocates and leaders in the field of social justice education. The book investigates how these teachers continue to integrate the progressive principles they learned in teacher education into their own pedagogy despite state-mandated educational reforms and often hostile and conservative school cultures. More specifically, the book:

- identifies and documents the strategies teachers employ to deal with the contradictions of legislated standardization of school curriculum and their own professional preparation for curriculum inclusion and diversity
- explores the risks and tensions these strategies generate and the potential short- and long-term impact on teachers' personal and professional lives
- examines how mandated school reforms de-professionalize, and lead to many teachers feeling disempowered and demoralized
- ascertains the ways in which teachers' responses to school culture and policy affect the curriculum their students receive and the relationships they forge with colleagues, school administrators, and the diverse communities they serve

- explores the extent to which teachers' identities and social difference may be factors in their attempt to implement an equity-based curriculum in a politically charged school environment
- describes the unique contributions of UD graduates in their classrooms, schools, and other workplaces to curriculum and pedagogy, as well as in advocacy and activism
- analyzes the essential aspects necessary for building a cohesive program for diversity education and training in multicultural as well as multiracial settings

Additionally, this text illuminates important implications for educational policy-makers, school administrators, teacher educators, and social workers regarding how they may work more effectively with teachers in a politically potent school environment where mandated policy initiatives may be in conflict with the ideals of democratic schooling. By looking at how educational restructuring for the global economic marketplace dramatically impacts the pedagogical, social, and political conditions of teachers' work both within and outside of institutional settings, this book will help bring teachers' and students' perspectives into the ongoing global debates on contemporary cosmopolitan schooling in democratic societies.

Building Equity and Social Justice in Teacher Education

We explore teacher preparation within a framework of equity, diversity, and social justice by addressing the different perspectives of Urban Diversity (UD) graduates toward the program and how their perceptions grounded them in the principles and practices of democratically situated anti-oppressive education. More specifically, this book explores how teachers construct meanings from their experiential work in schools and communities of practice. We also tease out the relationship between their present reflections and actions and the political goals implicitly championed throughout their teacher preparation program. Concurrently we differentiate teachers' response strategies to educational reform in their various work contexts, the impact of tensions and contradictions on their personal and professional lives, and the salience of teachers' social identities (e.g., race, ethnicity, gender, social class, etc.) as intervening factors in the struggle for equitable schooling.

At this juncture it is necessary to define our understanding of several key terms in the book—"equity," "social justice," and "diversity"—whose common, though uncritical, usage has threatened both their meaning(s) and complexities.

EQUITY

The term "equity" is used broadly, but is rarely understood. The Equity Foundation statement from an Ontario school district provides a functional definition of equity that reflects our understanding and commitment: "Certain groups in our society are treated inequitably because of individual and systemic biases related to race, color, culture, ethnicity, linguistic origin, disability, socioeconomic class, age, ancestry, and nationality, place of origin, religion, faith, sex, gender, sexual orientation, family status, and marital status" (Toronto District School Board, 2007). Based upon this understanding, it is clear that all educationally based programs and policies, as well as pedagogical and curricular initiatives that aim to achieve a more equitable society, must remain cognizant of the numerous factors, dynamics, and extant *inequities* listed above in order to strategize how best to address the distinctly complex, yet interdependent, categories of individual and group identity that represent *real individuals and discernible groups* who have been and continue to be socially and politically—indeed systemically—denigrated. Attempts to operationalize equitable practices aim for fairness, but an equitable understanding of fairness often seems counterintuitive for many as it does not necessarily entail equal treatment. To be clear, equity often does not mean equality in treatment or actions, although the two terms are not mutually exclusive. Equitable practices begin with the assumption that we do *not* live in a meritocracy. Accordingly, for the marginalized, no amount of hard work and perseverance will equalize their opportunities for success when compared with individuals from the mainstream, dominant culture. Social structures, hiring practices, and the increasingly politically constructed standards set in North America and other racialized and ethnocentric societies are not equal and are, in fact, biased, discriminatory, and structurally inequitable. Understanding how marginalized and racialized individuals and groups are unequally integrated into our social, educational, and political structures necessitates changing the criteria by which the status quo equates fairness of opportunity and outcome. Consequently, fairness of treatment must be understood as fairness of treatment according to socially, historically, culturally, and politically contextualized needs. In the words of Blye Frank, who conducted an equity audit for the Elementary Teachers Foundation of Ontario, "[t]his may include equal treatment or treatment that is different, but which is considered equivalent in terms of rights, benefits, obligations or opportunities" (Frank, 2006).

The difficult task is discerning what specifically needs to be done to create an equitable system. In the context of education, an equitable school and classroom is an *inclusive* one in which all voices and experiences are valued, regardless of physical ability, ethnicity, race, religion, sexual orientation, gender, and/or family structure. "Inclusive education calls for the integration of the individual, family histories, concerns, and practices in to the larger societal collective, etc. Inclusive schooling practices must be both 'critical,' culturally, socially responsive and relevant and must seek to engender empowerment and transformation in the lives of all learners" (Dei, Wilson & Zine, 2002: 4). The scope of equity pedagogy is nicely summarized by Christine Bennett in *Genres of Research in Multicultural Education* (2001):

> This movement aims at achieving fair and equal educational opportunities for all of the nation's children and youth, particularly ethnic minorities and the economically disadvantaged. It

attempts to transform the total school environment, especially the hidden curriculum that is expressed in teacher attitudes and expectations for student learning, grouping of students and instructional strategies, school disciplinary policies and practices, school and community relations, and classroom climates. (p. 183)

In order for this type of transformation to occur, learning and knowledge must be approached as interconnected emancipatory tools to be passed on for the purpose of raising consciousness. To become truly emancipatory, critical thinking must be engaged alongside a moral and ethical imperative that recognizes the inherent value of our undifferentiated humanity, a value that, paradoxically, can be illuminated only through the respectful recognition of difference. How do we know when our society and schools are more equitable? In the event of such an equitable transformation, many of the problems experienced by minoritized, racialized, and low-income students would be eliminated, leading to greater academic success and inevitably to more equal representation and achievement in educational, social, and political structures.

SOCIAL JUSTICE EDUCATION

Bell (1997) defines social justice education as both process and goal:

The goal of social justice education is full and equal participation of all groups in a society that is mutually shaped to meet their needs. Social justice includes a vision of society in which the distribution of resources is equitable and all members are physically and psychologically safe and secure. We envision a society in which individuals are both self-determining (able to develop their full capabilities), and interdependent (capable of interacting democratically with others).... The process for attaining the goal of social justice we believe should be democratic and participatory, inclusive and affirming of human agency and human capacity for working collaboratively to create change. (pp. 3–4)

In teacher education, social justice means educating teachers to directly contribute to bringing about these social changes. Thus, teacher education for social justice involves specific practices, attitudes, and information concerning individual, social, historical, and political actions and dynamics for teacher candidates. The sharing of this information and the co-operative nature of knowledge production in a social justice teacher education program fosters within new teachers particular ways of thinking about their roles as teachers. Also central is a commitment to critical thinking regarding the complexity of learning and knowledge in relation to social location, context, identity, and history. Teachers who embody social justice teacher education:

- maintain an awareness that their complex identities (race, class, gender, sexuality, language, ability, ethnic origin, and a myriad of other factors) continually shape and influence how they think about teaching, learning, politics, education, social difference, and social justice
- understand that their position in the social order is complex and often a result of the interactions between economics, politics, and power dynamics, racism, intolerance, and the reproduction of distorted thinking about difference and otherness
- have insight into the complexity of learning and knowledge, as well as the historical and contextual basis behind these conceptions/perceptions, keeping in mind that their students may value some forms of knowing and learning that have been traditionally dismissed from our dominant cultural belief systems
- believe that integrating their students' experiences, cultures, languages, histories, ways of being, ways of knowing, learning styles, and communities of origin into the classroom and the school are essential elements of good teaching

- see themselves as vital aspects of their students' communities and therefore participate in the healthy growth and mainte- nance of these communities
- understand their roles as teachers to be inspirational, nur- turing, empowering, collaborative, and humble, as well as focused on the overall well-being of their students; they do not see themselves simply as non-judgmental vessels through which the curriculum flows, knowledge experts, or represen- tatives of a common culture that their students are meant to emulate
- perceive themselves and their students as co-operatively involved in socially reconstructing a more equitable world
- acknowledge the political nature of education and know that their work in the classroom has potentially great social reper- cussions and therefore get involved in the politics within and beyond the school

Further to these goals for teachers, social justice teacher education programs aim to:

- increase minority representation in teaching
- broaden and deepen co-operation among universities, teach- ers, schools, parents, and communities
- expand the social, political, and historical parameters through which education is understood
- persist in insisting that our society is inequitably structured and that this must change

DIVERSITY
When diversity is referred to in this book, it is done in a manner that expresses a multitude of interrelated diversities:

1. *Diversity of curriculum:* how it frames knowledge, history,

and particular peoples; its organization, the expectations for its implementation, its aims, and the methods through which achieving these aims are to be assessed.

2. *Diversity of students:* their places of origin, race, class, culture, language, gender, sexual orientation, abilities, and learning dispositions.

3. *Diversity of teachers:* their places of origin, race, class, culture, language, gender sexual orientation, experiences in different schools, occupational background (before teaching), area of specialization, philosophy of education, and pedagogy.

- View all of their students and their diverse backgrounds as valuable and worthy of respect, attention, and inclusion in the classroom.
- Values divergent knowledge forms, teaching practices, and approaches to learning while constantly reflecting on why certain forms of knowledge (and types of experiences) are considered worthy of respect and attention while others are not.
- Commits to knowing their diverse students well beyond simplistic markers of difference such as food and celebrations.

Theoretical Context

This book is grounded in a critical democratic framework that values equity, diversity, and social justice. It is guided by a critical pedagogy approach that examines what is "taken for granted" (Simon, 1992) and raises questions about the social and political implications of the often unexamined daily practices of teachers. Over the last 25 years, debates concerning teacher preparedness to work equitably within schools and communities characterized by diversity and social difference have been well documented in the research literature (Britzman, 1991; Delpit, 1988, 1995; Liston & Zeichner, 1990; Sleeter, 1992a; Zeichner, 1996; Greenman & Dieckmann, 2004; Gay, 2002; *McAllister* & Irvine, 2000; Villegas & Lucas, 2002; Brayboy, Castagno & Maughan, 2007; Darder, Baltodano & Torres, 2009). How teachers who have been well prepared for diverse schools have responded and coped with policies and changes in the school system that are antithetical to doing anti-oppressive work has been left undocumented.

As a result of a shift in state's definitions of teachers' role, and curricula that increasingly reflect corporate interests, teachers' responsibilities in the classroom are being altered from getting to know and understand their students to "the role of operatives in a system which is managed centrally by politicians and their officials" (Hartnett & Carr, 1995: 46). Here they are faced with legislated curriculum that Cross (1998) describes as "linear, mechanistic, static, singular, prescriptive and preset" (p. 38); a curriculum that is disassociated from the lived experiences of students, particularly those marginalized by social class, race, ethnicity, gender, disability, etc. McNeil (2000) warns that the perverse effects of such legislated teaching and learning "reduce the public's possibilities for retaining democratic governance of schools once the controls are in place" (p. 265). Such a technicist conception of teachers' work, devoid of social or political contexts, provides limited opportunities for teachers to integrate *into* their curriculum and pedagogy their own insights, perspectives, and lived experiences (Apple & Weis, 1983; McLaren, 1998; Davis, 2000). Furthermore, a thorough analysis by Ball, Bowe and Gerwitz (1994) concerning how these reforms function in practice has shown that "in these situations educational principles and values are often compromised and quite often as a direct result commercial issues become more important in curricular design and resource allocation" (p. 39).

One central question is: Given the current climate of schooling in Western democracies such as Canada and the top-down imposition of curriculum standards, do teachers acquiesce to this higher authority, compromise their democratic principles to avoid conflict and confrontation, or negotiate space to practise equity and diversity in their pedagogy? Given teachers' pivotal role in either reproducing the status quo or transforming schools for inclusivity, diversity, and social justice, it is imperative and urgent that this research examine their pedagogical practices in given institutional, social, and political contexts. We need to examine the extent to which teachers can hold onto a coherent philosophical, moral, and political vision of school reform in light of its potential collision with state-legislated restructuring of schools.

Recent empirical research has documented an interesting range of teacher responses to this dilemma. Pre-service teachers often endure stasis, a tacit pressure to maintain the status quo within practicum schools; engage in "silences" on issues of equity and diversity; and simply wait until they "get their own classrooms," or for "teachable moments" (Grant & Zozakiewicz, 1995; Menter, 1989; Solomon & Allen, 2001). Some teachers, in their early years of teaching, become less committed to equity and social justice compared to their pre-service commitments (Louis Harris & Associates Inc. & Westin, 1991; Gomez, 1996). Experienced teachers have often resisted these reforms by being strategic in their classroom instruction as evidenced by McNeil's (2000) study, which demonstrated their resistance to imposed curriculum standardization and accountability. Their study found that experienced teachers conceive of their teaching in terms of two distinct curricula: the official proficiency-based curriculum, and the "real curriculum" or "curriculum of life" (Portelli & Vibert, 2001). Racial minority teachers in Lipman's (1998) study of race, class, and power in school restructuring strategically withdrew from what they perceived as an artificial initiative devoid of social context: "the powerful, mediating role of social context—the historical and current relations of power that shape social life and frame the limits and possibilities of educational change" were, in their minds, absent from the government-imposed restructuring agenda (p. 288).

This raises the very important issue of teachers' social identities as a factor in commitment and practice of equity and diversity education.

Canadian research on teacher response to multiculturalism and anti-racism conducted over the last fifteen years suggests that there is differential commitment based on educators' identities (Carr & Klassen, 1997; Dei et al., 1997; Haberman & Post, 1998; Solomon, Levine-Rasky & Singer, 2003). This factor is particularly important for this inquiry because of the ethno-racial makeup of the cohorts studied, the ethno-racial representational needs of urban communities, and the potential impact of teacher diversity on the schooling process.

Many of the problematics, themes, and questions that have emerged from the research literature on this complex subject are central to this text. The work of this book illuminates many of these queries. We seek to investigate the current social, cultural, and political climate within schools and the tensions generated between policy-makers and policy implementers, and how, given the contradictions between the legislated standardized curriculum and democratic schooling, in addition to the power dynamics pervasive in the hierarchical structuring of schools, teachers can negotiate space for emancipatory and inclusive democratic pedagogy. Furthermore, we explore how stakeholders can collaborate to reverse the erosion of democratic traditions in education and the concomitant disempowerment and de-professionalization of teachers and the teaching profession.

While there are empirical studies emerging from elsewhere (e.g., the United States) on teachers' response to school restructuring and curriculum reform (Lipman, 1998; McNeil, 2000; McLaren & Baltodano, 2000), this research provides a unique Canadian perspective and context. Equally original is the study design, which follows up on graduates over the long term (after five and seven years in the field) from a program with clearly articulated objectives of teacher empowerment for emancipatory schooling. A further dimension of its originality is the utilization of social difference markers of participants (e.g., race, ethnicity, gender, social class) to ascertain the importance of these markers in the pedagogical process. We wish to elucidate what effects these identifications have on teachers' commitments to equity. Also, we investigate the extent to which others' perceptions of these social difference markers impact the unique struggles that UD teachers face while doing social justice work.

The study reported in this book is directly applicable for teacher education and teaching, curriculum theory, intercultural education, the sociology of race, and critical race studies, all facets of multicultural and diversity education, social work practice, and prejudice reduction theory. For teacher education, specifically, the following areas are most salient: candidate selection and the importance of social identities; teacher education curriculum and scholarship regarding equity and diversity work in both local and global socio-economic as well as political contexts; and the exploration of intellectual and political support for teachers, such as building alliances with other progressive teachers, community activists, parents, students, and other stakeholders in the education process. Finally, this study is also useful for anyone working toward a clearer understanding of the field of equity and diversity in reference to the individual, institutional, and political challenges in doing this work.

RESEARCH PARTICIPANTS AND METHODOLOGY

The research focuses on 42 graduates from the Urban Diversity Teacher Education Program: 21 from the class of 1994–1995, and 21 from the class of 1996–1997. These two cohorts are ideal for this study since they self-selected into the UD program and represented the diversity of the larger group of 44 from which they were chosen in terms of race, ethnicity, gender, social class, and other social identities. They self-identified as being or belonging to the following categories: (White) European heritage, consisting primarily of American, British, Italian, French, Portuguese, German, Greek, Swedish, and eastern European backgrounds; and minority racial groups from a variety of ethnic backgrounds (for instance, Black, Jewish). Over the life of the Program, these groups have included such heritages as Aboriginal First Nations (Cree, Mohawk, Micmac, Ojibway, Lakota Sioux), Caribbean (Bermuda, Nassau, Jamaican, Barbadian, Trinidadian), African (Nigerian, Kenyan, Somali),

Middle Eastern (Iranian, Iraqi, Lebanese, Jewish), South Asian (Indian, Pakistani, Sri Lankan), East Asian (Japanese, Chinese, Korean), Southeast Asian (Filipino, Vietnamese), South and Central American (Guyanese, Mexican, Colombian).

The participants in this study were also working in diverse positions, including teaching in the arts, mathematics, and general junior-level disciplines, as well as working as librarians, equity instructors, and guidance counsellors. Most respondents, however, taught in the junior elementary range, although many stated that they had spent some years supply teaching before beginning permanent contracts. The vast majority of the participants still worked in the classroom. They discussed their experiences teaching from kindergarten to junior high school, and a small number of respondents had moved into such board-level positions as equity representatives for their district school boards.

Most respondents stated that they sat on various committees, including the equity, parent, and curriculum committees. The majority of the participants had furthered their education, enrolling in M.A. and Ph.D. degree programs, additional qualification programs in such areas as special education, completing the principal's course, and attending workshops dealing with equity and diversity, as well as leadership training in order to keep up to date with their changing work environments. With this in mind, many participants felt qualified in taking more informed, theoretically driven political stances on diversity initiatives at their schools.

This three-year study utilized qualitative research methods that combined data collection approaches such as in-depth interviews, focus group discussions, and computer online conferences with teachers in the study, classroom and in-school observations, as well as document analysis of participants' professional portfolios, teaching plans, and classroom resources. We also examined provincial and school district–generated curriculum policy documents that guided teachers' everyday practices within the school and classroom.

The qualitative approach we used generated a wide range of information with which to work. The interviews provided participants with an opportunity to reflect on their own experiences while giving meaning to the complexities and contradictions in their school settings. We also provided teachers with an opportunity to share their personal and professional experiences with others through group interviews, online conferences, and at the program's 10th anniversary reunion. The opportunity to share their experiences after graduation revealed a great deal as participants were able to reconnect with other diversity-conscious teachers. Each of these approaches allowed the participants to interrogate their social identities, the social and political context in which they teach, and their commitment to non-oppressive education and pedagogy, as well as to compare and contrast possible modes of negotiating through this terrain.

Interviews allowed participants to reflect on their lived experiences and to give meaning to the complexities and contradictions to which they must respond in institutional settings (Norquay, 1999; Gluck & Patai, 1991). Generating teachers' accounts of social equity issues has been quite productive using this interview approach (Connell, 1985; Ball & Goodson, 1985). Focus group interviews and online conferences offered the opportunity for research participants to share personal and professional experiences, as well as situating these experiences within specific schools and community contexts. These approaches create space to interrogate teachers' social identities, the social and political contexts in which they teach commitment to a diversity-social justice agenda, and the pedagogical and political skills they develop to navigate these terrains (McIntyre, 1997). Field observations in participants' workplaces provide researchers the opportunity to contextualize participants' perceptions of their practice and to triangulate these perceptions with data collected from documents and colleagues in their work environments.

Overview of Chapters

Chapter 1: "Preparing the Equity Teacher" introduces the Urban Diversity (UD) Teacher Education Program, which prepares teachers for democratic schooling in a diverse Canadian society. It begins by providing readers with the theoretical and conceptual foundations of the program and concludes with rich graduate narratives of UD graduates' strong "sense of mission and empowerment" to be change agents and to expand their teaching beyond pedagogy to embrace teaching as a political activity.

Chapter 2: "School Reform as Inequity: The Case of Standards, Standardization, and Accountability" articulates UD graduates' perception that standards-based curriculum reform, high-stakes testing, and the accountability rhetoric force teachers to prioritize prescribed standards over divergent knowledge forms and restricts their abilities to teach students to think critically. The inherent inequity in school reforms is assessed and the antithetical relationship between standardized testing and the promotion of social justice education emerges.

Chapter 3: "Challenges and Contradictions of the Equity Educator: Personal and Professional Impacts of School Reforms on Teachers" reveals how the discourse of accountability constructs teaching as a deficit profession. Teachers' desires to improve their profession are made clear, but so too is their resentment of the political and ideological forces denigrating their sense of professionalism. As well, their sense of being disempowered by a top-down, externally defined, and driven obsession with measurement is examined.

Chapter 4: "Identity Matters in Teaching for Equity" documents the significance of how teachers conceive of their social identity (i.e., race, ethnicity, gender, social class, and immigrant status) in relation to their motivation and commitment to equitable teacher practice in the context of school reform. Finally, this chapter engages how teachers' social identities are implicated in their teaching and discovers how they are working through the discordant tensions between how popular discourse defines social identity and the multilayered and textured lived experiences of identity.

Chapter 5: "Transformative Schooling" moves beyond the challenges of school reform and works toward building equitable, democratic classrooms within a supportive and inclusive environment. Three key strategies emerge as mutually supporting approaches: (1) creating a safe, nurturing, and inclusive classroom environment; (2) bringing the community into the learning context; and (3) facilitating choice and excellence among all members of the classroom.

Chapters 6 and 7 describe the unique contributions of UD graduates in their classrooms, schools, and other workplaces. Chapter 6: "Performing Curriculum and Pedagogy: Practices from the Workplace" introduces the practices of five UD graduates. In "*Hairspray* and Other Issues of Race," a graduate provides a safe classroom environment for her junior grade students to raise the uncomfortable questions of racial difference emerging from the movie *Hairspray* and other popular media. "Studies and Stuff: Engaging Community" describes the utilization of the community centre as a location for engaging children in culturally relevant learning. "Girls, Sports, and Border Crossing" is a brief essay that highlights the challenges of using sports to build bridges across socio-economic and racial boundaries. "Making Literacy Work for Everyone" describes in detail how a newly appointed literacy coordinator and primary curriculum chair engaged her students, other teachers, the principal, superintendent, city councillor, police, firefighters, and news anchors (among others) in a successful quest to create a school and community-wide focus on literacy for kindergarten to Grade 3 students, while "Africentricity and Other Progressive Practices" provides hands-on ideas for working with social difference. Chapter 7: "Advocacy and Activism: Progressive Curriculum and Pedagogy beyond K–12" focuses on how teachers transcend standards-based curriculum while proactively engaging children and their families in the process. In "Until Difference Makes No Difference," a school board equity officer charts his plan, which moves from a traditional to an advocacy approach grounded in human rights codes.

His work includes empowerment coaching for teachers who are equity advocates in their schools, developing student leaders as advocates, and networking with groups in communities outside schools. "The World of TV Learning" describes programming and online resources that enhance learning at home and promote the rich cultural diversity of the province of Ontario. "EDSJ Has to Be the Way!" explores how a coordinator and instructor within a university-based teacher education program learned how to build an inclusive classroom environment among the teacher candidates through activities, readings, and strategic conversations. "Becoming an Agent of Change" is the first-hand account of a UD graduate from a stigmatized community who, in addition to helping develop some notable equity-based curriculum for grades 1 to 8, became the student achievement officer with the Literacy and Numeracy Secretariat. She details a community-based literacy initiative as well as her experience in building a critical mass of teachers to eventually support her school-wide equity initiative. Finally, "Looking for 'Charlie Brown' in the Classroom" explicates the rigorous self, social, historical, and political reflections of a teacher educator who continues to draw strength and purpose from a deeply disturbing Grade 1 experience with a racist teacher. Also outlined are essential questions that serious social justice educators must ask themselves about their classroom practice.

Notes

1. Since this time the OTQT has been eliminated and replaced by a mentorship/induction program. Interestingly a report by Portelli et al. (2011) demonstrates once again how this new program (due to its centralized design and top-down implementation) is likely to reproduce status-quo inequities in the classroom.

CHAPTER 1
Preparing the Equity Teacher

JORDAN SINGER

The efforts of progressive teacher educators to prepare teachers for diversity and social justice pedagogy have gained some momentum over the past decade. The once dominant assimilationist and other homogenized notions of education are gradually giving way to multicultural curriculum in teacher education scholarship and practice. Notions of equity and social justice in teacher education have also captured the imagination of enlightened educators committed to building a more just and democratic society (Solomon, Allen & Campbell, 2007: 207).

In response to the traditional "cultural encapsulation" of many teachers, calls for teacher education programs to engage with a multiplicity of diversities and prepare "culturally responsive teachers" have increased. A successful social justice–oriented teacher education program, most agree, would be characterized by discernible changes in teacher attitudes and actions regarding social differences both inside and outside the classroom. How these changes can be recognized and understood will be outlined throughout this book. Achieving these often profound changes to teachers' perspectives and actions, it has been theorized, could be achieved only through a progressively based pedagogy framed in an inclusive, culturally responsive curricular design that elucidates manifestations of diversity, components of critical thought, social and political dynamics in historical context, and explicitly articulates and advocates for a clear vision of social justice commitment and action. Programming would have to involve placing teacher candidates with people who encompass a vast range of real and constructed differences, including race, ethnicity, class, culture, sexual orientation, and physical disability. Such potentially novel encounters would have to occur in an environment where *ideally* everyone involved (1) is made aware of the goals of the program; (2) promotes the understanding of and respect for diverse cultures; and (3) supports teacher candidates' intellectual, emotional, and experiential growth.

The Urban Diversity Teacher Education Program at York University, Toronto, Canada, comes quite close to achieving the ideals outlined above, and thus we turn to examine the rapidly changing context(s) within which this program began and now operates.

Present-Day Context

Canada's experience with diversity distinguishes it from most other countries. Our 30 million inhabitants reflect a cultural, ethnic, and linguistic makeup found nowhere else on Earth. Approximately 200,000 immigrants a year from all parts of the globe continue to choose Canada, drawn by its quality of life and reputation as an open, peaceful, and caring society that welcomes newcomers and values diversity.[1]

Between the 2001 and 2006 censuses, Canada's population grew by 1.6 million or 5.4 percent. The majority of this growth is attributed to new immigrants, primarily from Asia, Africa, and Latin America. The accelerated pace at which "visible minority" immigrants are settling in Canada is dramatic. In the census, visible minorities (other than Aboriginal peoples) are defined as those who are non-Caucasian in race or non-White in colour. In 1981, the total percentage of Canadians who identified themselves as visible minorities was 4.7 percent. In 2001, this number almost tripled to 13.4 percent, or a total of 4 million people. The preferred destination for new immigrants continues to be Ontario, where 2.2 million visible minority individuals comprise 19 percent of the population and 54 percent of all visible minorities in Canada.[2]

This increasing diversity is reflected in the many agencies, institutions, government bodies, working groups, and non-governmental organizations that are animated by official policies, commissions, and laws related to diversity at the local, municipal, provincial, and federal levels. Canada also has an official multicultural policy that is legally embedded in the Canadian Charter of Rights and Freedoms, the Canadian Human Rights Act, the Employment Equity Act, the Official Languages Act, the Pay Equity Act, and the actual Multicultural Act. Canada is also very involved in promoting multiculturalism at the international level through international conventions.

Thus, there are many forums to attend to issues of discriminatory practices regarding Canada's diverse citizenry. Taken together they protect freedom of thought, conscience, and assembly, as well as access to social services. The problem is that despite all of these policies and institutional spaces/places that express idealistic sentiments, provide assistance, and make rules that are sometimes supported by the weight of law, discriminatory practices continue to be a common daily occurrence for many of Canada's citizens.

The situation was much the same in 1994 when the increasing inequities of outcome for racialized students and new immigrants in schools were becoming increasingly clear (Working Group, 1992). Fortunately, at this time, the Ontario Ministry of Education recognized that something had to be done immediately to address the academic disparity within schools, and issued a challenge to teacher education programs to develop a program more relevant to the province's growing racial and ethnocultural diversity. York University responded by supporting the development of a progressive teacher education program, the Urban

Diversity Initiative in 1994. Today that initiative has become the Urban Diversity Teacher Education Program.

CONSIDERING THE PARAMETERS OF DIVERSITY AND SOCIAL JUSTICE IN TEACHER EDUCATION: ENVISIONING THE ENDS TO DESIGN THE MEANS

In the process of thinking through an effective and uniquely progressive social justice teacher education program, it was first imperative to identify what needed to be done to create a more equitable education system, one that would have equality of academic outcome for *all* students. In theory, an equitable school/classroom/system is an *inclusive* one in which all voices and experiences are valued regardless of social differences. More specifically, in the words of Dei, Wilson & Zine, (2002):

> Inclusive education calls for the integration of the individual, family histories, concerns, and practices in/to the larger societal collective. Inclusive schooling practices must be both "critical," culturally, socially responsive and relevant and must seek to engender empowerment and transformation in the lives of all learners. (p. 4)

Attempting to design an educational environment that exemplifies equitable practices and ideally accomplishes the seemingly monumental task of justly recognizing and acknowledging the numerous disparate races, ethnicities, cultures, sexual identities, exceptionalities, and differences within school curriculum(s) and teacher pedagogy seems improbable, although not impossible.

Understanding how the public education system's parameters move beyond the traditional markers of home and school into the larger realm of social institutions and political machinations became necessary in thinking through how to change individual, social, and institutional inequities. This meant that bringing about equitable practices and outcomes in our schools by creating inclusive environments required not only transforming individual classrooms, schools, and teachers, but also boards of education and university-based teacher education programs. Furthermore, such transformations necessitated working simultaneously toward changing mainstream culture, popular opinion, and the overall political landscape.

A logical place to begin this transformative project was at the source where teachers themselves learn to teach. Developing a transformative teacher education program presented numerous challenges, the most daunting being raising teachers' awareness of how biases inform their teaching practices. As the designers of the UD program knew from past experience and research, their teacher candidates would not participate in transformative teaching without a change in consciousness and commitment. Part of this process would entail a historical, sociological, and psychological understanding of where, how, and why deeply held biases exist. Raising their awareness of the existence of these biases and of the consequential implications of these biases on their teaching practice was essential because without teachers' acknowledgment, understanding, and substantial commitment to equitable and inclusive educational practice, the aims of social justice education cannot be achieved. Indeed, in our previous book, *Teaching for Equity and Diversity: Research to Practice* (Solomon, Levine-Rasky & Singer, 2003), a cross-Canada survey of teachers revealed much complex and powerful resistance to doing anti-oppressive work, which was substantially related to teachers' racial, cultural, and social class locations. Also, many had misconceptions about the meaning of equity itself, and often believed that any type of focus on race was counterproductive. Moreover, we found that many teachers' classroom practices contradicted their claims of commitment to engaging with the practices of progressive education.

Resistance to doing this work and the misconceptions/perceptions about its complex meaning(s), in addition to the contradictions between teachers' articulated beliefs and their classroom actions, underscore how these social locations profoundly affect our comprehension—often unconsciously—of what equity is, and how in turn these perceptions impact what we do in our classrooms. Considering these difficulties became essential in building an effective social justice teacher education program. Of note here is that all stakeholders—including the faculty of education, teacher candidates, students in schools, parents, colleagues in the field, principals, and even those representatives of government agencies calling for progressive programs—continue to resist the transformative and political aspects of the program.

The Urban Diversity (UD) Teacher Education Program

GENERAL AIMS

The main aim of the program is to integrate equity, diversity, and social justice into all aspects of the theoretical, experiential, and practical aspects of the program. Our specific objectives are to: (1) provide an environment in which teacher candidates of various racial and ethnocultural groups and abilities have extended opportunities to develop teaching competencies and professional relationships in a collaborative environment; (2) integrate issues of equity and diversity into the curriculum and pedagogy of the teacher education program and in the classrooms of practicum schools; (3) prepare teacher candidates to work in urban environments that reflect society's diversity; and (4) develop collaboration among practicum school staff, the candidates, and teacher educators from the university in order to form a community of learners.

The UD program immerses teacher candidates in explorations of "difficult knowledge"[3] areas such as race, ethnocultural identity, class, gender, sexual orientation, and ability. Additionally, the candidates are encouraged to become leaders in their school communities through the mandatory community involvement aspect of its program. Furthermore, Urban Diversity candidates are required to examine and analyze the explicit and implicit linkages within and between theory and practice in relation to all aspects of the teaching and learning process, including a socio-political, historical, and contextual understanding of schools and the schooling process. As a result of these intellectual and experiential requirements, students begin to think and integrate the concept of praxis in their contemplations of what they do in the classroom. In the UD program, praxis is understood as "the dialectical union of reflection and action: it is the notion that theory and practice are inseparable" (Finn & Finn, 2007: 141).

One unique aspect of the UD program is the wide range of racial and cultural diversity of its teacher candidates, which accurately reflects the diversity of Toronto. Such representation is not the norm in *North American* teacher education as the vast majority of teacher candidates accepted into these programs continue to be overwhelmingly White, middle class, and of western European heritage.

The UD program candidate recruitment is allied with York University's Access Initiative (a policy/practice designed to attract groups traditionally underrepresented in the teaching profession). These recruits include: people of colour, Aboriginal/First Nations peoples, refugees, immigrants, and people with disabilities. The initial intake structure of the program required that half of each cohort be from cultural and racial minority groups, and while this intake structure has changed, the cohort has consistently maintained an approximately 50 percent racial and cultural minority student base. By June 2008, the program had graduated over 1,000 teachers.

The primary goals of the Urban Diversity program are as follows:

1. Provide an environment in which teacher candidates of various racial and ethnocultural groups can develop teaching competencies and professional relationships in a collaborative manner.
2. Integrate multiculturalism, anti-racism, and other equity and diversity issues into the curriculum and pedagogy of the teacher education programs and in the classrooms of co-operating schools.
3. Develop collaboration and partnership among co-operating

school staff, representatives of community organizations, York's teacher candidates and teacher educators, forming a "community of learners."

The UD program draws on the aforementioned theoretical and practical work and minimally requires:

- a critical examination of teacher candidate cultural and racial identity
- a problematization of the *power and privilege* inherent in the culture of whiteness
- an examination of one's cultural and racial biases
- a critical analysis of curriculum(s), both tacit and hidden, that recognizes that while the curriculum is designed to teach something specific, it simultaneously also denies and silences particular frames of reference and knowledge bases
- an explicit treatment of how the factors above influence one's teaching practice

The linkages between the engagements above with pedagogical practice are essential as the social reconstructionist philosophy of the program aims at developing "conscientization" (Freire, 1970) among its graduates. Conscientization refers to a type of learning that is focused on perceiving and revealing social and political contradictions. Conscientization also includes understanding one's responsibility to take action against the oppressive elements in one's life and/or the lives of others that oppress their freedom of thought and action.

A fundamental aspect of this type of socially enlightened consciousness is the desire to work toward ending all forms of inequity. In fact, the utilization of critical pedagogical theory is not just about developing critical thinking skills, nor is it "merely about deconstructing texts but [it is] about situating politics itself within a broader set of relations" (Giroux, 2004: 499). Through building such a pedagogical environment, the UD program creates an atmosphere in which students can acquire, interrogate, and produce knowledge for societal change (Banks & Banks, 1995).

The program ultimately aims to produce "culturally responsive teachers" (Ladson-Billings, 1995; Gay, 2002) who utilize "community reference pedagogy" (Schecter et al., 2003). Teachers are aware of and value the wealth of cultural capital that their diverse students bring with them, including their divergent experiences, realities, identities, and learning styles. An indispensable part of this process entails exposing teachers to particular texts, individuals, and experiences that invariably demonstrate that equitable practices often rub against the grain of our Western zeitgeist, most status quo teacher education programs, teacher attitudes, mainstream culture, curriculum design(s), and traditional pedagogical methods. Learning from these struggles, culturally responsive teachers use the insights gleaned from these experiences to transform inequitable reproduction practices by tacitly educating their students to think critically about the moral, ethical, and therefore socially just implications of what forms of knowledge and experiences are most valued in our society and why. As Gay (2002) articulates, "Culturally responsive teachers help students to understand that knowledge has moral and political elements and consequences, which obligate them to take social action to promote freedom, equality and justice for everyone" (p. 10).

By utilizing these disparate though interrelated strategies and instructional practices, the Urban Diversity program aims to produce "transformative intellectuals" (Giroux & McLaren, 1986) who can "adopt a more critical role of challenging the social order so as to develop and advocate its democratic imperatives" (p. 224). Transformative teachers are aware of societal inequities and they see schools as sites of political struggle. They focus on the relationship between knowledge and power, and the relationship between their students' knowledge and their political agency (Finn & Finn, 2007: 51). Specifically, these teachers "create spaces where parents, students, community members, and teachers can become collective actors with the ultimate goal of building powerful social movements that change policy and consciousness" (Finn & Finn, 2007: 51).

CONSTRUCTING THE FOUNDATIONS OF EQUITY IN TEACHER EDUCATION

The UD program consists of courses that are theoretical, foundational, and practical: "Urban Education" (formerly "Foundations and Models of Education"), "Human Development and Socialization," "Communication and Community Development in Education," "Teaching and Curriculum," "Teaching Language/Math," and "The School Practicum." The "Foundations and Models of Education" and now Urban Education course(s) set a philosophical grounding for the program. These interdisciplinary courses are rooted in such disciplines as history, sociology, cultural studies, and comparative education, and are influenced by critical theory, critical race theory, whiteness studies, as well as cognitive and developmental psychology. The course work is interdisciplinary in nature while introducing and integrating the meaning and importance of interdisciplinarity. Moreover, these courses develop an inclusively oriented knowledge base for thinking critically about meta-cognition, issues of thought itself, teaching, learning, schooling, democracy, identity, diversity, equity, social difference, oppression, and social justice. Together with "Human Development and Socialization," as well as "Communication and Community Development in Education," these courses provide the theoretical foundation for classroom practice. (See Appendix 1 for detailed course themes.)

UNIQUE PROGRAM FEATURES
Progressive perspectives on teacher identity

Teachers who know themselves well are in a much better position than teachers who do not know themselves well, to treat students and their families with respect and fairness. If you know why you react to different people the way you do, you have some control over your reactions and can learn to modify them, question them, or grow beyond your present boundaries. If you do not know why you react as you do, interpersonal differences lead to frustration and conflict. (Grant & Sleeter, 2007: 15)

As Grant and Sleeter (2007) point out, teacher identity is a crucial part of educating for social justice. This component of the UD program helps teacher candidates reflect on their own ethnic or racial identity formation, and examine how attitudes, beliefs, knowledge, and world views are developed concerning those who are socially classified as "Other" or different in Canadian society. More specifically, this component helps teacher candidates *locate* and interrogate the status of their own identity development and consider how this may influence their perception of other learners, their own process of learning to teach, and their own, often unrecognized, teaching style and educational philosophy. This theme will be developed more fully in Chapter 4.

Inter-group dyad partnerships

At the time of the cohort group under study, teacher candidates of various racial and ethnocultural backgrounds had the opportunity to work in a dyad team. This combined the sharing of experiences, perspectives, and traditions with the goal of breaking down racial/ethnic barriers and own-group cleavages while encouraging a space for teachers of different backgrounds to engage collegially in long-lasting, increasingly prejudice-free association with, and appreciation of, each other's perspectives, norms, values, and traditions. Additionally, these partnerships provide good modelling and representation of anti-oppressive educational practice for students, schools, and communities.

A service learning approach to teacher education: Community development and engagement

Opportunities must be made for students to work in communities where they can spend time with economically and ethnically diverse populations.... (McLaren, 2003: 170)

Community field experiences help teachers to view pupils not as isolated individuals in classroom, but as members of total family and community environments. (Solomon, Levine-Rasky & Singer, 2003: 133)

One vital aspect of the UD program is to extend candidates' learning from the university and school environments to service learning in the wider community of the practicum school. This involvement in the community connects the social and cultural foundations of education to a critical analysis of schooling, civic responsibility, and community action.

Another key consideration in developing democratic classroom relations is the deep recognition of the importance of students' communities of origin. Students are situated beings who are part of a historical, socio-economic, cultural, and political context. As such, their communities and families are important facets of their identities. Teachers' sensitivity to social difference, empathy to the needs and experiences of diverse student populations, and advocacy for social change are brought together under the banner of community building. Community in this respect reflects from outside the classroom in, and inside the classroom outwards.

Education, as a democratic project, treats students as integral members of a particular context—a family, a circle of friends, a community. Social justice–oriented teachers, therefore, do not treat their students simply as autonomous, isolated individuals, but rather as citizens and individuals in larger social contexts. As one graduate of the program related, teachers often see themselves as "liaison[s] between communities and students, between communities and parents, between parents and administration, between communities and administration, between administration and students" (Mary). The fostering of connectedness with community, students, and parents is instrumental in forging democratic spaces within the classroom.

The UD program's commitment to inclusive schooling recognizes the student as a socially embedded individual and thus attempts to draw from the out-of-school context, which provides much meaning for students. Boyle-Baise (2005) insists that "[t]eachers who practice culturally responsive teaching validate students' life experiences. They teach to the whole child as a student, family, and community member. They utilize the cultures and histories of minority group students as teaching resources and they question universal versions of truth" (Boyle-Baise, 2005: 448). She adds that families are rich resources of knowledge and a key source of learning in terms of life skills, moral teachings, cultural information, and historic memories (Boyle-Baise, 2005: 448).

As with all aspects of the program, the service learning approach is interwoven and integrated throughout. The community involvement component of the teaching practicum course explicitly requires students to identify a need within the communities where they teach. It may be academic, health and safety-oriented, recreational, cultural, social, and/or political. Having identified a need, students are responsible for attending to all of the necessary requirements in setting up a program (or contributing to an existing program) and implementing a project that they have envisioned will address the need they have identified. In the past, these programs have been as disparate as assisting underrepresented parents to be heard by school councils, teaching essential computer skills to parents, and working at drop-in centres for at-risk youth. The programs are designed to last beyond the time when teacher candidates finish their direct involvement. Indeed, some of the teacher candidates' programs have been so successful that they have continued many years after their inception and others are now funded by a local government agency. In sum, the key principles, practices, provisions, beliefs, and dynamics of the program include:

- issues of social justice and progressive education are fundamental in all aspects of the program, including theory and practice
- praxis is fundamental to the process of teaching for social justice

- identity matters for teachers, for students, for teaching, and for learning
- students are intricately linked to their communities, and it is a teacher's responsibility to know and get involved in these communities
- society and therefore schools and the schooling process are fundamentally influenced by race, ethnocultural identity, class, gender, sexual orientation, and ability; accordingly, teacher education must critically address these complex issues
- careful examination of the formal and informal curriculum, evaluating ideological and political influences and how these findings interact, intersect with, and interrupt teachers' perspectives
- practical information, resources, and guidance on how anti-oppressive educational practice may be integrated into regular classroom activities
- holistic integration of diverse ethnocultural information and resources that have been traditionally marginalized
- forging partnerships between parents and schools to foster a "greater sense of critical empowerment for all" (Dei et al, 2000: 31).
- insight is gained and meaning is constructed through students' experiential work in communities of practice, and we require teacher candidates to reflect on how their teacher preparation helps them to work for social transformation

Constructing Meaning from Program Experience

Whether teachers were learning to name their practices, dialogue about practice with colleagues, or convince administrators of socially just practices, theory gave them a language of practice that connected their practices to their beliefs and therefore widened the circles of understanding and influence. (Finn & Finn, 2007: 149)

Congruent with Finn and Finn's (2007) research on teachers, the UD program recognizes the significance of building a language of social justice. This section explores some general issues about teacher preparation within social justice framework. We address the different perspectives of UD graduates toward the program, as well as their perceptions about how their teacher preparation grounded them in the principles and practices of democratically situated anti-oppressive education. More specifically, we explore how teachers construct meanings from their experiential work in communities of practice, and how they reflect on the ways their teacher preparation helps them to work for social transformation.

According to our findings, attitudes toward the UD program were quite complex. Most UD graduates were committed to the idea that an education grounded in the principles of inclusive education and anti-oppressive pedagogy was invaluable to their professional and personal growth as it provided a critical-theoretical and practical lens with which to interrogate their experiences. One teacher candidate summed it up well, saying that this type of education is "a crucial foundation to any teaching experience" (Eric), while another added that such a theoretical foundation is infinitely more important than "having enough lesson plans" (Marisa). What becomes increasingly clear throughout this book, as evidenced in UD teachers' own words, are the profound and lasting effects that this program has had and continues to have on their lives, as well as their professional identity.

TEACHERS' CLASSROOM VOICES

Responses during open-ended interviews clearly revealed teachers' perceptions and feelings about the UD program. One exclaimed, "The program really made me see things in a new light," while another spoke of a desire to "spread the word" to his colleagues concerning anti-oppressive education. Still others who entered with an informed political perspective found the principles of the program and the information learned within UD to be inspiring:

> I went into teaching for political reasons, and a desire to change the world for the better and to level the playing field for certain students in the classroom. And I felt even more grounded in those principles coming out of the program. When I got my first teaching job, it was actually an integrated arts position and my intention was to use that position to teach an equity curriculum, essentially with the arts as a vehicle, and I had a lot of support in doing that. (Ming)

A large number of UD teachers spoke of their desire to transform their schools into more equitable environments. The personal and professional challenges in attempting to dramatically alter the monocultural landscape of their schools are profound and require teachers not only to be knowledgeable professionally and politically, but also to maintain a strength of purpose and a courageous attitude: "I felt as though it [the UD program] was a fountain of knowledge, and that I was given all of the tools I needed. I felt very refreshed and felt as though I could conquer the world" (Carine). Another teacher speaks of the strength of his commitment and purpose:

> For me going in, I felt very inspired when I graduated from the program and very empowered because it gave me the knowledge to take to the classroom. And, yes, there were times where I was faced with a lot of negativity. However, I felt it my goal as a teacher is to go in and inspire. (Zora)

The integration of praxis throughout the UD program means that graduates often forget that inclusive education practices are not the norm: "It [the ability to integrate diversity in teaching] has become so ingrained you don't realize it's something special anymore" (Shannah). Of course, once in the field, UD teachers saw that their progressive ideas and perceptions about their students and communities were at odds with many other teachers' perceptions and beliefs.

MOVING ALONG THE EQUITY CONTINUUM

Different teachers enter the program at different levels of preparation. While some are already committed to certain social justice issues and aware of some aspects of progressive education, others need more preparation. As one teacher remarks:

> I don't think it [diversity effort of other teachers] was grounded as much as, say, some of the work that I was doing because I felt that the work I was doing was theoretically informed by the work in the Faculty [of Education], and I also had a personal interest in it, and I think that by doing the academic work, I found a way to weave it in more rather than just addressing it every so often. (Marcus)

Another participant refers to teachers having different levels of awareness. She comments on how teachers' perceptions and actions move along a continuum wherein teachers' ongoing experiences challenge them to move beyond status quo positioning. The notion of "continuum" articulates teachers' unfolding understanding and integration of progressive education. As she puts it:

> [I]t was really about moving [other teachers] along the continuum, and that was something that we learned about. So my objective was recognizing that all teachers were on different levels of a continuum and how we were going to move them along. (Virginia)

The structure of the program provided a forum for discussion and dialogue about difficult knowledge and challenging issues, as well as providing them language with which to express themselves:

> I found myself much more confident in taking part in those discussions with the background that I had. I felt I had something to say as opposed to sitting there and not wanting to say something that is politically incorrect. I felt much more confident about where I stood and whether that was an okay place to be in relation to these issues. (Amelda)

Another teacher reflects on how the program provided him with the necessary language to express himself:

> The program was the perfect foundation for me because it just verified all the things that I knew as a social worker and as an artist; [it] just sort of cemented everything. And politically it empowered me personally to be able to handle vague notions around where I sort of feel that certain people were getting away with certain things. The program gave me a little bit of language to be able to start from. It's been verified continually. (Eric)

Clearly, these teachers benefited from being provided with a theoretical understanding of others' potential positioning along a continuum, as well as having discussed difficult issues in depth during their teacher education. Accordingly, their theoretical, practical, and experiential backgrounds allowed them to engage confidently and strategically with others by utilizing informed dialogue. For these UD graduates, having the appropriate language and past exposure to complex social justice issues provided them with a politically powerful means of dealing with conflict, which often arises in discussions involving anti-oppressive issues.

Most teachers also contended that their preparation endowed them with the knowledge and sensitivity to teach children in urban situations.

One participant insists that every university should model their teacher education on the spirit of the UD program: "Urban Diversity shouldn't be a specific program that you can apply to. It should be embedded in all teachers' training" (Vera).

Each student who enters the UD program brings varied insights, values, expectations, and experiences. Their distinctive positions not only contribute to the diverse makeup of the UD program, but also greatly influence how they conceptualize the education to which they have been exposed. When they enter the program, many teacher candidates have an idea of why they went into teaching and what constitutes "a proper education" and "good teaching," but most often these ideas are still in development. As the program progresses, their perceptions of the purposes and methods of education, in addition to good teaching, become clearer as the theoretical information provided within the curriculum helps them to more precisely conceptualize their ideas and beliefs. We will now explore the educational philosophies and commitments of UD graduates and how these ideas can be traced to their preparation.

DEVELOPING A PHILOSOPHY OF EDUCATION

The emergent philosophies of education that novice teachers develop range widely in both depth and scope and can be understood partially as a reflection of each participant's own life experiences. Also apparent in their developing philosophies is a dedication to the critical praxis, a result of their teacher preparation and the influence of their subsequent teaching experiences. These philosophies are embedded in the language of memory and remembrance as we trace these recollections over a period of about six to eight years.

Teachers reflected on the changes in their philosophies of education, and on the distinct ways that particular experiences have impacted their perceptions. Specifically, these reflections focus on how their perceptions have been expanded both by education and a growing awareness of the issues encompassed within inclusive education for social justice. Moreover, these recollections describe how these altered perceptions have impacted their families, the manner in which their preparation has influenced their empathy and sensitivity toward others, and the intellectual and emotional experiences through which they have come to understand equity as a fundamental aspect of fairness and social justice as the foundational building block of inclusiveness. What follows is a sampling of these reflections and how the Urban Diversity program fostered these perceptions as our UD graduates commenced their teaching careers.

DEVELOPING A SENSE OF MISSION

Most participants reflected on what they referred to as their mission statements (personal philosophies described in the language of action) in terms that are also couched in the language of equity and social justice. What follows are some representative ideas expressed by the teachers when asked about the importance of being grounded in a philosophical praxis that facilitates equity work:

> Maybe it goes back to philosophy even though it wasn't fully formulated when I first started. You have to have a philosophy, you have to know what your place is in this whole scheme of things because you can have so many different positions and whatever positions you take, it's going to affect how your classroom works, how the curriculum is put forth, and how the kids accept it and how you interact with parents and how you interact with staff and administration. So you have to be grounded in those things because that's what's going to carry you on a day-to-day basis. (Cynthia)

Several teachers described what they felt needed to be done in their classrooms to express their mission, for example, making sure that all of their students were recognized in discussions and represented in curriculum materials. Several expressed that they felt that it was their responsibility to educate other staff members if they were not aware of or practising progressive pedagogy. UD graduates articulated many other aspects, thoughts, and descriptions of their practice that relate directly to their philosophies of education, including:

- the importance of providing a classroom that is a safe and open forum in which to discuss difference
- an ecological approach situated in the community outside of the confines of the classroom; this approach facilitates learning and recognizes that a great deal of learning occurs outside of the classroom
- the creation of a democratic classroom is paramount to doing equity work, and the experiences of one's students should be a common starting point for discussions within the classroom

A common theme among the majority of our participants was a commitment to a culturally relevant pedagogy:

I was using the students' own experiences as a springboard for my program and really wanted to make sure that it reflected them in a very genuine way. I did not want to do a multicultural program in a really tokenistic way. I was very opposed to that kind of teaching style. (Ming)

Another teacher tied together teachable moments, progressive pedagogy, and democratic values with the importance of student participation: "Issues come up and that's how we talked about racism, that's how we talked about stereotypes and about prejudices. It was all through real experiences that were valid for the students" (Zora).

In their descriptions of how their philosophy related to doing equity work, UD teachers suggested that equity should be visible from the moment you walk in through the doors of a school—that equity is part of the environment, part of the curriculum, and part of how one perceives the school—and that inclusive educational initiatives should be aimed at a deeper, more genuine understanding of Others. Also, several insisted that for a goal of inclusivity to be achieved, every contextually viable teachable moment should be used to promote critical thinking about social difference and, accordingly, for diversity initiatives to really take hold, they must be school-wide. As one participant notes, "It has to come from the whole school, it can't just be one person, and you can't just do it on your own; you can't do it in a shell and a vacuum" (Max).

The development of a philosophy of education proceeds at varying paces, and for some, the realization that they do have an educational philosophy occurs as a result of retrospectively discovering which practices are synonymous with one's philosophy and which are opposed:

> I don't think I had a philosophy at the time. I developed one as I went along. It developed in the first year and by the end of it, I could reflect on what had happened. I realized I do have a philosophy that guided how I do things; I don't know any other way. Even though I see teachers doing things completely differently, I couldn't emulate them; I could only do what had been embedded in me during that year that we were in UD. (Cynthia)

Many UD teachers remain unaware that they have developed a philosophy of education and become aware of the strength of their convictions only after discovering that these ideals can anchor them in the face of exhaustion, burnout, or frustration.

> At the time I remember [the course director] talking a lot about knowing your philosophy of teaching, knowing why you teach because you would have moments where you didn't want to do it anymore, and you needed an anchor. I remember thinking what a waste of time until I was in the situation where I felt like [whisper] *I can't do this*. It comes together to help form that foundation which makes *you* a pillar so you stand when you think you can't stand. (Jeanine)

Theses reflections indicate the often powerful feelings many novice teachers have both within and when they emerge from the Urban Diversity program. Throughout the year, they have been immersed in thinking about social difference, otherness, and social justice, only to find that the realities of the schools where they work are very different. Aware of these experiences, the program attempts to develop an expanded sense of patience and scope in teachers' understanding of equity work, especially in preparation for the significant resistance they will face.

Strategies for Change: Facing Resistance

> The one thing that I learned from the UD program is that you may have ideas, but going in full guns blazing and saying this is the change that I need to make very often backfires. It's a subtle process that develops over time. I just started to do things by introducing different theme ideas to students that maybe they weren't necessarily comfortable with or maybe they had heard a little bit about, but didn't know a lot. (Desmond)

Making changes in a school is indeed a "subtle process that develops over time." Most teachers feel that their training in the UD program has been instrumental in helping them develop patience when attempting to "rock the boat." As one astutely recognized, walking into a school and making demands for change based on what she has learned from the UD program is not the best way to initiate change. She mentions that being an observer at first and teaming up with others who are like-minded is of great importance:

> I think as far as colleagues go, you started with the people that you either can learn something from or [who are] ready to change or [are] excited about doing something different. And

> I certainly wasn't going to take people who hadn't a clue what
> equity was. (Marisa)

In a general way, this process of learning to bide one's time and form alliances can be both strategic and emotionally intelligent. Learning about who is on your side or like-minded is important, although it is also necessary to remember that perspective expansion and action is often the end product of an intellectual and emotional process/transformation that often takes time. Therefore, those who may not think likewise now, or who are not willing to act in solidarity with progressive teachers, may change over time, depending on many factors. One major factor that can contribute to these teachers' transformation is the prolonged efforts of progressive teachers to expose them to what they themselves have been exposed to during their teacher education.

PREPARATION AS PERSPECTIVE EXPANSION

This section explores the promise of the Urban Diversity program to help emergent teachers to stimulate awareness of themselves and of Others as they begin to perceive other perspectives and experiences. This ability to put ourselves in others' situations is central to the sensitivity preparation that is at the core of a teaching program committed to principles of equity education. Included in this section are teachers' perceptions of their own struggles to develop a sense of self-awareness, their perceptions of how their emerging understandings impacted their extended families and friends, and finally their perceptions of how their training facilitated a more sensitive and congenial attitude toward colleagues both during the program as well as during their first years as teachers.

> I think the awareness was the biggest thing for me and constantly searching for that knapsack, that thing inside me that I had always taken for granted and made me miss something. And I am still doing that. I don't think I will ever get over doing

that because I don't think you can if you are committed to learning.... I try still to critically look at everything that's going on
around me, and the things that are coming out of me because
you just sort of close your eyes for a minute or slack off, and suddenly it's there or you've missed something or let something go
by and it is kind of a nauseating feeling. So I think the awareness
is the biggest thing. (Amelda)

Complicating the process of expanding self-awareness are intense
feelings, thoughts, beliefs, and experiences that emanate from teachers' socio-cultural locations as part of the middle-class, often dominant, social group. These powerful ontological inclinations exist, in part,
below the level of consciousness, and often arise when teachers prepare
to work in urban inner-city school communities. Indeed, many teachers are surprised by the powerful cognitive-emotional dissonance that
occurs when these often unacknowledged aspects of themselves collide
with their perceptions of themselves as politically committed, equity
conscious, teachers and professionals.

When I went [into the Urban Diversity program] I thought
that I was a good candidate for this, I am very open-minded,
I'm accepting of everyone, and, yeah, I had this wonderful little
world in my head. I wasn't one of those people. I didn't have a
racist thought in my head. I didn't have any issues with people
of colour or anything. I didn't find out I was racist, but I realized that just in growing up the way I did, and growing in the
life I did, just made me ignorant of a lot of the ways that people
lived.... [Through the UD program] I looked at the world with
such different eyes. I look at everything, including the curriculum, and when going into schools, looking at the walls in the
schools to see who is represented and who isn't, seeing how
people are interacting, and not only in classrooms, out in public.
(Amelda)

Teachers indicated that their education in the UD program often resulted in differences of ideas, opinions, and beliefs that stirred up family discussions: "I was asking them [family members] questions that helped them to evaluate whether [odd colour jokes] were appropriate. It was a very delicate thing to start because I was coming out of school; I didn't want to come across as that [high and mighty], although I am sure I did sometimes" (Amelda). An expanded awareness and sensitivity to how intolerance is reproduced extended not only toward family members but also their colleagues in schools. Grappling with difficult knowledge helped to build trust in the classroom while participants were still in the program, and gave them the language and conviction with which to confront difficult knowledge after they graduated. Typically, during the beginning of the program, students learn how to speak and listen to one another with a growing sensitivity toward discussing issues that often create great tension. After the first semester break, the level of trust and community among the teacher candidates increases to the extent that many are able to discuss delicate matters in greater depth, and with much greater personal honesty and interpersonal sensitivity. Incidentally, this process is constantly monitored by staff who, to the best of their ability, attempt to create the pedagogical conditions necessary to bring about these changes in interpersonal, intercultural, and interracial communication and understanding.

These narratives reveal a unique picture of graduates emerging from the UD's progressive educational approach. The experiences that these graduates have undergone, the types of reflections they were asked to engage in, the forms of academic and professional activities in which they participated, and the direction they received from course and practicum leaders all helped them to expand their perspectives. Next, we take a look at the ways that their teacher education helped solidify for them the perspective that equity is a fundamental aspect of fairness and that social justice is a foundational building block of inclusiveness.

Equity as Fairness and Social Justice as Inclusiveness

Central to the UD mandate are the principles of equity and a commitment to social justice. These principles are the driving force of the program. It is therefore not surprising that most participants discussed these concepts as being formative in their teaching practices. On the surface, some participants felt that equity was about fairness and giving each student what he or she needed. However, it is not clear whether or not these students have differentiated equity from equality. Treating everyone equally is not necessarily an equitable practice and, as pointed out in the introduction, equity often involves treating people differently in order to counteract systemic inequities of the past and present. In order to examine whether or not the organizing principle of graduates' pedagogy and curriculum represents the educational preparation received in the UD program, it is necessary to delve a little deeper into teachers' comments.

> Social justice to me means that we are working together to meet each other, and to see eye to eye in a just society, and you have to build it from the foundation up. Its understanding is the basic core. Equity, I see as respect…. So in full equity, I have to take into account where that person is coming from, what they bring to the situation, and how we can work together with what they have brought. (Amy)

These interpretations, and others like them, reveal the complexities underlying an understanding of the principles of equity and social justice. While on the surface they may seem to be straightforward definitions, a deeper study of the implications of these concepts reveals layers of significance that are contextual, meaning-laden, and difficult to pin down. While the participants acknowledged that equity and social justice entail fairness to each individual, this fairness and inclusivity must be embraced within the context of responsibility to a larger group in order to be equitable. One teacher surmises that equity for her means "To treat people in a way that you are recognizing them as individuals in their own right, but also within the larger context of recognizing that everyone has a particular responsibility to the larger group" (Desmond). Responsibility to Others comprises a crucial aspect in the UD program as we simultaneously prepare and empower teacher candidates for their future leadership roles, which entail political action to extend this work beyond the immediate.

Teaching as a Political Activity: Preparing Agents of Change

Another cornerstone of the Urban Diversity teacher educational approach is a conception of teaching as a political activity. Given this type of preparation, many graduate teachers saw themselves as social change agents and political advocates. In fact, all of those we interviewed—whether from dominant or minority groups—perceived their education as embedded within their social identity and, in their analysis, as a result of their pedagogical practice. Some envisioned their role as filling in those things they had learned during their teacher education that were missing in their schools. Most of them saw their mission as change agents and became increasingly active in the school and even at the board level. Various teachers found that their ability to apply the knowledge and tools acquired in UD largely depended on the school setting and whether or not it was homogeneous or diverse. They felt that the racial and cultural multiplicity of the student population makes the most difference, whereas it is harder to educate students about diversity issues in a homogeneous school because students lack knowledge of other races, and UD teachers subsequently regarded them as very close-minded. Some entered the field with a mission to provide and educate teachers, staff, and administrators with new perceptions and expectations of their students. In one teacher's words:

I think initially I saw myself as a change agent, and so I went in there thinking that I could change the school, that I could help all the children there and, more specifically, the ones within my class, but certainly make them feel included, make them feel valued, respected. (Donnette)

I saw a space where I could start in my own classroom and over the years was able to become more of a change agent in the school and even in the board. My focus has always been anti-racist and equity teaching. That's always been a personal passion and why I went into the program to begin with. (Sakshi)

I felt that the Urban Diversity program really did ground me in a lot of equity materials as far as curriculum and around issues of social justice, and I, too, found that my mission was to be a change agent in the school. (Virginia)

UD teachers identified as change agents and actors with the knowledge and responsibility to engage in anti-oppressive education. They spoke often of their approach to integrating progressive educational practices within their classroom pedagogy. They articulated how their preparation grounded them in integrative teaching practices that simultaneously appreciate differences and similarities. The preparation they received gave them a sense of urgency in their teaching and the knowledge that what they do has political ramifications.

One UD teacher commented that the way in which the program broke down the politics of schooling, its history, the institutional culture of schools and schooling was seminal. He argues: "It made me political. I realized that I had to be political and I saw the value in that. I think that if you don't become political, somebody could politicize you because they know what they are doing." (Eric). His belief in the importance of understanding teaching as a political act also implies the politicization of other teachers: "We might as well get it out in the open and let teachers know that teachers are political beings" (Eric). Another graduate noted the importance of teachers seeing themselves as advocates for their students: "I think they [teachers] have to be more political, they have to be advocates, and they have to look at the long-term effects that they have on students and on society" (Donnette). The political nature of their work was echoed by Virginia:

> I think teachers have to start seeing that their roles are political. The very fact that you are educating our youth and that you bring into the classroom and teach your own biases, or that you have special privileges as a teacher, wherever you are on that spectrum, it comes across to your students within your classroom, so it is a very political role. I think they have to be more political; they have to be advocates; and they have to look at the long-reaching effects that they have on their students and on society. (Virginia)

Part of being political involves strengthening teachers' convictions and a corollary desire to speak up about discrimination. For one particular teacher, speaking up occurred while she was learning about what inequity looks and sounds like, and while she was just beginning to understand how to strategically protect herself and make a difference. What makes this teacher even more courageous is that she was in her practicum placement within a cross-race co-teaching partnership.

At one point in their partnership, both teacher candidates became very upset after consistently observing that their mentor teacher had an extremely negative attitude toward her poverty-stricken students and students of colour in an inner-city school. It was clear to these teachers that their mentor teacher had "written off" these students because of their backgrounds. Her negative attitude was not only obvious to these teacher candidates, but also to the students in her classroom. Unfortunately, this situation is common among many middle-class teachers who work in urbanized environments and find themselves unwilling and unable to effectively teach these racialized and poverty-stricken children. The teacher candidates in this dyad were unsure of what to do and how to act in a situation where they had little power and where children were being hurt. After much contemplation, they decided that it was their responsibility to get advice from the principal. Key to their plan of action was to document what occurred in the classroom. Amelda describes it as a key professional learning experience:

> I think that affected the way I've dealt with people since then.... I remember probably in the past being in situations where somebody might say something that was inappropriate and getting that kind of uncomfortable feeling, but not really doing too much about it, just feeling uncomfortable. After that year, I was much more apt to say something. (Amelda)

Preparing Students for a Democratic Society

Fundamental to the notions of equitable practice for social justice is a vision of democratic pedagogy that opens up spaces for dialogue; reduces social oppression; and works toward a more informed, respectful, and inclusive way of living with our differences. Progressive education is based on the interdependent aims of preparing beginning teachers to teach democratically and to learn how to equip their future students to strive for a democratic society. There are three aspects of democratic education that teacher candidates perceived as central to an education grounded in democratic ideals: (1) stimulating awareness both in teacher candidates themselves and in the students with whom they interact; (2) being effective role models; and (3) facilitating respect for communities from which students originate. Here we outline a sampling of UD graduates' visions of democratic education.

Stimulating Awareness

While beginner teachers are grappling with ways to deepen their own understanding of inclusive education, they are also working in class-rooms to help students develop a critical awareness of the interrelation-ships between the challenges of globalization and the everyday complexi-ties of dealing with a heterogeneous world. Central to their democratic vision was the ability to see beyond one's immediate context as part of an awareness of other perspectives. As one teacher exclaims, "I could be teaching social studies, I might be talking about Aboriginal cultures or First Nations' cultures, but then I'll say that this is one perspective, here is another perspective, and then I might talk about how when you read a newspaper, you have to realize that you are likely to get just one perspec-tive" (Chantelle). As another participant notes:

> I think the biggest challenge in our school right now is trying to develop greater critical thinking. And actually there are very deliberate things that we are doing right now to bring that in. Being involved in anti-racism is one part of the whole, which includes environmental issues. We started off with [an] environ-mental video in geography and it was very successful; and one we started this year that's an anti-racist video which is a co-curricular venture with the history department. (Eric)

UD teachers argue that along with teaching critical thinking, it is impor-tant to help students reflect on things that are happening in the world around them and to introduce different points of view. One reflected on the value of asking questions: "my goal for [the students] is to challenge them, to make them question things that they believe right now so they can look at things more broadly and not so squarely" (Katerina). Another connected the significance of critical thinking to school culture. Initially, he observed that critical thinking was lacking among the students them-selves in his new school, but after well-coordinated school-wide initiatives to increase critical thought were put in place, the results were obvious and gave the entire school environment much greater depth.

Also, appreciation of the value that diversity brings to everyone is synonymous with a democratic education in the context of a multicultural and multiracial country such as Canada. In practice, many UD teachers described this as "awareness-raising" pedagogy. They described the importance of informing those students who live or go to school in homogeneous environments that they live in the most diverse city in the world and contextualizing their students' location in a somewhat homogeneous, culturally sealed bubble.

One teacher passionately expresses her vision of a democratic society: "I need to tell you that I think the hope for this truly democratic society lives with teachers, but I think they have to change teacher training, they have to change teachers' colleges. I think if you want to change the culture of teaching, you've got to start with the teachers; they've got the greatest impact and to do a much better job means they need to be better trained" (Jeanine). These teachers all opined that the lack of an inclusively based democratic education at home and at school contributed to students' lack of critical thinking. In all cases, the teachers perceived that it was their role to extend an understanding and appreciation of social difference and otherness to their students and to their students' homes. Generally, UD teachers argue that while stimulating students' awareness remains the teachers' responsibility, it is crucial that adequate teacher education be provided to teachers so that they can be best prepared to deal with the challenges confronting them in the classroom and to help their students develop the critical awareness needed to become responsible democratic citizens in the classroom.

A Community of Respect and Respect for the Community

My first mission was to ... respect the different communities that a school serves. (Shannah)

In addition to stimulating critical awareness in students and acting as role models for them to emulate, teachers perceived the value they placed on the inclusion of community within the classroom as central to an education grounded in democratic ideals. Rather than simply focusing on the students in the classroom, UD teachers recognize the importance of community both as the space from which their students arrive each day, as well as a rich resource from which to draw. They felt that respect for the different communities served by the school should be taught, and that students should be encouraged to connect directly with their immediate environment. "It is important to create a good relationship between the school and outside community. This can be achieved by inviting community members to the classroom to speak with the students about their knowledge and experiences." Donnette speaks to the fact that students cannot be isolated from their socio-ethnic, geographic, and familial context. To do so is to devalue their identity, family, culture, and often their race and ethnicity. Moreover, UD teachers maintain that this understanding must be premised on an integrated and respectful rather than an additive and deficit-oriented notion of community. An appreciation of the values and knowledge base that students bring with them to class is crucial in fostering and demonstrating respect for their students' communities of origin and the importance of trying to ensure that the children saw themselves reflected in the school culture and curriculum.

In the same way that the social justice teacher strives to make students feel empowered through fostering a sense of belonging to a community, she or he also helps include parents within the classroom:

> We have the opportunity to build a direct relationship with people who, for the most part, trust us. You know, you are going to get your parents who are going to curse and carry on, but for the most part, if you can get parents in and show them that what you want to do is partner with them for the success of their kid, there

is not one parent who doesn't want their child to be successful. We need to come up with better ways to make parents feel welcomed and true partners, and it means giving them a voice in the curriculum, giving them a voice in some of the policies. (Jeanine)

Remarking on involving the parents in the political process at school as a way of fostering inclusion and community, one insightful UD teacher states:

I would really try to get the parents all involved with regard to the parent council and school council. Encourage them to come to the school at anytime, go into your child's classroom, see how the teachers are teaching them, and be actively involved. And third, I think I would just want students and teachers and parents to know that my door is always open any time they want if they have a concern or a question or if they are not sure about anything, come and see me. (Frank)

By bringing parents and the community into the classroom, students feel less of a divide between their lives at school and their lives outside of school. Through forging such partnerships, a synergistic integration between school and community is built and maintained, helping to break down the traditional sense of alienation many parents from marginalized populations, immigrant families, and inner-city communities feel with regard to schools, schooling, and the educational system. This kind of empowerment in turn can act as a catalyst to help students feel more welcome in their schools and feel more of a sense of belonging, a key feature of democratic schooling that can further students' desires to engage in dialogue, critical thinking, and change.

Discussion: Theorizing Education for Equity and Social Justice

Through their preparation in the UD program, teachers were grounded in the theoretical and practical issues and challenges of fostering inclusive and equitable educational environments. As a result, they developed a praxis-oriented mission statement that represented their progressive pedagogical aims; in other words, they documented in detail what they wanted to accomplish, how they might accomplish their aims, and what success might look like. With the tools gleaned from their own progressive teacher education, they approached the workforce empowered with confidence and visions filled with being leaders engaged in advocacy work. They wanted to initiate change and were armed with a democratic commitment to challenge students who would, in turn, confront and alter the status quo reproduction of power. To do this, they engaged in a plethora of strategies in their classrooms that were often first encountered in the UD program where they were encouraged to develop their own philosophy of education and a commitment to action that led them to assume various leadership roles. These qualities were indirectly and sometimes directly passed on to their students, who often became enlightened carriers of the inclusive principles of living in a democratic and pluralistic society.

The model of progressive teacher education in the Urban Diversity program has made these teachers more aware of their own cultural assumptions, more sensitive to cultural differences, and more knowledgeable about their students' communities and cultures. If such a model were adopted by other teacher education programs, our schools would be much less engaged in assimilative modes of schooling as its teachers would be more responsive to the unique needs of individual students from diverse backgrounds. The experiences relayed by graduates of the program who are now engaging in equity and diversity work in their respective schools prove the significance of such a program.

Notes

1. Department of Citizenship and Immigration Canada, Canadian Heritage: Multiculturalism website (2008), http://www.pch.gc.ca/progs/multi/respect_e.cfm, p. 1
2. Government of Ontario, Office of Economic Policy: Labour and Demographic Analysis Branch, *Factsheet 6* (November 2007), http://www.fin.gov.on.ca/english/economy/demographics/census/cenhi06-6.html
3. We are using Britzman's (1998) concept of "Difficult Knowledge" in this book to refer in a general sense to knowledge that incites the ego to defend and/or revise its contents. In other words, knowledge that fundamentally challenges our identity—who we believe we are, what we think we believe in, and, by implication, how we understand and value "Others" at both a conscious and unconscious level of recognition.

CHAPTER 2

School Reform as Inequity:
The Case of Standards, Standardization,
and Accountability

R. PATRICK SOLOMON AND JORDAN SINGER

Just remember that it's the kids we are teaching, not the curriculum. (Sakshi)

Over the last few decades, mainstream initiatives to reform education have put into practice standardized measures in an effort to increase the quality, rigour, and accountability of public education. In Ontario, and increasingly in other parts of Canada, there is a deeply entrenched mindset that standardizing education is a logical course of action that will improve the quality of schooling. Indeed, in many parts of the world, efforts to standardize different aspects of schooling have become commonplace. Cooper and Jordan (2003) point out that there have been three main waves of educational reform over the past two decades. The first wave of reform focused on raising standards and did little to change the fundamental nature of teaching and learning, "schools were simply asked 'to do more of the same, but just do it better'" (Cooper & Jordan, 2003: 385). The second wave of reform focused on the redistribution of power within the school system as it aimed to decentralize control of curriculum, budgets, and staffing to principals, teachers, and parents. The third and present wave aimed to recentralize and redistribute many key aspects of control over education to locations and people external to the daily machinations of schools. Furthermore, the current wave of reform is also based on a fundamental shift in how some educators and policy-makers view the purpose of education. This shift in perspective, influenced by neo-liberal and neo-conservative ideologies as well as business interests (as detailed in the introduction), views the function of education as preparation for the workplace and the generation of capital. The current wave does not bode well for a progressive and democratically centred educational perspective where issues of social justice and equity are taken seriously. As Cooper and Jordan (2003) have asserted, anti-racist and other emancipatory pedagogies are *not* embedded in the present wave's understanding of the purpose of education.

Central to the current reform movement is the desire to equip newly graduated teachers and their students with the necessary skills and technological know-how to become more competitive within a market-driven international economy. To do this, an attempt to standardize the knowledge that students receive across all the provinces and territories has been undertaken. National standardization reflects a belief that everyone should receive an identical education and be subject to the same assessment procedures. Thus, a student living in Alberta, for example, would receive an almost identical education as a student living in Ontario. It is thought that by providing an identical education for everyone, everyone will benefit equally.

A wave of standardization in Ontario began in 1995 with the election of a Conservative government. A new curriculum was introduced for grades 1–9, and a provincially standardized report card was created. In 1996, the Education Quality and Accountability Office (EQAO) was established. This arm's-length body of the provincial government was formed with the expressed intention of evaluating and reporting on the quality of publicly funded elementary and secondary education in Ontario. System-wide testing and the dissemination of the test results to the public began. Standardized testing commenced in 1996–1997 with Grade 3 reading, writing, and mathematics tests. This was followed in 1998–1999 with Grade 6 reading, writing, and mathematics assessments. In 2000–2001 mathematics tests for Grade 9 were administered, followed by the Grade 10 Ontario Secondary School Literacy Test in 2002.

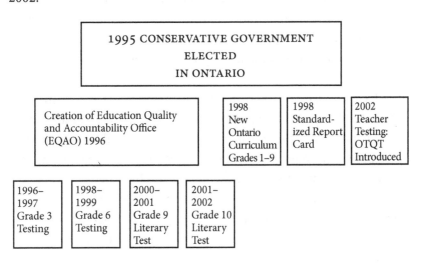

FIGURE 2.1

While these reform initiatives are intended to raise standards of education, it is unclear what impact so-called improvement measures have on the perceptions and practices of teachers grounded in the principles of equity, diversity, and social justice. This chapter focuses primarily on Urban Diversity (UD) teachers' perceptions of the notion of standardization, both in terms of a standardized curriculum and the push to standardize teacher preparedness through qualifying tests, induction, and mentorship programs. In so far as the population of teachers who participated in this study were demographically, ethnically, and socially diverse, their perceptions of the issues of standards and standardization also diverged. Here we focus on the particular perceptions, which we found were generally based on UD teachers' different understandings of what it means to standardize education and how standardization might impact their equity work. While some were very critical of standardization in general, others were more discerning in their judgments. Also, while most UD graduates spoke negatively about standardization with regard to teacher preparation and the standardization of the curriculum, others were somewhat more favourable. Less representative were those who were generally indifferent to issues of standards and standardization. Permeating UD teachers' reflections was the notion that standardization as a policy and as a practice was antithetical to issues of inclusive education.

We have divided this chapter into two sections. Each part includes UD teachers' perspectives on standardization in its different manifestations, including how they see it impacting their general teaching performance, as well as their personal and professional attempts to teach for equity and diversity. In Part 1, we address teachers' perceptions of the province-wide standardized test and we explore teachers' perceptions of the new curriculum itself. In Part 2, we elucidate teachers' contradictory and conflicting perceptions about a relevant yet extremely contentious example of standardization that has recently become central to the history of pedagogy and policy in Ontario: The Ontario Teacher Qualifying Test (OTQT). While we have divided the chapter in this manner for deconstructive purposes, it is important to note that UD teachers' perceptions of these different aspects of standardization need to be understood in a holistic way. The main themes we explore in the first part of the chapter include: (1) how the standardized curriculum produces conflicting and contradictory responses in UD teachers; (2) key challenges associated with the standardized curriculum; (3) teachers' understandings of how the standardized curriculum and standardized testing neglect issues of equity and multiculturalism in society; (4) insight into how the standardized curriculum bureaucratizes learning and teaching; and (5) liberatory practices that can make the integration of equity and social justice issues possible. In Part 2 of the chapter, the main themes we reveal include: (1) UD teachers' general perceptions of standards and standardization and how these strictures impact equity work; (2) their perceptions of the government's impetus for initiating standards-based policies; (3) how they interpret the value of a high-stakes test for evaluating teacher performance; and (4) their insight into the impact of standardization on teachers' attitudes toward the profession of teaching.

Part 1: The Inequities of Reform: Standardizing Student Knowledge

We focus on UD teachers' perceptions of standards-based reform in the context of the Ontario curriculum, which came into effect in 1998 to replace the common curriculum (1993). The stated impetus of these reforms was to raise educational standards. Thus, designing a demanding curriculum that would challenge students and develop the necessary knowledge and skills to meet provincial, national, and international standards was the main goal of these reforms. To acquire this uniformity, the curriculum would consist of a set of clear and distinct standards that students would have to achieve. These performance indicators specified and identified students' present level and placed them within a four-tiered rubric. In addition to these changes, students in grades 3, 6, 9, and 10 would have to write standardized tests in literacy and numeracy, which were created by the Education Quality and Accountability Office (EQAO). In their attempts to implement the standardized Ontario curriculum and the EQAO standardized tests, UD teachers reported many difficulties. We will now explore these problems in detail. Teachers who participated in this study perceived the general impetus behind the Ontario curriculum as antithetical to education grounded in the principles of equity, diversity, and social justice. While most participants spoke negatively of the curriculum, many simultaneously indicated that their teacher preparation helped them find ways to strategically modify the Ontario curriculum and engage in teaching that honoured anti-oppressive principles. Here we focus on UD teachers' perceptions of the extent to which the standardized curriculum affected their thinking and teaching. The main themes we uncovered included perceptions of how a standardized curriculum produces conflicting and contradictory responses in teachers; key challenges associated with a standardized curriculum; teachers' understandings of how a standardized curriculum neglects issues of equity and multiculturalism in society; teachers' perceptions of how standardization bureaucratizes learning and teaching; teachers' observations of how a rigid curriculum can stifle anti-oppressive education; and, finally, strategies to modify the standardized curriculum for social justice aims. We will explore how these themes intersect and converge to produce a particularly powerful picture of how the UD teachers in this study imagined the Ontario curriculum and how they struggled to traverse its measured landscape.

PERCEPTIONS OF THE STANDARDIZED CURRICULUM
Contradictory and conflicting responses to standardization in the classroom

What follows are some generally positive responses to the Ontario curriculum:

> I like the curriculum, although I just think it's too much.... I like it because there are definite skills that the students need to know. It's very obvious what the students have to know by the end of Grade 5—math skills, language skills, but the question is: Do they have to know all the different systems in the human body? Is it really important? Are they going to remember that 20 years from now? So it becomes hard to avoid getting into that expectation trap. I have to meet every single expectation, the students have to know all this information, and it becomes a trap for teachers.... But I can feel the pressure to meet all of them. You don't report on all of them, but that doesn't mean you are not working on all of them or the majority of them. (Max)

While the tone of the preceding narrative is somewhat positive, it reveals what most UD teachers expressed in some form or other as an underlying aversion for the standardized curricular measures. However, it is important to note that this distaste exists alongside the desire to approach the curriculum in a more positive way, as indicated in the following three quotes by the same person at different times during her interview: "The curriculum expectations are there to help those teachers who maybe aren't exactly sure as to 'What should I target specifically?'... I think you need to be creative using the documents, so I see it in a more positive way" (Stella). "For some teachers, it [the curriculum guide] can be viewed as a good resource tool, a very good basis to start" (Stella). "I find that it is a very restrictive document" (Stella). Over the course of the entire interview, this teacher revealed that her feelings and thinking about the curriculum were both conflicting and ambivalent, alternatively describing it as a guide for those who "maybe aren't exactly sure" what to do, as a creativity promoter, as a good resource and starting point, and, at one point, as a "very restrictive document." At first glance, these comments seem to indicate that the teacher is simply contradicting herself. A closer look, however, reveals the extent to which she, like many UD teachers, feels torn about how to approach the new documents. Above all else, these teachers expressed their commitment to facilitate a curriculum that offers a high standard of education for all children. The same teacher declares: "I really do believe that everyone in Ontario should have equal education, and I think that was the main premise for creating these documents. How do we get everyone in Ontario, everybody in Canada, on the same page so to speak, doing the same things?" (Stella). Similarly, another teacher indicated that it is important to have high standards, and that a curriculum that would assist teachers in helping students to attain higher educational achievement levels would be welcome. "I'd feel much more comfortable going in and knowing at least the guidelines of where I need to be by the end of the year.... I think a standardized curriculum and testing might help at some point to explore areas of potential growth in schools. I think learning outcomes are fine" (Amelda). Although this teacher had mixed impressions of the standardized curriculum, she showed support for it as a guide, as a means to demonstrate deficiencies in the schools, and as an instrument to control what is being taught in the classroom.

The preceding comments from several teachers accurately represent many of the voices that were heard. Their comments delve into the complexities involved as teachers struggle with how to approach the Ontario curriculum. Central to this struggle is the conflict between their desire to develop a curriculum that *does* indeed achieve high educational outcomes, and their simultaneous suspicion of standardized measures to achieve such outcomes. In other words, while maintaining high educational standards is a focal point for these teachers, there remains the deeper and more poignant question of whether it was necessary to standardize almost all facets of education in order to achieve this goal, and if by doing so, this goal might never be reached. In sum, most UD teachers felt overall that the current direction of standardizing curricular material was actually not conducive to achieving higher educational outcomes for students because the new curriculum (1) is not developmentally appropriate; (2) is "very restrictive" and riddled with contradictions in structure and content; and (3) is premised on political rather than educational aims. Regarding this last point, UD teachers believed that the reason why the new curriculum does not seem to coincide with actual teaching activities and the daily work of classroom teachers is precisely because the "standardization" initiative was politically and not educationally motivated. "What is completely contradictory to me is I believe that the reform has actually very much discouraged accountability. It has helped the teachers to simply follow a prescribed method.... I think the objective [for creating the standardized curriculum] was a political objective, not an educational objective" (Jailin).

Key Challenges Associated with the Ontario Curriculum

One of the central concerns that UD teachers had with the Ontario curriculum was that the expectations were overwhelming. Given the context in which they were expected to work, teachers vehemently described how the Ontario curriculum's imposed expectations were not only unrealistic, but also very limiting. Issues regarding the number of content expectations, of time and time management, of the bureaucratization of education, and of insufficient resources were central to teachers' perceptions in this regard.

CONTENT EXPECTATIONS

Representatives in this study describe the Ontario curriculum as overwhelmingly dense in the sheer number of content expectations it laid out. Thus, they articulated, its focus on discrete bits of knowledge was not conducive to enabling children to delve deeply into any particular area. "I think the curriculum expects a lot. And to have to cram that into eight months is difficult, and if kids fall behind, well, I'm sorry, that's the way it is and it's really unfair.... The expectations are just wild. There are too many. I'd rather let the students understand something very well than to get a little bit from here and a little bit from there" (Perron). For many teachers, having to satisfy the large number of content expectations means teaching in a very rigid manner under limiting conditions:

> I think the curriculum is a bit limiting. If I'm trying to address curriculum content in a meaningful way, it's hard, it's a challenge. I get frustrated sometimes because I would like to spend some more time on a certain subject. (Marcus)

> The curriculum is so intense and it is so full and so structured [that] there is little deviation. And there are no expectations in there that even deal with diversity. I mean, sure you can stretch it, which I do, but there is nothing in there that really deals with

it in an obvious way so it's been very difficult to justify doing equity work. (Chantelle)

UD teachers were under the distinct impression that if they did not cover the expectations, their students would fall behind in upcoming years. As a result, many indicated that they were forced to "teach to the curriculum" so that they would not have to endure the pressure of being perceived as the weak link in the so-called chain of excellence in addition to creating undue hardship for their students in the future. "You don't want these kids to fall behind because now they are young and you want them to keep up ... so you have to meet all of what is required in the curriculum so they can make the transition to the next grade" (Perron). Having to "teach to the curriculum" often meant that one had to leave out important teaching topics and discussions that are not explicitly stressed in the curriculum.

> I think what happens is teachers become overloaded, and what starts to be weaned out are all of things that have to do with teachers taking more time to look into issues of diversity, multi-culturalism, and doing all different celebrations and discussing different cultures. That's the first thing they start to wipe out, and that's where I think the overload of the curriculum is causing stress because a lot of us are not teaching exactly, I think, how we would like to teach. We are so worried about making sure that every point is covered. When the curriculum first came out, I had checklists and was checking every strand because it was so overwhelming. You lose the natural flow of teaching because you become so stressed about the curriculum. (Zora)

The preceding quotes are representative of the prevalent notion that, as a result of the expectations indicated by the Ontario curriculum, teach-ers must constantly prioritize what *is* indicated as important within the curriculum and eliminate almost everything that is *not*. Often what become ignored are the humanities, such as art, music, and drama, in order to focus on math and language skills. Unfortunately, as a result of the added pressure of meeting numerous expectations unrelated to the humanities, math and language are often taught in isolation rather than in an integrated, interdisciplinary, cross-curricular manner. Most of the UD teachers found that the overextended curriculum affects both teachers and students in negative ways, leaving them all feeling quite stretched and devoid of much of the joy that they experience in teaching and learning. Moreover, they advocate for fewer expectations, which would allow them the time and energy to focus in depth and in more detail on fewer ideas, topics, and themes rather than doing a quick survey of innumerable minutiae.

TIME AND TIME MANAGEMENT
Related to, and indeed stemming from the number of content expectations laid out in the new curriculum, are the issues of time and time management.

> I find the curriculum wants you to do a million things—not necessarily very well—so there is not enough room to have student engagement in there. Social and critical engagement about a subject, combined with inclusive education and critical thinking, takes time. I think that's the frustration that I have: How do I take the complex things and fit it into 25 expectations? I know [how] to get there, but it's a challenge and I've been teaching now for going on eight years. (Marcus)

This teacher raises the very salient point regarding the relationship between time and learning. The process of learning tends to be latent and as this teacher remarks, sometimes "students just don't get it," especially when they are rushed through "a million things." When time considerations become paramount to the learning project, it becomes exceedingly difficult to do justice to any type of learning that involves deep and critical engagement, but especially to learning that involves issues of equity and social justice. Several teachers in our study suggested that the only way to prioritize social justice content was to try and integrate diversity when the opportunity arises on a daily basis.

ISSUES OF INSUFFICIENT RESOURCES AND BALANCING DIFFERENT TEACHING DEMANDS

The issue of insufficient resources is not unique to the new curriculum, and having to balance a litany of teaching demands has always been a part of teachers' working lives. The fact that the introduction of new curricular documents was not accompanied by what UD teachers considered adequate resources (both financial and otherwise) was an immense concern. The lack of resources placed substantial, additional demands on teachers. What follows is a sampling of teachers' thinking about this subject.

> You've given me this wonderful curriculum and you said, "Okay, here, teach this, and teach about the Islamic influence and Muslim influence during the medieval times." Great! Give me something to help me because, unfortunately, a lot of books that might be readily available in another country we don't have here. (Sandra)

> A lot of the teachers are happy to embrace the curriculum. There aren't enough workshops, there is little being offered to them.... There is no money, the school boards say there is no money, and administrators say there is information out there, but it is not being passed down to the people that need it so we can facilitate the curriculum. (Katerina)

> When the government switched to the new curriculum, I had all these units. I was looking at them in the summer and I was

trying to think what can I use from these excellent units into the new curriculum and there was nothing, absolutely nothing. The students are not embracing the new curriculum at all, and I would say that's across every subject area. It's just not there. I mean, in social studies, for example, in Grade 6 we might be talking about First Nations' culture, but it's related to global trade, it's not encompassing equity and diversity. I was looking at their history from a world perspective. It's in isolation. (Chantelle)

Insufficient information and financial resources, compounded with the tight time schedules and the overwhelmingly dense curricular expectations, present a difficult situation for teachers in terms of their pedagogical freedom. UD teachers also indicated that even when the curriculum does prescribe content that teachers feel *could* be meaningful, it is framed in an isolated manner. As in the statement above, if First Nations culture is represented in the curriculum from the perspective of global trade, then their culture is being introduced and depicted in isolation from its politically and historically relevant context within Canada and North America. The introduction of this topic (First Nations culture) in a socially, historically, and politically decontextualized manner means that the most likely focus in a classroom (which does not have a social justice–oriented teacher) will be on the transmission of discrete bits of knowledge to students, here concerning First Nations trade. In addition, if important topics of study are introduced in such a decontextualized way, it becomes very challenging to integrate curriculum resources for multiple uses. The most prevalent consequences of these real and perceived restrictions, which were mentioned in our study, is that teachers feel it necessary to skip over content that they believe is important from an equity perspective if it does not lend itself readily to immediate consumption and/or curriculum outcomes. Often, as a result of this tension between their desires and the curriculum, graduates feel overwhelmed and underprepared. Unfortunately, this is a situation that has the potential for new teachers to be perceived as deficient *if* they do indeed spend the time necessary to discuss important issues in depth and in context, at the expense of decontextualized information.

The UD teachers feel the curriculum is also eroding their capacity to engage in teaching as an ongoing learning project. Instead, many feel that the curriculum is forcing them to become mere technicians "programmed" to follow a given guideline in "a prescribed manner." Others indicate that the content of the new curriculum has impeded teachers' ability to teach in more engaged ways, and that this, in no small measure, is a result of a lack of funding. "The curriculum does restrict the integration of inclusive education, especially because so much money has been cut. We are not able to get the books that we need to really promote those issues" (Teresa). The cuts to which this teacher is referring are those outlined in Chapter 1, which were made by the Conservative government during their Common Sense Revolution. At that time, the government withdrew $1 billion from the education budget. Our UD teachers drew parallels between a curriculum that negates the "human" aspect of teaching and learning with the politically motivated overhaul of the Ontario curriculum by a government openly hostile to education.

As teachers attempt to balance the demands of the curriculum with other teaching obligations, they simultaneously struggle to honour the impulse to teach in ways consistent with their anti-oppressive stance and that benefit the students with whom they are entrusted.

> I know that part of my job to empower is to have them become critical thinkers and be mindful of different issues. But also I know that I want them to be able to write a paragraph because they have to be able to pass the standardized test. I have to empower them, but my way of empowering them is to go slower. (Marcus)

> You have to give your principal an outline of what you plan to do at the beginning of the year, but I basically wrote what they

wanted to see. Just because something is on paper doesn't mean it's right, and I really felt that in my heart, so I decided to do something different than what I wrote down. Many teachers are doing this—it's just not me. (Teresa)

It is significant that many UD teachers perceived the demands of the standardized curriculum and the demands of having to teach real children to be at odds as teachers had to "bring themselves back" and "remember" that it is the "kids we are teaching and not the curriculum."

Engaging in Equity Work: The Antithetical Relationship between Accountability and Democratic Education

Participants have serious concerns about how standardization adversely impacts the equity teacher's ability to engage in sustainable social justice work. A great tension between how standardization promotes prediction, measurement, and accountability, on the one hand, and how equity initiatives integrate issues of democratic education, on the other, is central to these concerns. UD teachers feel that the Ontario curriculum devalues issues of equity and social justice. Paramount to these perceptions is that teachers feel they are being driven either to approach equity work as an epiphenomenon to the content specified by the curriculum or to, conversely, find ways to reconceptualize the curriculum in order to integrate issues of progressive pedagogy.

STANDARDIZED TESTS: EQAO

One of the challenges UD teachers expressed concerned the standardized tests implemented by the Education Quality and Accountability Office (EQAO). Nezavdal (2003) has characterized standardized tests as upholding the modernist philosophy of a "factory model of education." Nezavdal also argues that the function of a standardized test can be viewed as a form of "educational ethnic cleansing." In particular, the achievement of marginalized students is *at risk* when standardized tests privilege the dominant group's ways of knowing.

We offer a sampling of some of the general types of comments about standardized testing:

> I'm not very big on standardized testing or outcomes because I find them to be lacking in the real purpose of education. (Martin)

> We don't know a formula for how kids learn, but you know how to support learning and the education reform is not about that. There is a lot of misinformation that goes out to the community. That's very disempowering, demoralizing. (Marisa)

> I feel awful administrating the test—kids asking for help and you can't help them. (Shannah)

> Standardized testing is not going to ever be able to address all the issues or all the different aspects of intelligence that the students are going to bring. So while I understand the need for it, I can't understand how it's going to be executed and done in a way that's going to satisfy everybody or help everybody. (Amelda)

> To have them sit for five consecutive days, writing a test that is asking nonsense questions, is ridiculous. I don't see what point it proves. It doesn't go into their report cards, it's a waste of five days, it makes the child feel extremely stressed, and it makes them feel negative about themselves. (Perron)[1]

These comments indicate the extent to which most UD teachers disapprove of standardized testing. Most participants in this study felt that standardization as an attempt to equalize the ways in which different people are treated, and the concept of equity, which denotes equal treatment as not necessarily equitable, were in conflict. Standardized tests were seen as inequitable and biased since they did not reflect the abilities and backgrounds of all students. The participants were also clearly concerned about the emotional effects of high-stakes testing on students. Not only did they find that such testing is culturally biased, favouring those who have the cultural capital to decode the various content aspects of the test, but it also privileges those who are accustomed to taking tests. At the same time, it forces teachers to "teach to the test" in a narrow, reductionist manner which often requires rote methods. Consequently one's ability to integrate content and diversity across the curriculum is profoundly hindered. Some participants felt that testing puts English as a Second Language (ESL) and English Language Literacy (ELL, formerly English as a Second Dialect), students at further disadvantage because of their lack of familiarity with the language of the test, as well the tests' inherent cultural bias: "The entire test is language-based, the entire thing. It doesn't matter whether it's math or language, it's entirely language-based. So if you are just acquiring the language, that's already a disadvantage" (Perron). What follows is a sampling of comments that demonstrate how, in the opinion of our teacher participants, standardized tests as they are currently implemented are culturally and racially biased:

> I think the standardized testing is culturally biased. I remember administering it. I went for EQAO training and I taught Grade 6 for three years, so I was part of the first wave of teachers that were administering this test, and there were so many things that were on that test that the students had never even heard of; so many different words, such as "regatta." Some of these students have never even gone camping, and there were questions on different equipment that you have to take camping. I think that they are trying to make everyone equal in that sense of the testing, but it's impossible to test kids this way and get a true reflection of their ability. I think that by standardizing everything, it is not going to give a true reflection of these students' ability in that sense if that's where they want to go with it. Kids are going to

end up missing out and suffering as a result of that, and you are not going to get true results of these students' ability. (Francis)

A lot of them are reading passages that they cannot relate to. They have no idea what they mean. They can read the word, they can comprehend the passages, but they just don't have that personal experience that allows them to relate to it. (Eleni)

On the whole, UD teachers spoke about the assumptions embedded within standardized tests: that all children have the same knowledge base and similar prior experiences. The EQAO tests and similarly standardized tests focus on uniformity and sameness as opposed to valuing diversity in the classroom and honouring experiences that students new to Canada bring with them to our classrooms.

THE STANDARDIZED CURRICULUM

Concerns regarding cultural biases were not restricted to the EQAO standardized tests, but also permeated discussion of the Ontario curriculum as a whole. Generally speaking, conversations about the curriculum centred on its Eurocentric cultural bias and its lack of explicit focus on issues of anti-oppressive education. Two teachers provide us with a snapshot of these opinions:

I believe very strongly that the curriculum is a biased curriculum. The Ontario curriculum is inherently biased largely by its omissions. It has encouraged teachers more and more to go inward. Teachers feel like they have more work than they can possibly do, and so they are inherently much more resistant to any idea of doing something that they perceived as extra.... What the government wants to do is to say you can only do what they fund, and most of diversity education is outside the realm of their funding. Therefore, we are in contravention. (Jailin)

Books that address equity and social justice issues tend to cost more than the other books. It's just like when people of colour start doing "regular" things, and for some reason the price of the books go up. (Vera)

Each of these comments highlights the ways which the Ontario curriculum explicitly and implicitly devalues issues of diversity. As the teachers put it, a curriculum that is "biased largely by its omissions" makes it very challenging to integrate issues of equity. Moreover, books that deal with diversity issues are much more expensive than the books normally found in schools, pointing to yet another way that economic realities stand in the way of diversity initiatives and anti-racist education. In addition, since schools were allowed to purchase textbooks only from a prescribed list of approved resources, the onus is on the classroom teacher to be creative and "find spaces of entry" into anti-oppressive ways of thinking and knowing. The UD teachers maintain that the Ministry of Education created a limited curriculum with a lot of "redundancy." One teacher related her experiences while on an anti-racist committee, during which she discovered some very interesting things about the curriculum:

The last year that I was on the committee we wrote a document called *Blurred Vision*. It looked at the Ontario curriculum from an anti-racist perspective.... We deconstructed it from that perspective, and we found that the Conservative government policy-makers have taken out any material or issues relating to diversity. The examples in the Ontario curriculum are very Eurocentric, so we mentioned that in the document. It doesn't tell teachers they have to integrate. For instance, when they talk about pioneers, they talk about [how] the majority of the curriculum is based on European experience. There are two expectations I think that has to do with Aboriginals and how the Europeans helped the Aboriginals. Even the music curriculum and the drama curriculum—there's a wealth of examples that you can use from different diverse communities [that are] all taken out. It's all Mozart and other European artists. So I guess it does restrict a teacher because from reading the curriculum as a teacher, I just have to teach the expectations. (Vera)

Having participated in the analysis of curriculum documents from an anti-racist perspective during her career as an educator, she notes that a fight continues against Eurocentricity in the curriculum. The participant points out that a closer look at the requirements in schools themselves reveals that teachers are not required to seek out diverse material to present to their students. She also notes that previous curriculum materials that dealt with equity, diversity, and social justice have been removed from the "new" curriculum. In consequence, she concludes that the "censored" and fact-heavy requirements of the curriculum restrict teachers' ability to raise diversity and equity consciousness with their students. The removal of content from the curriculum that deals with more than superficial multicultural practices of celebration and food is for some not only tragic but highly suspicious. One teacher asks: "How is it that we have such a multicultural, diverse society and it's not reflected in the curriculum where the expectations are prescribed? It doesn't make sense. We are known worldwide for our multiculturalism, [so] how is it [that] in classroom[s], where our foundations are set as learners, as members of society, that this isn't reflected?" (Alykhan). Comments similar to this reflect the disenchantment many participants have with the new curriculum and how it undermines a more critical understanding of multiculturalism in Canada. Significantly, many UD teachers still work to integrate issues of social justice within their classroom curriculum despite the explicit omissions mentioned above. Conversely noteworthy is that some teachers tend to justify their lack of equity work by appealing to the curriculum's implicit ruling on this aspect of teaching and learning by its omissions.

THE BUREAUCRATIZATION OF LEARNING AND TEACHING

The perception of an increased bureaucratization of education accompanying recent market-based reform deeply informed teachers' critiques of the Ontario curriculum. That schooling is being reconstructed according to economic and business paradigms deeply troubled them while adding further challenges to their work. Many UD teachers believed wholeheartedly that instead of resulting in higher efficiency and accountability, the bureaucratization of education is producing a mechanistic system that reduces teachers to mere technicians and students to "widgets."

I believe that the reforms have actually very much discouraged accountability. It has helped the teachers to simply follow a prescribed method.... My strongest objection is that I believe standardizing the curriculum and the testing suggests that the kids are widgets, are little boxes that all function and act the same, and that no matter where you are in the province, every kid needs the same information, needs it at the same speed, and will be able to regurgitate it back to you in roughly the same way.... What I am trying to say is the very notion of putting a tremendous amount of knowledge-based education into a young child and expecting everyone to do it relatively the same regardless of their background, their language, who they are, and where they are from and then purposefully underfunding any possibility for real remediation and help is totally anti-humane and anti-child. (Jailin)

Many teachers feel students are being programmed. Now, that you have to follow a certain guideline, you have to be a certain type of teacher to achieve what the government wants you to achieve instead of why you truly went into teaching. We went into teaching to guide students to be the best they can be, to see the world from a different perspective, to educate them in all areas.... A lot of teachers are feeling that, no, they have to follow

a script, and a lot of good teachers are leaving the teaching profession because it's being controlled. (Katerina)

The UD teachers commented on how the humanity of the education process and the people within it seemed to be lost through the
bureaucratization of education. What they say is entirely missing from
this business perspective is the importance of day-to-day contact with
students and the understanding that learning also occurs outside the
classroom.

A key repercussion of educational bureaucratization is that the
increased paperwork requirements inundating the educational system add extra challenges to teachers' work, including their capacity to
engage in equity work.

> For me I think the real frustration is the way education is going
> in terms of how teachers are treated in the profession and that
> comes from above. It has to do with the province and the board.
> I think because there are so many things that are expected of us
> and there has been so much cutbacks, that's the frustration for
> me. (Vera)

The frustration that teachers have toward the bureaucratization of
education is compounded by the related issue of what they perceived
as insufficient resources alongside having to balance different teaching
demands, which further complicate their ability to traverse through the
dense landscape of the new curriculum.

Resistance and Liberatory Possibilities

The work that UD teachers do in relation to anti-oppressive education
can be viewed through two competing lenses: resistance to engaging
in equity work and, conversely, finding creative ways to liberate the

curriculum and infuse aspects of democratic education, both of which will now be explored.

OBSTACLES TO EQUITY WORK: RESISTANCE

The UD teachers cited some obstacles that impeded their ability to effectively engage in equity work in the classroom, including time constraints as a result of imposed standardized testing in specific grades, financial cutbacks, and the density of the curriculum documents. Several teachers express representative views concerning these obstacles:

> I would love to do more diversity work, but I find that especially in Grade 3.... We're teaching for eight months and all the other grades have 10 months within which to teach the curriculum. We have eight months because we are preparing students for the EQAO.... There isn't enough time to do what I want to do more of, and that is the most difficult thing. (Perron)

> You try to integrate equity issues into different parts of the curriculum in order to address the expectations, but what I'm finding is more difficult is the actual cutbacks within the system. You lose programs, so you lose the ESL support, you lose the special education support, so it makes it harder for certain students and it makes it harder to deliver the curriculum to them because your help is gone, and without the help, it really is next to impossible to deliver the program no matter how resourceful you really want to be. (Sharlene)

> It's easy to get sidetracked by the sheer number of expectations you are supposed to cover, so it's definitely not impossible to continue to do work of anti-oppressive education, but you really have to look for those entry points because in the middle of a very fast-paced math unit, you have to take that time to try to go and integrate a lot of these issues. (Sakshi)

Although most teachers in this study reflected critically about the difficulties of integrating issues of diversity and social justice into the curriculum, they also observed that some teachers used the fact that the curriculum does not specify equity issues as an excuse not to do anything perceived as "extra." In addition, they also shared the perception that if progressive ideas are not explicitly delineated in the Ontario curriculum, then these ideas will not be addressed by the classroom teacher:

> I think it's kind of an excuse to say that you can't teach equity issues because of the standardized curriculum. (Marisa)

> Teachers are somewhat less willing to look at diversity issues because they are overwhelmed and because they now have a better reason not to.... The students are being used as political pawns at the moment. It doesn't respect their dignity, it doesn't help them. We are already saying we are not teaching in a diverse way; we are not teaching in a way that celebrates the difference of our children because we are turning education into something that is different from what it was meant to be. (Jailin)

> A lot of teachers alongside me felt that we just needed to keep an open mind in regards to teaching to bring more examples of things into the classroom about diversity and equity and we were able to do that. But some teachers think that it is another piece of paper; they feel they have too many things on their plate already in regards to teaching and they don't want anymore. Just because the government is imposing the curriculum upon them, they've already put up a wall, they've already said, "Well, we don't want to do it and we don't have to do it when our door closes. It's our classroom and we are in charge." I find that they put up a wall when they have to look at the equity issue. They feel it is not necessary, they feel it is questionable.

And this is unfortunate, but I think it's because of lack of time, lack of funding, lack of knowledge, and lack of experience in some ways. (Katerina)

According to Giroux (1983), resistance can be understood as oppositional behaviours that draw attention to inequities and injustices in an effort to dismantle the social and institutional structures of schools. The resistance to engaging in equity work is a theme that permeates the findings of this study. The key markers of resistance include viewing the teaching of inclusive education as an "add-on" and feeling immobilized by a curriculum that has been imposed by the government in a top-down manner. As a result, teachers view equity work with skepticism because it is not explicitly addressed in the curriculum documents. Resistant acts, however, are not only oppositional, but may also be political acts of change because such recalcitrant behaviours are an attempt to replace the objectionable structures of schooling with new structures that will better serve the needs of the resistant groups (Solomon, 1992). Understood in this way, those who continue to do equity work despite systemic obstacles resist the status quo imposition of power that is transmitted through the new curriculum (and teachers' attitudes regarding the importance of taking an anti-oppressive stance) in order to move forward their vision of reconstructing education for those who are presently underserved, underrepresented, misunderstood, and whose experiences and histories are made invisible by the new curriculum.

LIBERATORY POSSIBILITIES: MAKING SPACE FOR INCLUSIVE EDUCATION

While most of the teachers we interviewed acknowledged the difficulties and challenges associated with integrating progressive pedagogy into the curriculum, many found ways to engage proactively with the Ontario curriculum. It is significant that those who resisted integrating equity issues into the curriculum largely attributed this resistance to the restrictive nature of the curriculum, while those who declared that they were able to integrate issues of social justice expressed an opposing perception, which is that the curriculum was largely open to interpretation. What follows is a sampling of voices explaining how they understand the dynamics between the curriculum and their ability to communicate a social justice orientation in the classroom:

> It restricts you in the amount of equity and social justice things that you can bring into the classroom, but you can still bring those things in. (Yvette)

> I can't say I felt really restricted by the curriculum. I don't think the curriculum encourages anti-oppressive education, but I didn't feel restricted because I knew I could bring it in. (Jeanine)

> I don't find the curriculum marginalizes equity issues.... I think that most teachers know at some level about integrating values into the outcomes is increasingly important in terms of what's been measured in terms of accountability. (Marisa)

What is clear from these narratives is the creative ways in which Urban Diversity graduates have found to intuitively and intellectually interact constructively with a narrowly focused curriculum. The graduates have integrated and infused concepts of democratic education in unique and practical ways. What these narratives establish is a firm dedication to critical education and the confidence that if one is committed, one can always find a way to remain true to one's convictions. When asked whether they felt demoralized by the restrictions that the curriculum imposed, this is what many said:

> In terms of the curriculum, I feel no restrictions at all. I teach the curriculum, but I just bring in so many different things. In terms of just the changes and school reform, there's been so

many changes and there's been so much downloading on us. I don't feel demoralized or disempowered because I think I just have to put in extra effort to get things done. I know that I have the equity policy, I know that people know my work in equity that when I bring something forth, they'll say, "Okay, it must be something that's going to be good and benefit the students." So it's just more energy and more work for me to do, but I don't feel disempowered. (Vera)

I honestly welcome the new curriculum and I was probably one of the few, but I ran with it. From the Faculty of Education we were taught to integrate all the subjects across all subjects. So I took a summer and integrated it across the curriculum and I brought the diversity and I welcomed the curriculum because to me, it was so open-ended that I could put in and integrate a lot of diversity and equity that wasn't in the curriculum before. It just opened up the doors and I thought, wow, this is just like a godsend to me. I was able to do it across the subjects and bring in all the diversity and equity and still teach the curriculum. So for me I just loved it. I have nothing negative. It's a lot and just the concept of it and the way it was downloaded on teachers was not very effective because people felt so inundated and over-whelmed. (Virginia)

Several other teachers argued that they did not experience the standardized curriculum as restrictive. Indeed, many UD teachers report that they were well prepared to locate progressive books and other appropriate resources. In addition, they planned field trips and other excursions that would enhance their ability to deliver an inclusive program. In sum, these teachers view the Ontario curriculum as open for interpretation and as a guideline rather than a rigid prescription for action, noting that each classroom is different, and therefore it is up to the individual teacher to "interpret the information" and tailor it to his or her classroom contexts. Tellingly, many expressed the caveat that you do not have to publicize your approach.

Also central to their perceptions was the notion that passion, dedication, and hard work were needed to modify and augment the curriculum. The idea of the "good" teacher as one who was competent, experienced, and grounded in progressive pedagogy remains the focal point, as one teacher relates:

> I think if you are a good teacher that anything the government throws at us is manageable because we know teachers that are passionate about education would always make sure their students are being assessed and being assessed properly, and are getting the materials that they need for those students. If you are passionate about education, you already put students first, so throwing the new curriculum at us is not going to really do anything if you are competent. (Francis)

That the "good" teacher or the equity teacher can unshackle the curriculum does not negate the overwhelming perception that the curriculum does indeed devalue issues of equity and social justice. Generally speaking, teachers who participated in this study have related again and again how standards-based educational reform works against the teaching profession, devalues learning in complex ways, and places further obstacles in front of those who are working toward a socially just society.

The UD teachers' frustration with the new curriculum confirms DeStigter's (2002) insistence that the standardization movement, with its focus on high-stakes testing, limits creative possibilities and is based on a desperate attempt to control a complex and rapidly changing world in which there are far too many human and learning variables for a test to address. The findings of this study can be framed by Kohn's (2003) theoretical critique of the current trends in educational reform in which he asks why some theoretical positions are considered safe while others are constructed as social engineering. The latter usually contain more radical ideas, while the former remain unquestioned as these ideas/positions rest on so-called conventional wisdom or what is often referred to as common sense. Kohn calls for a refusal to accept the debate around standardized tests as it has been framed and insists that we must determine the source of the fierce demand for accountability and question its underlying assumptions. He maintains that it is especially important to consider who benefits and who loses when accountability, as constructed through the standards movement, becomes the primary focus of education. He warns that the discourse about accountability seems straightforward, so the values informing this discourse are masked. This is and continues to be the case regarding school improvement initiatives in Ontario over the past decade. There is consensus among educators and researchers that the government of Ontario failed to improve schooling because of misguided policies and poorly implemented initiatives that might otherwise have been worthwhile. Furthermore, these policies have been developed and enacted without sufficient attention to empirical research providing evidence of what actually improves teaching and learning (Leithwood, Fullan & Watson, 2003).

Teachers in this study have raised major concerns about the impact of the standardization movement on the nature of what is taught and learned in the classroom, the complexity with which issues are discussed, and the ability to attend to a more progressive form of education that values the diversity of our students in an equitable and socially just manner. As Anrig (1987) warns, the key to helping minorities is not to change the test, but to change how minorities and others who are socially different are educated. A no less important factor in the equity equation is that we must also change how those outside the dominant culture are perceived and represented.

Part 2: The Inequities of Teacher Certification: Standardizing Teacher Knowledge

> ... I don't think [standardized testing] will create better teachers; it will actually create people that are conforming to the level of consciousness of the people who are creating the tests, and they are certainly not my teachers. (Martin)

PERCEPTIONS TOWARD ISSUES OF STANDARDS AND STANDARDIZATION
In many professional fields, graduates must be evaluated through various forms of assessment to ascertain their readiness to enter a particular field. Education is not an exception, contrary to what is often reported (mostly by those in support of major education reforms), as rigorous teacher preparation programs are designed with a variety of assessment tools to evaluate teacher readiness to enter the classroom. While many of these evaluative tools take place during the pre-service education period itself, some take place after teacher candidates conclude their teacher preparation or while they are in the first few years in the field. In 2002, an initial teacher certification test (OTQT) was launched in Ontario that purported to measure professional knowledge, as well as the teaching practices of those who had just finished their pre-service education. As a standardized evaluation tool, the OTQT purported to measure teacher readiness to enter the field while ensuring that teacher preparation across Ontario was comparable.

The teacher qualifying test was received with mixed and contradictory responses as some favoured a test that would purportedly give education the type of credentials afforded to other professional fields. Some new teachers presumed that their training, testing, and adherence to standards will make them better teachers than their more experienced colleagues. Most, however, had very negative responses to the test as they were highly suspicious of the test's intentions, its predictive value, and the impact it would have on teachers' attitudes. The constructed necessity of having teachers' competency tested resulted from the intensely negative depictions of teacher professionalism that accompanied the school reform movement with its emphasis on standards and accountability. This discourse, as you will recall from the introduction, scared the public into thinking that teachers were incompetent (Berliner, 2005) and that our schools were broken. They also carried within them the assumption that competency in the dynamic, human interaction–centred field of education could be measured with a paper-and-pencil test.

Since 2005, the OTQT has been replaced with the New Teacher Induction Program (NTIP) in hopes of designing alternative modes of teacher evaluation that are more reflective of teachers' knowledge and performance. At the time of this study, however, particularly when the first cohort of Urban Diversity graduates (class of 1994) were being interviewed, the issues regarding teacher testing and the OTQT were very much alive in the participants' consciousness and are reflected in their responses and attitudes toward standardization in general. In this part of the chapter, we explore these perceptions.

GOVERNMENT RATIONALE

The UD teachers' general perception of the governmental intentions and mandates was one of distrust, suspicion, and alienation, which inhibited a meaningful dialogue between the two essential stakeholders. This impasse was exacerbated by teachers' perceptions of the lack of contextually representative tasks in the test (mostly indicating the dynamics of teaching and learning in a classroom environment) and the predictive value of these tests, which were thought to presciently adjudicate teacher performance in the classroom. Normalized notions of accountability, which were constructed by the dominant discourse at this time, disallowed any criticism of holding teachers accountable through testing, creating a no-win situation for those opposed to the test. In fact, much of the research in defining quality teaching (based on action research) is progressive in nature and outcome-based. However, this work doesn't count in dominant discourses of accountability, which exclude activism and discount teachers fighting against racism (Cochran-Smith, 2001).

What we found revealed a low morale among many teachers, which is, in part, directly related to how the government negatively framed the reasons for high-stakes testing of both teachers and students. Hextall et al.'s (2001) study of the implementation of "skills tests" for entry into the teaching profession in England also found that teacher candidates worried about the negative effect of the testing on professional morale and recruitment. While teacher testing could be positioned as a way of increasing public respect for the teaching profession, much of the teachers' concerns point to increasing disrespect for teachers. The reason for this growing negative perception of teachers is because the government claimed the test was necessary as many teachers lacked the basic skills to be good teachers. As a result, much of the public viewed the test as an indictment of teachers' lack of skills and professionalism. Consequently, rather than improving teacher quality and professional esteem, the tests had the opposite effect, which, as many have argued and proven, was the government's intention all along—that is, the government wished to demoralize teachers and break their unions, giving it almost complete control over the entire educational enterprise and its sizable assets.

PERCEPTIONS OF TEACHER TESTING

In this section, we explore the perceptions of Urban Diversity graduates on the teacher qualifying test. Conflating their negative perceptions is the view of teacher testing as a demeaning attack on teachers' competence and professional capabilities. Two UD graduates respond:

I resent the fact that they are forcing it [the OTQT] on us. (Josie)

The OTQT is seen as a slap in the face. (Jonelle)

In terms of teacher preparation programs, UD teachers felt strongly that initiating any type of high-stakes testing would be inequitable as it would privilege those from the dominant culture, while simultaneously changing the focus of pre-service preparation. Testing represents the competencies of the dominant group. As a result, the values of those teachers from minority groups may be compromised through testing that fails to recognize their distinct competencies.

> Instructors can't teach to the test, and students can't learn with the premise that you are going to prepare for the test and that's all, and I'll think about diversity later when you get in. You can't do that. The Faculty of Education is an environment in which you develop your philosophy of education, and in order to develop your philosophy of education, you have to hash it out.... You have to understand equity; you've got to figure out what is your place in that, what is your position on racism. And that philosophy helps your style of teaching and your structure of teaching. So if you only prepare for a test so to speak because I am talking from the students' perspective, you are missing out on developing an integral part of what you can possibly be as a teacher. (Chantelle)

While this comment is representative of most participants in this study, some UD teachers responded positively to the notion of standardized testing, suggesting that it is important to ensure that teachers are accountable and remain abreast of current teaching methodologies, ideas, and pedagogies. OTQT was also seen as a way to elevate the status of teachers, aligning the profession of teaching with professions that write official board-certified exams, such as engineers, lawyers, and doctors. This possible justification of OTQT is rooted in a desire to ensure that the teaching profession maintains high standards. However, this argument was tempered with the notion that a written test is a one-day event that could undermine the entire year in a teacher preparation program. As such, it does not seem fair to base academic success solely on one's performance on a paper-and-pencil exit exam. Indeed, while some of the UD teachers in this study viewed testing in a positive light, equating teacher qualification testing with more highly esteemed professions, Coulter and Orme (2000) warn that defining the teaching profession along the lines of other professions, such as doctors or engineers, distorts the moral dimension of teaching by using inaccurate, distorting, and deceptive language, such as "clients," "consumers," "efficiency," and "accountability." The usage of this language to describe education also subsumes student identities as fundamentally linked with their economic utility. Once this occurs, not only is the fundamental democratic character of education at stake, but so too are the social and cultural identities of students, who will increasingly have difficulty defining themselves outside of an economic perspective (Baez, 2007).

The research literature also supports participants' concerns about the dangers of teacher testing reinscribing racial inequalities within the profession. In particular, warnings of the adverse effects of teacher testing on the number of minorities entering the profession have been persistent (Daly, 1987; Weiss, 1987; Hood & Parker, 1991; Hill, 1996; Parker, 2001). A case in point is Albers's (2002) description of a disturbing experience she had as a teacher educator when five pre-service teachers (all African-American) out of a class of 17 failed a teacher qualification test: "In just four short hours, a teacher test called the Praxis II nearly destroyed the qualities in them that we most value in teachers: confidence, knowledge of content, and desire to work with students in a culturally responsive way" (Albers, 2002: 123). Clearly, teacher testing presents dramatic challenges in terms of a social justice agenda.

Politics above Pedagogy?

Most UD graduates perceived the Ontario government's attempts to standardize public education as an anathema to what they had been taught in teacher education. UD teachers further argued that government-initiated testing does not represent the experiences of teachers in their local communities. Most of their comments reflect a growing mistrust between education and government that has become increasingly evident in recent years. Several indicated that the OTQT reflects the gap between the profession of teaching and government bureaucratization, a gap that is becoming more pronounced as the move toward the marketization of schooling gathers momentum.

> I get frustrated because I know that the government has their idea of what the ideal teacher and the ideal classroom is, and that is just not the reality. I just wish policy-makers would come into the classroom and into the schools more. They talk and you see them on the news and in the commercials, and I just shake my head because they have no idea really what the needs are. (Juanita)

Other teachers indicated that the OTQT was simply "a source of money," which has little bearing on teacher quality. As a result, a sense of suspicion and mistrust underscored many respondents' reflections, as indicated below:

> The OTQT is just like the provincial test that the students have to take. It doesn't have any bearing on the report card, it doesn't have any bearing on what kind of a student they are or what kind of person they are. It's just something the government wants them to do for the government to meet their own agenda, whatever that agenda may be. (Gail)

Another teacher questioned the extent to which education is controlled by the government:

> To be a politician in this world, you have to act in a duplicitous fashion, and so I don't think it's safe to base educational standards on the dictates of duplicitous politicians. (Martin)

The reform-based standards movement has created a climate where following rules in lockstep is valued over divergent thinking, as evidenced by the following narrative:

> A lot of people are being fast-tracked into administration.... These are people who tend to be rule followers because the whole system is big and rule-bound as opposed to being values-bound. There is not a lot of flexibility in the system and there is not a lot of support for administrators who are not rule-followers. And then the people who are being rewarded and promoted are people who implement rules and who do things by the book.... I think the people that are being chosen for that are being chosen because they will implement policy. (Marisa)

Some graduates feel the government purposefully misleads parents about the teaching profession. Fudging the numbers concerning class size was cited as a key example of policies in conflict with the reality of the classroom. For example, while the "new" government formula purported to cap class size at 24 students (clearly intimating that many classes exceeded 24 students), most teachers observed that this number was, in fact, already the average found throughout the school system.

The Test's Lack of Predictive Value for Teacher Performance in the Classroom

For a test to be considered valid and useful, it must have predictive value. However, most teachers in our study were confident that high-stakes standardized tests were not reflective of, nor could they predict, one's effectiveness or ability in the classroom. As many teachers confidently stated, it is impossible for a written test to determine whether or not a person can teach well because one of the most important aspects of teaching is building relationships and supporting the social-emotional development of young people. These are aspects that a paper-and-pencil test simply cannot evaluate. Instead, the test is seen as a tool to enforce conformity from teachers, and shape them into non-critical employees, essentially functionaries who would follow the party line. The following narratives indicate the extent to which UD teachers questioned both the intended purpose of the certification tests and the authority it endows on those who write these tests:

> Some teachers can write a nice little essay and then go into the classroom and do very different things. I've met people who blatantly make racist comments about certain students, but they have an excellent evaluation because on the day someone went to evaluate them, they put on a nice show. (Sakshi)

> All kinds of people pass these teacher tests, but it doesn't necessarily mean they will have good relationships with their students and their families, which really is probably the most important thing. If there isn't trust between a person and another person, then there can't be any transmission of knowledge. (Martin)

Clearly, our teachers remain suspicious of the role that standardized testing plays in maintaining the status quo, and question whose interests the maintenance of this status quo preserves. In both quotations, respondents draw on a common critique of the so-called professionalization of teaching. This critique points out that the most important moral and performative facet of teaching is the ability to foster and maintain informed and respectful relationships among teachers, students, parents, and administrators. These facets are complex dynamics born out of personalities, emotional intelligence, and educational philosophies. Such complexity cannot be easily quantified and needs to be understood and assessed over time in a variety of contexts by a number of people.

Like the UD teachers in this study, educational researchers and theorists have exposed the assumptions that underlie the foundations on which teacher testing is based. Cochran-Smith (2001) insists that there is no connection between test scores on standardized teacher tests and classroom performance. Others have also maintained that the best way to evaluate teaching is to observe teachers in the classroom context (Daly, 1987). Indeed, teacher testing is contrary to emerging, research-based trends in teacher evaluation that are participatory and include differentiated systems, multi-year cycles, and active teacher roles (via portfolios, professional conversations, and student achievement results) (Danielson, 2001). Thus, standardized tests are reductive in how they describe the complexity of work done in schools (Appleman & Thompson, 2002). Verloop, Van Driel, and Meijer (2001) contend that the quest for "effective" variables that can be tested to ensure quality teaching fails to understand and respect the extremely complex enterprise of teacher practice while yielding few generalizable results. The consequence of this quantitative and reductionistic thinking is that teaching is increasingly viewed as mechanistic and fragmented (via the variables tested). Subsequently, a perception that negates a notion of competency inclusive of the *intangibles* of good teaching, such as caring and perseverance and cross-cultural competency, is elided. Consequently, there is little possibility of a correlation between test performance and job performance (Flippo & Riccards, 2000).

A review of Ontario's teacher assessment program, along with the Massachusetts teacher testing program, suggests that current standardized teacher tests also leave much to be desired when it comes to evidence of psychometric validity. The review concludes that despite the questionable psychometric validity of these types of tests, it is the political validity that determines the public's acceptance of such tests (Miles & Lee, 2002). Also, research has shown that there is no evidence that the implementation of teacher testing in Massachusetts has resulted in better teachers (Fowler, 2001). Thus, the concerns of our participants are well founded, and the fact that many of these issues were precipitated before the standard-based reforms were put on the government agenda reflects the troubling trend of neo-liberal and neo-conservative forces ignoring established research for political and ideological ends.

Teachers' Demoralization and Disillusionment toward the Teaching Profession

Here we outline and elucidate UD teachers' sense of demoralization and disillusionment regarding teacher testing. Most teachers we interviewed felt that high-stakes testing, such as the OTQT on which teacher competence, value, and quality are premised, was extremely demoralizing as it becomes the yardstick upon which teacher performance is evaluated. The following are some representative responses:

> You are not valuing what a teacher is educated to do, which is to teach. (Sakshi)

> The teachers are going to feel like (1) they are going to be checked on at all times; (2) their education prior to becoming a fully fledged teacher is considered not adequate; and (3) that the government and society is now controlling what should be taught instead of the true essence of what education is supposed to be: the quest for knowledge.... My perception is a lot of teachers feel demoralized, feel questioned, and they are going to reassess whether they should even go into teaching. (Katerina)

Feelings of demoralization, victimization, and a general perception that teacher testing hinders teachers from doing what they enter the field to do—to teach—permeate teachers' reflections.

High-stakes exit exams have the potential to either dissuade those considering a career in education or dishearten those who are already in the field. Indeed, many of those we interviewed indicated a desire to leave the educational field because of the impact that the reform in general has had on their work, and in particular the fear that more insidious efforts of standardization will continue to haunt education. Classroom teaching at one time may have been viewed as a lifelong career, but that may not be the case any longer. Burnout and the pressure to conform to rigid (and counterproductive) standards are leading teachers to search for alternative career options. This reality is often contrasted with a notion that some teachers will stay in the profession for more pragmatic rather than altruistic reasons, such as securing a full pension and/or valuing their summer vacation above all else. The notion of entering teaching as a lifelong vocation seems to be eroding as many are considering leaving the field of education to enter others where they can earn more and still work with children in less stressful environments. Concurrently, many who would have considered entering the field of education in the past are reconsidering their options, given the current reform climate. In spite of the level of demoralization and disillusionment, or perhaps because of it, many participants in our study consistently demonstrate a passionate commitment to resist high-stakes testing.

The concerns about professional morale, resulting from the discourse of teacher testing, point to important negative consequences often hidden in the discourse of accountability. Apple (2001a) encourages a critical consideration of teacher education programs and to the larger context of social field of power in which they circulate. Apple asserts that while standards-based reform are well intended, the motives for market-oriented and uniform standards for students, teaching, and teacher education may not guarantee positive effects in the real world of schools. Thus, in order to avoid dangerous consequences, Apple insists that reform efforts be situated within an honest analysis of the entire context within which schooling and teaching are implicated. Flippo and Riccards (2000) examine the negative effects of the Massachusetts teacher testing policy, which, when implemented, had a harmful effect rather than an encouraging influence on teacher performance and the teaching profession in general. The extremely high failure rates resulted in a great deal of negative press and discouraged people from pursuing a teaching career. Of particular note are the consistently lower scores of minority teachers, which point to an inherent cultural bias in the test. In sum, the UD graduates who participated in this study consider the discourse of accountability as a major contributing factor behind the increasing feelings of low morale among themselves and their colleagues.

The high administrative costs of teacher testing cannot be justified when results do not actually contribute to improving teaching (Leithwood, Fullan & Watson, 2003). Beyond the fact that the test lacks validity, predictive value, and economic justification, there are also other hidden effects on teachers and students concerning the development of teachers' educational philosophy. Appleman and Thompson (2002) suggest that subjecting teachers to many standardized tests may result in their loss of a critical stance toward high-stakes testing because there is a strong tendency to teach the way one has been taught and to believe, if one has been successful in such a system, that it is the "correct" way to assess the skills under scrutiny. If there is a tendency to teach the way we have been taught, then high-stakes testing of teacher competency through paper-and-pencil tests may contribute to a technicist-oriented paradigm of learning.

In the preceding sections of this chapter, we explored UD teachers' perceptions of standardized testing in general and the OTQT as a particular case of high-stakes testing. We outlined UD teachers' perceptions of the inequities associated with the teacher testing, especially the ways it privileges those with the social and cultural capital to decode such tests. We outlined teachers' suspicions about what they perceived were the government's ulterior political and financial motives for launching the high-stakes standardized tests. We indicated the extent to which teachers found the paper-and-pencil test riddled with contradictions that prevented it from being an adequate predictive measure of teacher performance within the classroom. Finally, we followed narratives that revealed teachers' demoralization and disillusionment about the education profession, given the direction that educational reform has taken with standardized measures such as the OTQT.

The frustrations and concerns expressed by teacher practitioners committed to a social justice orientation begin to expose and unravel the untested assumptions on which recent school reform has been based. This allows for an opportunity to revise a vision of school improvement that takes into account the real experiences of teachers and the research-based trends emerging in academic literature. Most assuredly there is growing momentum for reclaiming educational reform from neo-conservative and neo-liberal political agendas, and committed teachers' concomitant desire to move education in a more critical, democratic direction where a more socially just understanding of the true purpose of teaching and learning extends beyond reductionist, stilted, and expedient business-oriented measures of learners' abilities. Thus, opening up the horizons of the educational field to a paradigm where students are viewed as engaging in a life-long project of potentiality, as opposed to a one-dimensional landscape of probability, remains a possibility.

Notes

1. At the time of publication, testing now occurs during three full days or two half days and two full days.

CHAPTER 3

Challenges and Contradictions of the Equity Educator: Personal and Professional Impacts of School Reforms on Teachers

R. PATRICK SOLOMON AND JORDAN SINGER

I found a way to include equity and diversity because I had to. It's who I am; it's who my students are, and I wouldn't be an effective teacher if I didn't find a way to include equity. (Virginia)

Burnout among progressive educators is growing as the number of personal, professional, and systemic obstacles to a social justice orientation increase. Many of these obstructions are linked to the dramatic reforms contained in the Ontario curriculum—student standardized testing and an increase in politically oriented bureaucratic demands. Indeed, the teacher's role in the classroom today resembles that of a procedural facilitator whose primary purpose is to transmit what the curriculum deems as *appropriate* information to students in order to help them meet specific outcomes and succeed in standardized tests.

Disempowered teachers point to a lack of available resources and conflicts with other teachers, administrators, and community members as further obstacles to their attempts to create and teach within an inclusive schooling environment. Engendering social justice perspectives in teaching and learning is also compromised by an alarming number of teachers and administrators who consider this work to be voluntary at best and, at worst, as the *actual cause* of disparity, racism, and inequity. Moreover, when this work is undertaken, the approach is usually "celebrational," focusing on ethnic foods and costumes rather than on anything in depth. Adding to these disconcerting dynamics, we have found, perhaps not surprisingly, that regardless of how this work is taken up, it is almost always relegated and/or identified with a core group of committed teachers who are more likely than not to be minoritized teachers. The result is further marginalization of these teachers and the progressive work they are committed to doing.

In this chapter we examine several consequences of current educational reform on the attempts of Urban Diversity graduates to create progressive pedagogical classrooms and school environments. In the first part, UD graduates discuss how the increasing bureaucratic demands on their time have resulted in physical exhaustion and burnout. UD teachers also describe an unwelcome sense of detachment from diversity issues as a result of being forced to refocus their energies on those larger goals set forth by recent educational reforms, a disengagement that is exacerbated by a lack of resources for engaging with issues of equity. In the second part of this chapter, UD graduates reveal the resistance and disapproval they encounter from their colleagues, administrators, and community members. In attending to these obstacles and the reactions of teachers to these impediments, this chapter describes the major barriers to progressive education by examining in detail how current educational reform, coupled with insufficient support for the diversity teacher, creates often impenetrable barriers for the sustained development of equity-based democratic education in schools.

Impact of Education Reform of Equity Pedagogy

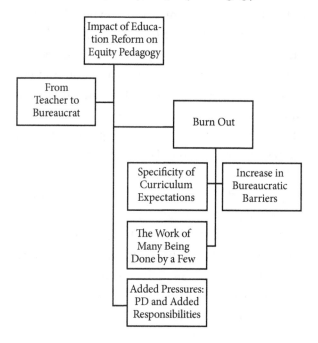

FIGURE 3.1

FROM TEACHER TO BUREAUCRAT

There is a common perception among almost all teachers that their jobs are becoming increasingly burdened by bureaucratic demands, which is especially true for progressive educators. As discussed in Chapter 2, the new standardized curriculum documents play a part in teachers' perceptions of themselves as "bureaucratic facilitators." Also contributing to this sentiment is that many teachers consider the curriculum to be overwhelming in its scope, disconnected from many students' experiences and structured in a way that stultifies critical thinking. Further compounding teachers' sense of frustration is the added pressure of ensuring student success in passing standardized tests in grades 3 and 6.

In consequence, equity initiatives are often left out of the classroom in favour of meeting curriculum requirements. The new and excessive requirements, our participants report, create extra work for teachers, resulting in their being overwhelmed and "too busy" to integrate equity work. In fact, a vast majority of the teachers in our study observed that most new teachers were almost exclusively concerned with following curriculum documents to the letter, in addition to preparing their students for standardized testing, rather than attending to any of their responsibilities concerning equity and diversity education. For more experienced teachers, this tension results in pressure to drop diversity education from their classrooms in favour of preparing students to pass the standardized test. Often this pressure works in tandem with teachers' propensity to revert to past, more familiar and comfortable ways of teaching. The common point of reference here is the belief that there is not enough time in the day to do everything that is demanded of them to fulfill their professional responsibilities and to do what they believe strongly is in the best interests of their students. These challenges exert great pressure on teachers' motivation and desire to teach for inclusion and also on their sense of themselves as professionals. Furthermore, regarding oneself as a professional in terms of fulfilling particular mandated duties may conflict with the core values that constitute what they consider good teaching. In other words, their sense of identity, which is connected to what makes a good social justice teacher, conflicts with what the curriculum both implicitly and explicitly identifies as good teaching.

UD teachers indicate they feel like passive recipients of a mandated formula. This perception leads to a decreasing sense of agency, which affects their sense of themselves as professionals. They cite several noteworthy examples below, which demonstrate how the increasingly bureaucratic model of teaching and learning removes much of their power to make decisions. However, there is disagreement among teachers regarding their roles, especially when the demands of "accountability" and "standardization" challenge their personal ideology and/or professional beliefs:

> What a number of people are saying is that you have to com-
> press the curriculum and get everything done before May, that
> teachers are hard-pressed. Parents, colleagues, or administra-
> tors were saying there isn't time to talk about gay and lesbian
> issues…. Make sure the students can read and comprehend and
> draw inferences and so on. So teachers give up on equity issues
> because they don't have the time. They are trying to complete the
> curriculum. (Marisa)

Teachers in this study explicitly speak about the troubling and
pressure-filled climate of teaching, of being weighed down by school
reform, and the negative impact on their ability to foster a progressive and democratically oriented classroom. Often cited as particularly
draining and as an example of how the increasing bureaucratization of
schooling impacts social justice work is the increase in paperwork. As
one teacher clearly notes:

> The climate of teaching right now is that you are so bogged down
> with a lot of paperwork and a lot of other things that you have
> to do. So I can see how it's so easy to say that this is what's in the
> curriculum, so let's just teach that and not put in that extra effort
> to include equity and diversity work. (Vera)

Our findings reveal that teachers have been increasingly marginalized
from school budgetary decisions, a further indication of the bureaucratization of the profession. In fact, equity initiatives now require a
great deal more paperwork than in the past. The handling of monetary
funds, it should be noted, is also caught up in the discourse of accountability. Some teachers wonder if administrators' concerns with budget
cutbacks are a convenient excuse to discontinue doing any progressive
work. In effect, most equity initiatives undertaken by teachers are more
and more in the hands of a top-down bureaucracy that discourages,
rather than supports, social justice programs:

I'm not quite sure if it's because of a budget restraint or it's just the way this principal does things, but I did an International Women's Day conference for the junior grades and I had to write up a whole proposal: What I was going to do, and why I was going to do it, how it was going to affect the students, and how it is linked to the curriculum, whereas before, it would just be okay [to] go ahead and do it. (Vera)

What becomes clear is that while many teachers continue to do equity and social justice work, their commitment has faltered due in part to an increase in paperwork and pressure from colleagues, including administrators, both of whom emphasize meeting the curriculum expectations. As a result, many formerly committed teachers are dropping anti-oppressive education from their classrooms because this work does not meet any specific curriculum requirements. The overall effect of this top-down business environment has made teachers feel demoralized and reluctant to engage in progressive pedagogy.

To be sure, this assembly-line paradigm of schooling has a history of criticism that is re-emerging in current debates around school reform (see Nezavdal, 2003). Anderson (2001) raises a concern about the effects of a depoliticized discourse of high-stakes testing entering public schooling discourse, arguing that "we may end up legitimising a discourse that further marginalizes more authentic attempts to link educational equity issues to broader social equity issues" (p. 329). Sheldon and Biddle (1998) concur, stressing that "schools are *not* businesses run for profit, teachers are *not* assembly-line workers, and students are *not* commodities to be turned out with specific skills installed and ready to take their place on the assembly lines of America. Rather, schools are complex organizations, with many goals, whose success is often hard to measure" (p. 165; original emphasis).

The social justice educators in this study are negotiating and resisting the reality of being caught between their commitment to social justice, their desire to be professionals, and their understanding of what it means to be a good teacher, the latter two interrelated personal and professional considerations having been pre-defined by a discourse of accountability and a curriculum focus that contradicts and seriously impedes the possibility of teachers acting as agents of change. Another example of this occurs through the governance of funding as it seems that in the vast majority of cases, whenever teachers initiate programs designed to focus on issues of equity and diversity, their efforts are disproportionately rejected by the bureaucratic process of funding allocation. Often these initiatives never get beyond the proposal stage as they are vetoed by principals who control schools' ever-decreasing finances. Notwithstanding the impact on teachers, principals' access to funding is also restricted by top-down school reform. One notable study in Texas, where test scores have become paramount in determining school quality, concluded that: "The role of principal has been severely limited, with greater authority to allocate resources for activities aimed at raising test scores, but with less discretionary power to undertake other kinds of work in the school or to have that work recognized" (McNeil, 2000: 262). Taken together, these restrictions on classroom and school funding, guided by external policy-makers fixated on test score improvement, exclude the possibility of teachers and principals utilizing their expertise to identify and directly act upon what needs to be done to improve their *specific* schools and classrooms. Moreover, this means that the voices of children, who are in need of much more than an improvement in test scores, are silenced as the decisions concerning what needs to be funded are made in the upper echelons of educational decision making and governance. The unmistakable message of this autocratic system is that teachers' and principals' expertise are unwanted and unrecognized even though, despite being abandoned and denigrated, they are still expected to "make it work" in their schools. The result of having all major funding decisions made at the top in tandem with a tacit disrespect for the decision-making abilities of teachers and principals has meant that significant change has been undermined by a top-down approach (Lupart & Webber, 2002; see also Sheldon &

Biddle, 1998). Of note here is the Ontario government's cynical removal of 5,000 administrators from the teachers' union (see Bill 160, Chapter 2). This removal, it has been argued, allowed the government to quell any discord between an ideologically driven plan for education and the possible empathic and experiential propensity of principals to understand the needs of teachers and their classrooms.

Clearly, the frustration expressed by teachers in this study is understandable given how they have been silenced by a system that has stripped their autonomy and power in favour of a vision formulated and managed by those who work well beyond the front lines of educational reform, and whose motives and educational expertise can certainly be questioned. As Lupart and Webber (2002) indicate, "Surely it makes good sense to place those at the centre of the teaching and learning process at the very centre of school change" (p. 35). This is particularly important for teachers working in environments that do not reflect some predetermined norm upon which policy has been framed. Another very real danger arising from a top-down management system is to encourage what Hargreaves (1991) referred to as "contrived collegiality." Within this type of environment, dissenting voices are most likely to be silenced.

ADDRESSING SPECIFIC CURRICULUM EXPECTATIONS
In an attempt to meet the expectations of the curriculum, teachers in our study report having little time to spend collecting and incorporating diverse and equitable material into their lesson plans. Often the standardized curriculum provides a rationale (or excuse) for not doing equity work:

> I think there certainly is a point that is easy to make—that teachers are somewhat less willing to look at diversity issues because they are overwhelmed and because they now have a better reason not to. (Jailin)

That "better reason" not to do progressive work is an almost complete lack of curriculum materials, outcomes, and expectations related to issues of diversity, equity, and social justice. Interestingly, her comment here is expressed ambivalently. She does not use the words "excuse" or "rationale" as we have, and she tempers her language with phrases such as "less willing to," implying either they were never willing to in the first place and/or some are still willing to do this work, although are less motivated to do so. She also empathizes with the overwhelming struggles teachers are having in meeting curricular objectives. Some of this ambivalence can be traced to a psychological-professional dynamic that we observed again and again in many of our respondents, which is the propensity of most teachers to gain a sense of security from covering prescribed outcomes while simultaneously lamenting the absence of expectations that deal explicitly with diversity. They also observe that the relationship between the curriculum and issues of diversity are viewed as an "either/or" proposition, whereby a teacher must choose between either adhering to the curriculum or working for social justice. Consequently, how teachers understand whether or not there is any choice or flexibility between either implementing the curriculum and/or remaining dedicated to progressive democratic principles affects whether or not they feel their autonomy has been irretrievably compromised by the present dictates of the educational system. When the curriculum is viewed as a literal map driving all teaching practice, some UD graduates perceive it as disempowering and demoralizing. Conversely, those who perceive and therefore emphasize the possible flexibility of the curriculum envision many creative opportunities to incorporate diversity-based pedagogy.

THE WORK OF MANY DONE BY THE FEW

Research by Goode et al. (2003) discovered that visible minorities are overrepresented by those who identify as activist leaders. Their study also found that these teachers are less likely than other teachers to agree that colleagues share their beliefs. In addition, activist leaders reported fewer opportunities for collaboration and professional development.

In terms of teacher attrition, activist leaders are "more likely to stay in education because they are attached to the kids, and all activists are less likely to stay in education based on good relationships with colleagues" (Goode et al., 2003: 16). Since teachers who identify as activists or change agents differ, not just by how they chose and understand their professional roles and duties (such as equity rep, equity committee member), but by a "deeper dispositional stance" (Goode et al., 2003: 17), the effects of school reforms may be felt on a more personal level. An illustration of this is the strong sense of collegial dissatisfaction that UD graduates in this study felt. These reports indicate how teachers with a strong personal commitment to social justice often do not distinguish between their personal and professional motivations. As a result, teachers feel a very personal loss of professional autonomy as a result of the top-down nature of school reforms. These feelings are intensified by a sense of both professional and personal isolation from colleagues. In consequence, teachers of colour in our study are at higher risk of burnout since they are the ones who most often end up taking on even more responsibilities when other teachers feel overwhelmed: "I think that certain teachers right now are so bogged down with the work that they think that it's not my job after a while, and it's only the Black teacher that has to get those kids to come into their office" (Eric). Teachers who self-identify as both change agents and visible minorities are overrepresented in this group. Often the extra responsibilities they take on either by choice and/or necessity greatly contribute to this group's sense of increased pressure. As Marcus shares:

> I need to learn that at this point it's not possible to do everything, and it may not be possible to slow everything down the way I want to because maybe I might get there in about 10 years, but at this point I sometimes think I put too high expectations on myself and I found myself getting tired sometimes and frustrated.

One teacher describes the burnout resulting from being "Ms. Equity," indicating she is a "one-person show." Other UD teachers describe being given control over equity initiatives by default. Yet another guiltily describes being able to address equity issues only four times a month with each class as a result of the rotary system. This sense of remorse and the realization that his interactions with students are limited inspired another to become a homeroom teacher:

> When you only see a class once a week, or four times a month, you realize that there is no context in the school where other teachers are doing this sort of critical work. So you kind of felt a bit frustrated because you realized there weren't other teachers encouraging critical reflection, which is probably one main reason why I decided to get my own classroom. (Marcus)

The burnout factor for the equity teacher can be exacerbated by the lack of immediate results.

> When you are Ms. Equity, there is a burnout factor. You get to the point that you get frustrated. You feel like you are banging your head against the same brick wall and it's not even chipping away. There are times that you question: What am I doing? Why do I continue to do this? Am I making an impact? In terms of burnout, I think there is a lot of burnout because teachers on the whole put a lot of time and effort and energy into their work, into their classroom, into preparation, marking, trying to create a good balanced program. And when you look at it from the perspective that you are adding equity in there and you are creating things that don't exist within the school, that's like another 50–60 percent of your time and you do burn out quite quickly. (Donnette)

While burnout is a constant danger, we are reminded by another teacher that even in moments of frustration, when we begin to question the efficacy of our work, we must keep in mind that equity and social justice learning unfolds over time; that learning is not immediate. Her wisdom not only brings solace to those who feel overburdened, overworked, and possibly ineffective, but also forces us to remember that learning is often belated, especially when difficult information is engaged (Britzman, 1998).

INCREASED BUREAUCRATIC BARRIERS

As mentioned above, many UD teachers trace their feelings of being overworked and overwhelmed to the increased number of bureaucratic barriers endemic within the new curriculum and the top-down nature of school reform and governance. They conclude that their resultant feelings of disempowerment and demoralization, in addition to a lack of support from colleagues and administrators, make it less likely that they will engage in progressive pedagogy in their classrooms. Another respondent speaks of a further responsibility that contributes to burning out—teachers' extracurricular commitments.

> I think time is a huge issue with so many commitments that you have in life. You want to be there for the community, but it is also difficult to sort of find the time. Your school work or your class work, your teaching, and then combine that with other sort of extracurricular community initiatives takes time. (Shauna)

Other respondents agree, speaking of an overwhelming workload:

> I hear a lot of complaints. A lot of teachers once again are very concerned with the workload. The workload, the stress load, and then I find that they put up a wall when they have to look at the equity issue. They feel it is not necessary, they feel it is questionable. And it is unfortunate, but I think it is because of lack of time, lack of funding, lack of knowledge, lack of experience in some ways. (Katerina)

Despite the frequently antithetical relationship between school reform and the ability to teach for social justice, a significant number of participants have not allowed their socially conscious work in their lessons to be compromised. While they agree that teachers have become increasingly inundated with bureaucratic demands, their ability to incorporate a variety of material in the classrooms has not been deterred. They point out that within the solitude of the classroom, there is the potential to deliver the curriculum at their discretion. Other UD teachers confirm that looking for creative ways to incorporate diverse material in their classrooms is a constant challenge, yet it is an endeavour to which they are committed.

Most teachers in our study discussed often ingenious ways of integrating diverse materials within a structure that works against inclusion. Deep sentiments in this regard are indicative of the depth of dedication these educators have to social justice-oriented education. More precisely, these teachers return again and again to their ongoing search for teaching materials that can traverse the seeming gap between systemic demands and the diverse realities of their students. Such work, many report, should not be considered as extra, but essential. Above all, they feel that it is natural for them to search for and turn to diverse materials when preparing for their classes.

While the perception that the curriculum can be viewed as a creative teaching tool, where diversity, equity, and social justice are valued, most UD teachers see the curriculum itself as discouraging democratically oriented teaching and learning and encouraging conservative teaching methods and topic choices. In sum, the increased number of required demands has most of our respondents struggling with how they can combine their desire to continue their progressive work with the daily demands dictated by the curriculum.

PRESSURES OF PROFESSIONAL DEVELOPMENT RESPONSIBILITIES

Pressures of professional development add to the stress levels of teachers and feelings of burnout. UD teachers are committed to ongoing professional development and often voluntarily take extra courses and workshops. They express a strong desire to continue enhancing their skills, and view teaching as a profession that demands ongoing and continued growth through workshops, additional qualifications courses, action research, and so on. Some have continued to take courses and attend seminars to keep themselves "in the loop" when it comes to current diversity practices. Additionally, one UD teacher claimed that, despite feeling not as connected to diversity issues as she once was, she believes it is up to her to "stay current." "Staying current" is a common choice for diversity teachers, and is an added demand on their time. Nevertheless, it is also intrinsic to their view of themselves as change agents committed to responsible social reconstruction.

Most UD teachers also express being weighed down by commitments to various forums, such as parent councils, diversity and equity committees, in addition to many other extracurricular responsibilities, including sports clubs and/or community development work. Given these demands, there is insufficient time to complete the expectations in the new standardized curriculum while also planning and seeking professional development to incorporate equity and diversity material in their pedagogy. While many plow through and continue as best they can, others focus on bureaucratic tasks and attend diligently to the standardized curriculum at the expense of diversity work. Over time, a sense of duty and increasing obligations take a discernible toll. Goode et al.'s (2003) research into retention rates of teachers shows that activist teachers work, on average, one and a half hours more per week than those who do not identify as activists. As well, activist teachers are more likely to be dissatisfied with the amount of support provided by administrators and colleagues, a theme that is consistent throughout this study. Significantly, Goode et al.'s study warned that while the multiple roles taken on by activist teachers allow for a greater sense of professional potential, these teachers are also more likely to want to leave the classroom earlier, although they most often do not leave the field of education (Goode et al., 2003). While activist teachers can have greater influence on schooling through administrative or academic positions, it is of great concern to think that they are not fulfilled personally and professionally in the classroom. The loss of these teachers in the classroom results in an inestimable psychological, social, and academic cost to the students whom they could have taught. In short, the various and significant pressures expressed by our respondents signal an imperative to support these teachers in a direct manner, especially in light of the added demands of recent school reform. This study suggests that without major interventions to support these teachers, the future of equity-based education is in jeopardy.

Obstacles to Successful Equity Work

As we have seen, there are a variety of obstacles to building inclusive classrooms and passing on the democratically based ideal of a more equitable world. Another barrier that our respondents revealed is the problematic rendering of diversity education as little more than a superficial add-on to the curriculum. In particular, this work is often positioned as "voluntary" and thus not valued as integral to the teacher's role. These attitudes, in addition to the above impediments to equity work, shape the negligible professional commitments to and negative connotations of a social justice teaching orientation. The result has been that meaningful diversity initiatives are time and again relegated to a core group of committed individuals instead of being integrated in the classroom, throughout the school, and into the realm of policy planning and the guiding of implementation frameworks. Unfortunately, as referenced throughout this study, the theoretical vision of education (including the aims of education), curriculum planning, as well as the power to implement school reforms, often emanate not from schools, principals, or teachers, but from business practices shaped by ideologically driven government policy-makers adhering primarily to dehumanized economic methodologies.

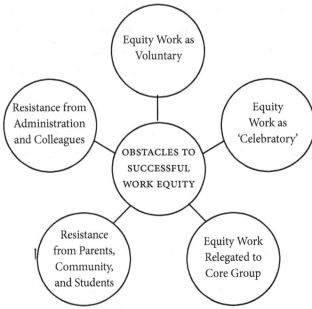

FIGURE 3.2

EQUITY WORK AS VOLUNTARY

Many respondents agreed that almost all their colleagues, including administrators, consider diversity and social justice work as voluntary work. Such an interpretation is highly detrimental to the larger, structural goals of equity education as the formation of a successful and progressive educational environment requires integration between teachers' pedagogical practices, the school culture, and the education system at large. Recognizing this, most diversity teachers remark that they continue to volunteer for any and all positions at their schools involving anti-racism, equity, and/or diversity in the hopes of broadening their systemic acceptance. As one UD teacher explains, in order to ensure that she had a hand in transforming the school community's perception of progressive education, she has "sat on just about every committee in the school" (Francis). Another shares her similar experience, remarking that:

I'm on the school improvement team. I purposely got on that

team to try to make some changes in terms of curriculum assessment procedures, staffing, and how we work together. This is my
third year on it. Slowly but surely, we are making little steps, little
milestones. (Zora)

She continues: "I'm trying to make myself active in certain roles so
that I could be more verbal and vocal," a stance that many UD teachers
took in the hopes of securing a place for progressive approaches to education in their schools. In many cases, the "equity committee" becomes
the de facto central vehicle for integrating diversity in schools. Understood in this light, participation on equity committees initially entails
exploring strategic ways to engage colleagues in democratic schooling.
The role of "equity representative" is another means by which diversity teachers can participate in change agency. While this is true, some
UD teachers spoke of these positions as superficial because most (1) did
not understand the work of these representatives; (2) viewed these representatives negatively; and (3) believed that their work was peripheral,
unnecessary, and sometimes harmful. To illustrate, our participants point
to the troubling fact that many teachers are faced with the obstacle of trying to implement change in a school that has no equity policy in practice:

I couldn't come in and change everything when people weren't
discussing things like racism and stereotypes and prejudices.
People weren't discussing Hanukkah and Kwanzaa and Rama-
dan. It was like [they] just didn't exist! (Zora)

These types of struggles highlight the lack of a systemic approach to
equity practices in our schools, as well as these positions' lack of power.
In order to be effective, principals not only had to be "on board" and
supportive of the work of these committees and representatives, but
also willing to encourage teachers to engage with these issues both personally and with their students.
Teachers who volunteer their time as equity representatives and/or

serve on equity committees take on a major undertaking. Often they must work hard just to introduce a diversity consciousness to their colleagues in the hopes of securing a commitment to social justice. Several participants related that forming anti-bias committees was an effective, non-confrontational strategy in building support for and promoting an ongoing awareness of progressive teaching and learning. Many others, who found themselves alone in their commitments, reported being viewed as equity and diversity *personified* at their school. Again, the marginal status of these positions further exacerbates the isolation felt by minoritized teachers who often volunteer or who have been delegated to fill these positions. The added workload and increased hours of these positions intensifies these teachers' experience of burnout.

EQUITY WORK AS CELEBRATORY, SUPERFICIAL, AND AS AN "ADD-ON"
Of great concern to many UD teachers is how equity is most commonly understood as a celebratory activity, often carried out in a non-integrated, isolated manner. In addition, they are very disturbed by the "equity and diversity" trend whereby people, institutions, schools, and governments claim they are doing this work, but are using these terms as slogans devoid of substance and understanding (see "Introduction"). As Paulette notes:

> I'm concerned about diversity initiatives just being a celebration as opposed to an everyday thing. The children in my class should always feel that they are well liked and loved and respected no matter who they are. So it's not that we are just taking the time out one day in a month to celebrate their culture, but they know that I don't tolerate disrespect to anyone because of them being different. (Paulette)

In the rest of her narrative, this teacher expressed how the lack of cross-curricular integration and the designation of special days or times to do this work made it almost impossible for many teachers to open up (let alone think about) culturally relevant, consistent, and contextually appropriate discussions of what she referred to as "the other -isms."

Several UD teachers also suggested, almost counterintuitively, that creating an equity committee in a school hinders the naturalization of equity, diversity, and social justice work in the pedagogical practices of educators. Specifically, one UD teacher argues that relying too heavily on these committees allows individual teachers to avoid doing the necessary anti-oppressive education in their own classrooms because, as is often the case, they believe that the equity committee "would take care of it." Moreover, after the formation of an equity committee and the building of some awareness and commitment among colleagues, an administrative change can undermine past progress, as Vera clarifies:

> When she [the old principal, dedicated to anti-oppressive pedagogy] left and the new principal came in, we had this equity committee where it was like saying, "Okay, we don't have to do equity anymore because the equity committee would put up things around the school. The equity committee will educate the kids through announcements. I don't have to do it in my classroom anymore." (Vera)

While this comment demonstrates the importance of having administrative support, it also illuminates how fragile the apparent progress in consciousness among one's colleagues can be, and/or how quickly teachers involved may again succumb to a sense of overwork by giving up what is considered "extra." In addition, this narrative makes clear that while schools may appear to be equity-conscious through announcements or other public gestures, often there are no equity and diversity initiatives beyond the existence of the committee itself. This example also suggests that schools can "celebrate" that they have addressed equity and diversity since they have a "special" committee when the committee is, in reality, only a hollow representation of equity, diversity, and social justice with little substance. These responses also suggest that equity representatives and equity committees, once accepted, are often rendered unable to promote any transformative change on a structural level.

Another issue closely associated with celebratory versions of diversity work is expressed in how some of these initiatives are or become little more than token representations of "otherness" in the school. One participant describes what happened at her school:

> Diversity and equity work has been relegated now to just Black History month or Chinese New Year. It's just celebrations now and the whole idea of integrating into everyday teaching is lost. (Chantelle)

Another participant, while discussing tokenistic displays of otherness, explained that the equity committee at her school considered their "display committee" to be the main fulcrum of the school's equity commitment. The committee's job was to put up monthly exhibits around the school *based on various themes* in an attempt to avoid tokenism. The ease with which authentic attempts at anti-oppressive education become and remain celebratory and reductionistic, rather than aiming for authenticity and an expanding notion of inclusion, has left many progressively oriented teachers frustrated and largely discouraged.

Knowing where to draw the line between tokenistic and/or celebratory visions of "otherness" and a meaningful integration of anti-oppressive education is not always easy or obvious. Also, to be effective, teachers' efforts in their classrooms should be part of a school-wide strategy. One participant explains that her principal's promotion of diversity in the schools has been troublingly superficial: "All the special days are announced through the PA system and we are celebrating in music and concerts" (Rachael), yet beyond being able to cite the topic of each special day and maybe a few facts related to this topic or theme, little more is done by anyone in any classroom. Another teacher considers her school in general, and the school's equity committee in particular, to be lacking in vision. She says that efforts at her school, which come under the guise of diversity education, such as Asian History month and Black History month, fail to effect any real change or provide any authentic learning beyond superficial awareness: "The staff and students were aware of them and they mentioned [the celebrations]" (Adrianne), but she goes on to say there was no real indication that these celebrations represented anything more than a survey of other cultures different from the dominant culture. The examples outlined above represent many similar narratives that were disturbingly common. In each, the construction of "us" and "them" remains unchanged, which is not surprising as this reflects the general lack of understanding, coordination, and commitment to issues of equity and social justice by most educators throughout our school systems. For any of this to change, students, teachers, and administrators need to recognize why many of these attempts at diversity education are counterproductive and how to meaningfully move beyond "celebrations" and the two-dimensional representations of others and otherness.

EQUITY WORK RELATED TO CORE GROUP
As a result of the peripheral "add-on" status of equity education, those who work diligently to bring these issues to their schools often become isolated and distressed. Often there are only a small select number of colleagues with whom these teachers can speak. As one participant relates:

> There are a number of colleagues that I felt I could talk to about those things or who were aware of issues. We could sit around a table and all of us would know. You would know who picked it up, and who didn't and the people that did you talked to. And then there were people that you didn't talk to. (Amelda)

This reluctance to speak with some staff members, given the negative status of their work, is completely understandable, although this may also limit opportunities to educate uninformed teachers about these issues while precluding the possibility of more teachers taking part in diversity initiatives. Another participant discusses her role within the core group of teachers making up the initial diversity committee at her school:

> I started looking for people that I could pull that were like-minded, and I got a group of about six teachers and we would meet in my portable.... So this group of six formulated the diversity committee. We put together an action plan, we took it to the principal, and we told him that this is what we wanted to do. We felt this was a need and then we asked whoever would be interested on the staff to come.... We ran that successfully for probably about four of the six years that I was there. (Virginia)

Some UD teachers envisioned how to expand the small core group of committed educators by planning how school dynamics could help them achieve their goals. In particular, one participant describes how the select group of "change agents" could impact other teachers:

> There were certain leaders in the school, and those leaders were the change agents. That filtered down to the teams, which were the teachers in the school and instilled change within them. And then it filtered down to their classrooms. (Sharlene)

The delegation of equity *duties* to a core group of people often results in the dilution of responsibility on the part of the teaching staff at large. Some respondents have voiced concern, noting that the creation of an equity committee at their school merely de-emphasized the need for integrating anti-oppressive education issues throughout the school. They commented that it was always the same teachers doing the work, so the whole school was never involved. Others emphasized the need for equity work to be seen as a preliminary step in the process of creating school cultures based on democratic ideals and equitable frameworks. By contrast, what our study illuminates is that the creation of a core group of people, focused on implementing diversity initiatives, is interpreted by both teachers and administrators as the end-game of equity and diversity efforts. The question for us becomes: How do progressive educators convince others to develop an equity consciousness, and how do we foster the understanding that equity committees are only the first step in a much larger process? Without seriously contemplating strategically how these questions may be answered, equity committees run the risk of being isolated, short-term attempts to solve systemic problems. Once any political aspect of the system changes or there is a change in the school administration, any progress made by the committee runs the serious risk of being reversed, dismantled, or reductively reconfigured.

Clearly, despite their rigorous teacher education program focused on equity, diversity, and social justice, UD graduates still faced many challenges in their classroom practice. Contributing to the already difficult struggles associated with this work, the increasing bureaucratization in the school climate (reflected in increased accountability measures) has further complicated attempts to integrate a diverse and equitable approach to teaching, learning, and knowledge in our schools. Rather, it has contributed to halting progress toward more progressive education beyond simplistic and superficial attempts. The myopic focus on standards, standardization, and outcomes has made it increasingly difficult to fight for equity initiatives within this narrowly defined notion of school reform. As Capper and Jamison (1993) have warned, "outcomes-based education ... fails to challenge the status quo and existing power relations in schools and society" (p. 43). Furthermore, not only do these constrictions pose serious problems for socially transformative educational ventures, but they also make it less likely for educators to address other problems concerning students' educational, social, and emotional needs and/or systemic shortcomings. A similar sentiment is echoed by Sheldon and

Biddle (1998), who caution that "[t]o the extent that accountability systems are seen as a panacea, they can distract us from dealing with the real problems of education" (p. 175). The concomitant emphasis on standards and accountability, in tandem with high-stakes testing, may also succeed in "sabotaging" the democratic goals of education (Cochran-Smith, 2005). Indeed, it is easy to see why the majority of the UD graduates are frustrated by the precarious positioning of equity and diversity in their schools. The marginalization of social justice in schools, as evidenced through the "extra work" needed to include equity and diversity in the new curriculum, the often superficial outcomes of volunteer equity committees and representatives, as well as the tokenistic ways that diversity initiatives are executed, if at all, raises important questions for teacher education programs aimed at preparing activist teachers for these sorts of challenges. Not only do they face the reality of extra workloads and the marginalization of their philosophical orientation to teaching and learning within educational environments, but they must also face a great deal of interpersonal resistance to their ideals as well.

Resisting and Opposing Diversity

PARENT AND COMMUNITY RESPONSES TO DIVERSITY INITIATIVES

In relating their encounters with resistance and opposition to their efforts to build inclusive classrooms, our teachers revealed a great deal of exasperation. Many parents feared that if time is spent teaching about cultures other than their own, the dominant culture would be ignored, invalidated, or even denigrated.

> [I] had a parent who would come in and help. And she was a combination of angry and upset and hurt. Her father or grandfather was a missionary; she basically felt that by celebrating Native Canadians, I was slanting the role of the Catholic Church. And it

took several meetings, including even an option with the lawyer from the board. It became quite a dicey issue. (Jailin)

Other participants spoke of the inordinate amount of power many parents and community members had, noting that if these stakeholders were resistant to diversity, equity, and social justice education, they could pose quite a threat to the possibility of building inclusive classroom environments. One teacher explains that this tension is heightened in schools such as hers, which is not multicultural. Despite a slight demographic change over her seven years at the school, she notes that it was made up predominantly of White, middle- to upper-class students and teachers whose homes were worth an average of $1 million. She explains the significance of these demographics:

I'm working with a lot of children that have stay-at-home moms and dads that make quite a bit of money, and sometimes issues of power become an issue between teacher and doctor, teacher and lawyer, teacher and someone in a higher status that wants to dictate how we are doing things, and why we are doing things. (Zora)

The participant goes on to add that parents at the school were used to older, more experienced teachers, and expected teachers to have 20 years of experience as opposed to being newly graduated. These parental critiques came out during discussions in which our UD graduate was made to feel as though her introduction of diversity and equity within the school "rocked the boat a little bit."

Another UD teacher also revealed pressures that arose when more influential parents who oppose the method and content of lessons where common perspectives concerning difficult historical issues are examined.

You know who else was causing trouble? Parent committees. We were trying to do a Heritage Day assembly, and I was coming at it from an anti-racist point of view, and a parent was coming at it from a superficial perspective. She didn't like the "stop racism" posters. It was quite a conflict between very different philosophical points of view. If you deal with strong parents, it's just as hard as a strong administrator. Sometimes strong parents get administrators on their side. (Sakshi)

This example of parental resistance to topics that engage in and reveal power imbalances suggests that certain parents make efforts to negate issues of power implicit in the "isms": racism, sexism, classism, ethnocentrism, ableism, hetero-normatism, and so on. In effect, this situates teachers' attempts at raising students' critical awareness and thinking about these issues as harmful and incorrect.

While opposition to these efforts exist, so, too, does support. However, this encouragement is often contingent on both time and familiarity. Notably, parental support appears to be more in evidence once diversity teachers have spent more time at the school and, in some sense, have proven themselves to be genuinely interested in the well-being of the students. As one participant notes, "I quickly won the parents over and they could see then that I was professional, that I had a strong background in education and obviously I could communicate with them" (Amy). Some parents also support the progressive teacher if the community and administrators at the school have purposefully recruited equity-trained teachers, or have become accustomed to this orientation in their new hires. As some UD teachers commented, schools, including parents and administrators, are actively seeking out teachers who will reinvigorate the school with fresh ideas, deliver more diverse lessons with "cross-curricular integration." Nevertheless, it is important to keep in mind that an initially positive start, as well as support from the community, colleagues, and administrators, is no guarantee of lasting encouragement. Instead, quite frequently, after being hired with the express purpose of fostering diversity initiatives, these teachers find themselves at odds with the school community once they attempt to put their ideas into practice. As one UD graduate remarks:

A lot of my parents and teachers, principal included, at first were very excited and very vibrant about doing a lot of critical multi-cultural activities. However, as we charged into it straight ahead, we realized that we were hitting a wall because a lot of parents and committee people, family, friends, and even people outside the schools were concerned about what was happening in the classroom. (Katerina)

Many parents are not accustomed to anti-oppression pedagogical approaches, and tend to encourage the conservative approaches of teachers who resist incorporating diversity and equity work into their classrooms. This is no surprise as a number of studies over the years have revealed that parents are more comfortable with a curriculum and teaching style that closely mirrors their own schooling experiences.

Resistance and opposition to diversity initiatives come in various forms and from different social, cultural, and linguistic communities. Often a lack of support for equity education occurs in diverse communities. To attest to this, the choice to oppose equity initiatives is often cited as a reflection of smaller homogeneous communities not wanting to mix within the larger heterogeneous community that comprises a school's demographic makeup.

There are lots of different ethnic communities [which make up our school] and they all sort of stay by themselves. They don't interact a lot. They stay very focused on their own community. For instance, the Somali community, they will stay by themselves. Then you've got the Vietnamese community, and the Caribbean Black community, and the African Black community. They don't seem to do things together. The only time that I see them getting involved with each other is at a school fair, which is a once-a-year thing. (Adrianne)

We believe that this example is exceedingly important to consider because we cannot assume, as many do, that the existence of a culturally diverse school community automatically results in support for a social justice–oriented teachers' pedagogy. In fact, comments from our participants suggest that multicultural and multiracial communities often do not support pluralistic-egalitarian and/or cosmopolitan perspectives, nor easily accept, identify, or communicate with each other. That is to say, there is greater incidence of homophily or "own group cleavage" than might be expected to occur in multicultural and multiracial communities.

Similarly, we take note of a final significant comment regarding how parents choose to interact with staff at school. While attempting to provide a reason for the lack of parental involvement at her school, Adrianne notes:

> I think a lot of parents come from areas in the world where teachers were seen in a different light, and they totally rely on teachers, realize that we are operating in a different system, and they focus on the fact that I've got him to school, now you can do what you want.... I would not even say that they are not supporting us. I don't think that they believe they have to.

Adrianne's insight here into possible parental motivations is significant for many reasons. Understanding how the backgrounds of some parents influence their attitudes toward teachers and schooling cannot be ignored. Also, her thoughts pinpoint the pitfalls of trying to interpret parents' motivations based on our particular North American or Western world view, which inevitably leads to assumptions and judgments about whether or not teachers and schools are being supported in general and, in this case, whether equity work is being supported by parents in particular. Parents' culture, linguistic origin, and individual experiences all affect how and why they choose to participate in the school culture and indeed what participation itself means and how it would appear. Often teachers do not consider how the role of the teacher and the school differs in different cultures, which results in teachers making negative judgments of parents who are seen as not participating in their child's education. Essentially, parents' seeming disconnection from their children's schooling may not be indicative of resistance or a lack of interest or support, but rather an indication of the amount of respect they feel for the teachers and school staff and of their own understanding of the autonomous role of the teacher.

Lightfoot (2004) reminds us about the importance of being aware of the discourse regarding parental involvement and the need to fully understand and appreciate class and cultural issues "because the metaphors and other imagery we use to apply terms such as parental involvement to particular groups are used so habitually that they become invisible, they are difficult to question and difficult to change" (p. 92). This is echoed in Diamond and Gomez's (2004) study of the class implications of African-American parent involvement. They argue that there is an interdependent relationship between social class, parents' perceptions of schools, and parents' educational orientations. As a result, what we perceive to be parent resistance may not be resistance at all: "Teachers and administrators in low-performing schools should also recognize that the frustrations expressed by working-class African American parents (in American schools) are often rooted in their desire for better schools. School officials should (whenever possible) acknowledge the legitimacy of parents' concerns and seek common ground with parents to facilitate school improvement" (Diamond & Gomez, 2004: 422). Keeping this in mind when thinking through our interpretations of parents' motivations is essential if we are to be successful in building more inclusive schooling environments where students, teachers, and administrators remain culturally responsive to the similarities, differences, and nuances of those members of our school communities whose backgrounds differ from those whose policies provide our interpretive frameworks of teaching and learning, including what parental involvement looks like and means. As we have seen, these policies echo monocultural norms and do not take account of the many diverse ways in which people engage with education as a whole.

STUDENT RESPONSES TO DIVERSITY INITIATIVES

Students, at times, also demonstrate their displeasure with diversity initiatives, although their reaction to progressive pedagogy is only touched upon by a small number of UD teachers. And yet, as one description makes clear, their opposition can be displayed in a most worrisome manner, especially if supported by teachers:

> [The head of the Art Department] takes [the students' artwork, which represents diversity], he puts them all up in the hallways, and you wouldn't believe it. The kids and the teachers rip these posters down, pull them down because they [are] so disturbed, and they don't want to deal with equity and diversity issues. (Katerina)

Another participant describes how students in her school are being trained to respond negatively to equity, diversity, and social justice perspectives. She explains that this is the case because students are merely learning to be obedient, and are therefore scared and unsure of how to ask critical questions concerning classroom materials. The school culture itself, she clarifies, explicitly condones the reproduction of social inequities through an emphasis on promoting "well-behaved assembly-line factory workers." She goes on to say that "although we talked about sort of pushing the students to achieve their full potential and making them really good readers, we weren't turning them into critical thinkers; we were in fact doing the opposite" (Ming). Instead, students are given mundane, rote-type learning tasks so there is nothing "dynamic going on." The description of this school is particularly interesting as it is one of Toronto's designated "model schools,"[3] which are supposed to be at the forefront of innovative teaching, community involvement, and, of course, improved standardized test scores. In addition, the school is also

French immersion and where the student demographic is split equally between Chinese and Portuguese. After sharing these observations, she wonders if a French-immersion environment contributes to students' resistance to anti-oppression education since the students are presented with more traditional pedagogies, and "the emphasis is on vocabulary learning, and language learning and the kids don't have facility with the language to have more sophisticated discussions" (Ming). While it is clear from her description that the overall school environment is not conducive to building an inclusive space, the interrelationship between student and school culture, language, pedagogy, and teacher perception, in this case, makes clear the complexity of factors that must be attended to in order to do equity work.

In contrast, another participant at a different school explains that her students come from families where critical questioning and politically oriented discussions took place regularly. This family dynamic, she hypothesizes, helped to prepare them for class discussions that engage in anti-oppressive issues. Markedly, this teacher went on to describe how important the support of her principal was in allowing her to tackle difficult issues within her class.

Other comments by UD teachers indicate that students' resistance to progressive pedagogy is not widespread. Some teachers state that their students enjoy the diverse materials provided to them and demonstrate genuine interest in learning about perspectives, politics, and opinions that were not provided in other classes. Another teacher notes that while the staff and administration are not supportive of her initiatives, the students have been supportive and are engaged by the new learning occurring in the classroom.

In one heartening example, a teacher describes her students' positive reaction to her progressive approach, explaining that in response to her teaching, her class has created a competition among the other teachers, forcing them to seriously consider including diverse topics in their lessons. Not surprisingly, though, the quality of the work done by other teachers at the school is questionable. Most commonly, rather than focusing on one significant Christian holiday, such as Christmas, teachers in her school are beginning to discuss a variety of significant religious events. While this approach mirrors the types of efforts we have previously been critical of in this chapter, these attempts, nevertheless, are hopeful as they demonstrate how one teacher can influence others, and how students have the power to expedite change among colleagues and the school culture at large.

In general, our participants insist that the majority of students at most of their schools are the most supportive of their attempts to foster progressive learning environments because "as long as you are doing something fun, it doesn't matter what you are doing, they are on board" (Zora). Another teacher notes that she thinks it is wonderful that her class, which is ethnically diverse, always works quite well together. She describes her school as being open to her democratically oriented teaching and reports that, as a result, more progressive pedagogies have been integrated into the school culture to a certain degree. She also comments quite proudly that student openness to diversity has resulted in greater curiosity and a deeper respect for religions in a non-judgmental way. We need to keep in mind that based on the description of the multitude of extracurricular activities and diversity initiatives at this teacher's school, this school is not representative of the majority. However, her example still strongly implies that where students are provided with access to integrated diversity, equity, and social justice work, they are more likely to respond to each other with more understanding and respect. Moreover, the multitude of extracurricular programs, diversity initiatives, and overall progressive environment at the school promote interaction among students, staff, and administrators, as well as parents and other community members, all of which go a long way in building a diverse, democratic, and harmonious school and community.

The tensions and complexities surrounding the challenges posed by student, parent, and community resistance highlight the interdependent relationships that affect school success. As Lupart and Webber (2002) insist, "School personnel cannot, it seems apparent, promote an overall improvement in students' skills and knowledge without forging stronger alliances with other segments of society" (p. 25). And while Goode et al. (2003) remind us that in order to serve students in high-priority schools, we must prepare social justice educators "to take on leadership roles and become involved at their school site in ways that transcend the classroom walls" (p. 19).

This study's findings caution against demanding more and more of teachers without giving them adequate support, and it also points to the pitfalls of expecting social justice educators to take on all the responsibility for students' success. Indeed, as Britzman (2003) has pointed out, there are great dangers in the common misconception that everything depends on the teacher, a sentiment that she claims is a "cultural myth." While teachers must work toward improving relations with the school's community, a mutual sense of responsibility must be fostered in order to create an environment that is most conducive to student and school success.

RESISTANCE FROM COLLEAGUES AND ADMINISTRATORS
Progressive educators also encounter opposition from their administrators and colleagues. Most UD teachers report that they have had to overcome obstacles ranging from overt to covert forms of resistance in order to remain true to their own democratic principles. For many respondents, this has meant refocusing their energy and moving away from large-scale, school-wide diversity and equity initiatives, and instead focusing on ensuring that their own classroom-based initiatives were integrated and carried out. Resistance from colleagues and administrators to equity initiatives has led other respondents to change schools, seeking a work environment that is accepting of anti-oppressive pedagogies and where other teachers are more "like-minded" and whose ideas are more "in line" with their egalitarian-pluralist mindset. Overall, a lack of support from colleagues and administrators is one of the greatest obstacles to engendering a progressive learning environment.

Collegial resistance

Collegial support for teachers is a necessity. When teachers who are committed to anti-oppressive education first enter a school, they look for like-minded colleagues. If these colleagues cannot be found, the equity practitioner feels physically, socially, and intellectually isolated. Responses to this sense of isolation differ. Some transform feelings of further marginalization into a stimulus to continue or begin new initiatives, whereas others may find it necessary to move on and find a more supportive working environment at another school. Regardless of teachers' responses to these feelings, a sense of being isolated among most colleagues persists.

> I think I didn't feel particularly aligned with other people in terms of what should be happening in the system. My school was considered to be a really good school pedagogically and a model school, but I just felt like the kids were learning to line up, they were learning to be obedient, they were learning not to ask questions, and that culture made me really uncomfortable on a fundamental level. (Ming)

In a profound way, Ming's description, which at first glance may seem like a typical teacher complaint, upon reflection reveals a deep connection between her personal and professional identity. In a simple and honest manner, Ming reveals how her educational philosophy is consistent with her ideological beliefs. Arising from her desire for students to learn to be thoughtful and empowered human beings, Ming's existential angst is triggered by witnessing a system that she finds demeaning to her students. These feelings are intensified as she realizes that her colleagues, who are considered good teachers in a model school, continue to participate in practices that she believes are doing harm to the children. We realize that this description may seem emotionally overwrought to some readers, yet the intensity of Ming's feelings is an essential part of her experience as a teacher. Understanding the profound sense of grief that some feel on a daily basis due to their beliefs and their positioning among colleagues is a significant aspect of this study.

It is not surprising that colleagues' support is an essential part of equity teachers' success as they are empowered when working in schools where both colleagues and administrators are supportive of their initiatives. While describing whether other teachers supported or opposed their social justice work, our participants shared ways of integrating progressive pedagogy into their lessons. Many mentioned a distinct lack of support from other teachers, claiming that this presents a major obstacle to their continued efforts at incorporating diverse material into their classrooms and schools. Their descriptions of opposition and challenges to their work contain many commonalities. Several commented that often many teachers who are initially excited about the prospect of incorporating multicultural activities become resistant as soon as the program gains momentum, thus revealing deeper attitudes that were previously hidden until awakened or incited. One teacher shared that her colleagues' continual opposition has affected her much more than parental resistance. While discussing her colleagues' attitudes, she reflected that "Diversity programs try to train us to walk into places like this [unreceptive schools], but you walk into a pretty good brick wall" (Mary).

While speculating on the dynamics of resistant teachers, some of our participants commented that a teacher's reluctance to see the value of other perspectives, including alternative or divergent teaching approaches, was directly tied to his or her inability to confront and deal with difficult knowledge. Sometimes the prevailing negative attitude among colleagues toward change or addressing these complex issues led them to ignore what the community wanted, needed, and strongly supported. As one UD teacher explains, "The wider community was more receptive and open and ready for change, but I found that the teachers weren't as receptive and ready, and that was a bit hard to take for me" (Yvette).

Many UD graduates describe other teachers' opposition as more often than not implicit and/or covert rather than explicit or obvious.

While their colleagues were not forthcoming in their actual rejection of diversity principles, our participants analyze their reluctance to participate in such work as indicative of their true beliefs. The ability of some teachers to reject participating in any or all of these programs, without administrative attention, also reinforces the idea that diversity teaching is a personal choice and not a systemic/structural commitment. As a result, the workload of the dedicated progressive teacher is increased. Other expressions of indirect conflict occur, according to several of our participants, after their philosophical/ideological differences about education are revealed to their co-workers. The form this subterfuge takes is a "behind one's back" attempt to undermine or thwart a teacher's anti-oppression work. For several of our UD graduates, other teachers' covert resistance to a progressive orientation was camouflaged in a critique of their pedagogical abilities. These barbs were apparent from the outset of their interactions, which, in the following case, began during a teaching practicum. Marcus explains:

> The host teachers again were upset with the student teachers who were trying to do social justice and equity work.... When they began to implement social justice work, they felt resistance. As a result, I had to negotiate through that. Their critique was never that they don't like equity or social justice because to say that doesn't look good. It would be something to do with pedagogy. (Marcus)

Another issue that appears to be deeply embedded in the narratives of the diversity teachers in this study concerns who anti-oppressive education should target. Some noticed greater resistance from their colleagues in schools where the student body was predominantly White. In these schools, they observed how teachers worked to maintain the status quo, for example, in the form of Christian-based plays. The presentation of a Christian play alone would not necessarily represent an insular and/ or closed-minded learning environment. However, the play, in a public school with no discussion of other religious or cultural beliefs, does indeed raise alarm bells as it indicates a myopic learning environment. Tellingly, in response to our UD teachers' concerns of religious and culturally centric programming, the teachers at this school claimed that the plays and subsequent lessons taught at the school are reflective of the community, so they could not understand the equity-conscious teachers' concerns and dismissed them as meaningless. UD graduates consistently spoke of confronting the mentality that progressive education, which values a diversity of experiences and beliefs, is only for students in communities generally made up of immigrants. Of course, the attitude that equity and diversity education, social justice awareness, and the introduction of diverse perspectives is only for those who are "different" from the normative White, primarily Christian culture reinforces an "us" and "them" mentality, fails to critically engage with perspectives different from those with which one is familiar, and does not prepare students for an increasingly diverse city as well as a world within which communications with others who are unlike oneself are increasingly the norm.

Many UD teachers choose to leave schools where collegial resistance is heightened.

> I didn't find teachers to be very receptive at all—they didn't like change. They didn't want to know that they couldn't read certain books in their classroom, they had certain structures, and they didn't want to accept any new ideas. I left that school, but what I took with me was the knowledge that just because I'm bright-eyed and bushy-tailed and ready to take on the world, that doesn't mean the rest of the world is. (Gail)

Experiences such as this can certainly be jading, but they can also be illuminating in terms of learning that one cannot always make changes in certain school environments. As we have argued, tensions with colleagues have an intensely personal and professional impact on social justice-oriented teachers. This presents particular challenges regarding social relations with their colleagues, which are unique to anti-oppressive staff members. Over time, some reported being able to challenge their colleagues' preconceived notions of progressive education through informal discussion as they became more comfortable with their colleagues and had established a rapport. Conversely, for many others interactions with the staff became more strained with the passage of time. One common experience and response among many of our participants was their deep discomfort with their colleagues' negative comments about parents. Negative comments were most often directed at the lower social classes, cultures of origin, and countries of origin. Assumptions generally were made about parents' lack of concern, lack of care, or general ignorance of education. These disparaging comments had a demoralizing effect and often led to UD teachers' reluctance to interact with colleagues, especially in the lunchroom (where most of these comments were expressed) as well as in common school spaces. So not only must these teachers struggle with integrating progressive initiatives in their class, but they also have to interact with colleagues who are resistant and who may be opposed to the ideals of democratic schooling. Sometimes the tensions are so great that they assume colleagues may have malicious intent in some interactions regarding social justice approaches, as one teacher intimates:

> But one thing that I find is sometimes colleagues will say if you bring up an initiative or an idea, they say, "Great, you do it." It's like they are looking for you to fail. (Sandra)

Tensions—whether apparent or assumed, implicit or explicit—can result in some colleagues refusing to participate in student projects with progressive aims. Although an explicit link between those who make negative comments about parents in the teachers' lounge and those who are unwilling to support progressive student programs has not been proven, there is a general feeling of negativity toward the teachers who initiate these projects. Thus, there is evidence of a mistrust that affects both personal and professional relationships among colleagues.

Resistance from administration

Many teachers also spoke of administrators being opposed to continued diversity, equity, and social justice work. Some administrators express resistance quite subtly. As one UD graduate explains in detail:

> I felt that my problem with school administrators was in relation to how I was perceived as a teacher. It's almost like when I was teaching the students about race and equity and anti-racism, that was okay, but in some respects, I was also encouraging students to be empowered in the sense that I was trying to develop social justice awareness with the students in the school; to raise different issues and questions within the school context. I think that when the issues became a bit more about the institution of the school that was critiqued, the principal became more critical about my professionalism. (Marcus)

This narrative highlights another way in which a lack of support from administrators can lead to professional recriminations about the work of the equity teacher. Essentially, staff members who take the initiative to promote social justice in the schools by, for example, volunteering for the equity committee are not only fully responsible for every aspect of this work, but may also be denigrated professionally when ideas that are perceived to negatively implicate the school arise from education grounded in democratic principles. As this sentiment was shared by many of our participants, it would be fair to say that, while administrators may be supportive of some diversity and equity initiatives, they are not necessarily receptive when diversity teaching critically implicates the school and educational system as a whole. This perception becomes more disturbing when one considers that the fears of exposing school-specific inequities may also reduce administrator support of these programs in the first place. Additionally, these comments suggest that administrators can become anxious that empowering students might mean disempowering the administration and their schools. Moreover, these observations and insights may explain the seeming contradictory and inconsistent support that some administrators give to social justice initiatives. Finally, notwithstanding the dynamic just outlined, we can surmise that if administrators perceive inequities as something that exists out in the world but certainly not in the school or in the school system, then their confusion or refusal to support these programs can also be better understood.

For one participant in particular, her commitment to equity, diversity, and social justice work has left her in the position of "scapegoat." She explains:

> The school administrators gave me the challenging kids, so I think they were setting me up for failure to begin with. But because I didn't have any issues with the kids, I gained respect.... I had an incident in my first year where one of my students and a student from another class was calling someone a "nigger lover." And because of that incident getting to the office, I was called down and the exact quote was, "This is what happens when you do what you are doing in class." So when trouble came concerning race and there were issues, I was the one who took the fall for it. (Chantelle)

In this case, Chantelle bases her perception of being set up for failure on previously negative interactions about her educational philosophy. She states that the administrator provided her with a particularly difficult classroom to work with in the hopes of undermining her efforts. While it is clear in this example that the administrator knew what she was doing in her class, it is also clear that he or she was not supportive of her efforts. The administrator's lack of support becomes clarified in the comment "This is what happens when you do what you are doing in class." The implication is that the work being done in her class incites or creates racist attitudes and behaviours that were previously not there or, if they did exist, they were not of any immediate concern or importance. The statement also identifies our social justice educator as the one to "take the fall" if any race-related incidents arise at the school. Blaming or scapegoating an educator as the source of racial incidents allows: (1) a denial of racial issues at the school; (2) a deflection of blame if racial issues become problematic at the school; (3) a rationale for inaction.

Another teacher spoke of how her principal feared the backlash of diversity and equity work. She observed that the principal's attendance at equity committee meetings signified a strong desire to know exactly what was going on in order to prevent trouble, rather than a desire for active participation or support of the initiative. Similar feelings of being watched over by administrators, who were not sure if they should support diversity and equity initiatives, were overwhelmingly reported. While oversight of sensitive work is understandable and often necessary, feelings of being spied on and being distrusted often led our teachers to take a more cautious and limited approach so as not to ruffle the feathers of their principals or other administrators.

Many participants make note of the important role administration has in the acceptance and implementation of democratic educational practices and new initiatives in a school. For some respondents, a new administration has meant the introduction of new ideologies and, in the best-case scenario, an openness to equity, diversity, and social justice. As one participant explains:

> My principal at the time was a major change agent. He totally transformed that whole middle school, and put education and understanding the students within the school first—everything about what equity education meant. The staff was extremely reflective of the students within the school. I felt at home. I was happy. I was content. (Sharlene)

In other cases, however, a change in administration resulted in resistance to and, in the worst cases, a dismantling of diversity initiatives that had once been in place. The same teacher explains:

> And now, after our administrator left in December, we got a new one in January and all hell broke loose.... I have to start thinking about how are we going to get it all back? (Sharlene)

Administrators, through budgetary and resource allocation decisions, also impact how school programs are implemented and thus affect how issues of equity and social justice are either attended to or left out.

> I think it's totally contradictory, but I think the curriculum looks like there is a lot of leeway, but at the same time there is not because your administrators come to you and say, "Here is the language program. You are going to be using these textbooks and here is the history book." (Sakshi)

Furthermore, while administrators may encourage more progressive types of teaching practices, this support can be undermined by resistant teachers on staff. As one UD graduate notes, more conservative teachers at her school believe that "the administration was irresponsible in counselling us [to use anti-oppressive strategies] and can't believe that they [the administration] are doing such terrible things" (Ming). Here, regardless of support from the administration, it is clear that some teachers will continue to oppose new teaching perspectives.

This chapter has revealed a strong thematic trend of tensions and confrontations among colleagues, which are experienced personally and professionally. These dynamics arise between teacher and teacher, teacher and parent, teacher and student, and/or teacher and administrator, often leading diversity teachers to become pigeonholed, stereotyped, demoralized, and even scapegoated as the cause of any negative perceptions of the school and school system. Furthermore, they may also be seen as instigators and inciters of racial incidents. In an attempt to avoid the effects of detrimental collegial relations, diversity teachers look to like-minded colleagues for support. Most importantly, they need a strong and supportive administrator. The importance of the administrator's role cannot be underestimated. As Sobel and Taylor (2003) point out, "Confronted by complex and seemingly perplexing social, political, and moral issues, the school principal, perhaps more so than ever before, plays a crucial role in developing sound educational programming" (p. 287). In sum, unsupportive and caustic collegial relations are a constant challenge to social justice educators that must be overcome.

Conclusions

Social justice educators feel overworked and under extreme pressure as they try to meet curricular demands while also fighting for a social justice orientation in their classrooms and schools. They confront resistance from parents, teachers, students, and colleagues. As a result of these major challenges, we concur with Good et al's research (2003) on activist teachers which states that these progressive educators are often more isolated personally and professionally from their co-workers, leading to frustration and even burn out. Many of these challenges are not new, and there is well-documented evidence that systemic inequities are pervasive in our school systems (Fordham & Ogbu, 1986; Hedges & Nowell, 1998; Hallinan, 2001; Solomon, Levine-Rasky & Singer, 2003; Portelli, Shields & Vibert, 2007). In many ways, the difficulties faced by UD graduates, once they assume positions within schools, is not surprising as real transformative change takes time and will require both a paradigm shift in the way we understand the purposes of education and a renewed commitment to democratic and socially just principles in our education system. Moreover, our research demonstrates that the recent climate of school reform has been particularly detrimental to the work of social justice educators. As Cochran-Smith (2005) insists:

From a social justice perspective, the purpose of education needs to be understood not simply as constructing a system where pupils' test scores and wise monetary investments are the bottom lines. Rather, the purpose of education also must be understood as preparing students to engage in satisfying work, function as lifelong learners who can cope with the challenges of a rapidly changing global society, recognize inequities in their everyday contexts, and join with others to challenge them. (p. 416)

Clearly, today's schoolteachers face an increasing number of institutional, social, and political factors and pressures that complicate their jobs. They are not only responsible for the measured growth of their students in reading, mathematics, and a variety of other subjects, but, from a social justice perspective, they are also accountable for the increasingly diverse needs of their students (Dearman & Alber, 2005). Given the sense of pressure and exasperation expressed by teachers in our study who are committed to teaching for equity and diversity within a climate of school reform, we believe it is imperative that teacher education must address the seemingly disparate goals of social justice–oriented teacher preparation on the one hand, and school reform on the other. While considering Zeichner's (2003) assertion that "[k]eeping the focus of proposals for social justice–oriented teacher education at the level of the teacher education classroom will not significantly impact the larger societal problem of inequality in education provision and outcomes" (Zeichner 2003: 509; see also Jennings & Smith, 2002), we conclude that in order to change this wider social problem, we must remain steadfast in our long-term plan to change these wider social dynamics by (1) persevering over time; (2) believing that the graduation of more progressive teachers will eventually change schools and schooling culture; (3) provide our students with more effective interpersonal, social, and political strategies to help them cope effectively with the challenges they face after graduation; (4) encourage our students to become involved politically both inside and outside their immediate school environments; and (5) maintain hope that over time, progressive teacher education programs will contribute to changing our wider social, cultural, and institutional landscapes.

The teachers in this study are working to be agents of change within huge constraints. They face challenges from: the new curriculum; the bureaucratization of teaching; a lack of resources; and resistance from parents, students, colleagues, and administrators. They are calling out for support, and how best to help them is a complicated matter. It is clear, however, that the current situation is not satisfactory.

Importantly, interviews with UD graduates indicate that not only are they committed to social justice principles, but many refuse to be disheartened by reforms that have been tacitly disempowering. These resilient progressive voices demonstrate a strong determination to implement and integrate equity into the curriculum. Choosing not to view specific expectations of the curriculum as rigid impediments, these educators instead interpret the curriculum documents as flexible enough to accommodate social justice and equity.

> I really didn't feel restricted by the curriculum and I thought it was just my mindset. My attitude was different. I embraced the curriculum because this is what I had to do, but then I found a way to include equity and diversity because I had to—because it's who I am. It's who my students are, and I wouldn't be an effective teacher if I didn't find a way to include equity. (Virginia)

The important perception that Virginia illuminates here is that although the curriculum is explicit in what has to be taught to students, it does not specifically stipulate how to teach; a creative shift in mindset can lead to imaginative ways in which one may integrate progressive teaching and learning environments.

One UD graduate expresses a concern that some teachers may use the curriculum expectations as an excuse to avoid equity and social justice issues because these issues do not appear in the text of the documents. She goes on to explain how perseverance is the answer to feelings of demoralization:

> Even though there's been so many changes and there's been so much downloading on us, I don't feel demoralized in that sense, and I don't feel disempowered because I think I just have to put in extra effort to get things done. When I bring something forth, they'll say it must be something that's going to be good and benefit the kids. I may have to go in a second and third time to get the okay. So it's just more energy and more work for me to do, but I don't feel disempowered. (Vera)

Both of these teachers believe that they can take control of how the curriculum is implemented, and therefore always see the potential for bringing progressive teaching and learning perspectives to their students. They teach us how a strong sense of efficacy, a search for creative methods, and a continued willingness to challenge the loss of professional autonomy can lead to success.

In our next chapter we turn to a more theoretical discussion of how teachers' social identity impacts their efforts to teach for equity, diversity, and social justice.

CHAPTER 4

Identity Matters in Teaching for Equity

ANDREW ALLEN

What is my cultural identity? What is my relationship to that identity? What issues are unresolved for me in relation to that identity? How will aspects of that identity affect what I teach and how I teach it? How do I feel about and how will I interact with each of the children before me, relative to my own cultural identity, background, education, values, and biases? (Dilg, 2003: 80)

Issues of social identity are extremely complex. How one identifies oneself and how one is identified by others is an ambiguous process. Identity is performed and experienced in elusive and complex ways, and for teachers, identity often influences how teaching and learning are understood and negotiated (Wenger, 1998). Defining a teacher's social identity is difficult since there are many intertwining identities through which one enacts and interprets one's social life. By social identity, we mean one's self-perceived racial, ethnic, religious, linguistic, and cultural in-group social affiliation or the social group identification that others assign to us.

In this chapter, we try to unravel some of the complexities surrounding teachers' understandings of how their social identities relate to their efforts in teaching for equity and diversity. We echo the distinction made by Brayboy, Castagno, and Maughan (2007) that teaching equitably is not the same as teaching for equality—socially just, equitable, or fair teaching practice is the means through which we can achieve equality, or sameness of opportunity, both in life and learning. By equality, we mean sameness and, more specifically, sameness of resources and opportunities. This concept of equality is the long-term goal of a just society: children, regardless of race, socio-economic class, or gender, should have access to the same resources and opportunity outcomes. It will become apparent that we have reached this goal when schooling and economic successes and opportunities look the same for all groups of children. A closer examination of test scores, schooling facilities for particular children, and life outcomes of children from different racialized groups demonstrate that currently there is no equality (i.e., sameness) in resources or opportunity outcomes (Brayboy, Castagno & Maughan, 2007: 163).

Given teachers' pivotal role in either reproducing the status quo or transforming schools for inclusivity and social justice, it was imperative and urgent that we examine UD teachers' pedagogical practices in given institutional, social, and political contexts. The central question raised in this chapter is: To what extent do teachers' social identities help or hinder the implementation of an equity-based, diversified curriculum? We were particularly interested in teachers' social self-identification and the ways in which their identity influences their understanding of issues of equity and diversity in their classrooms, and how such issues are taken up in their teaching practice. This chapter also raises the very important issue of teachers' social identities as a critical factor in developing commitment and practice of inclusive and democratic education.

Canadian research on teachers' response to multiculturalism and anti-racism conducted over the last decade suggests that there may be different levels of teaching commitment based on educators' identities (Carr & Klassen, 1997; Dei et al., 1997; Solomon, Levine-Rasky & Singer, 2003). This factor is particularly important for this study due to the ethno-racial makeup of the cohorts studied, the ethno-racial need for representation of Ontario's urban communities, and the potential impact of teachers' ethno-racial diversity on the schooling process. This chapter also offers insight into various factors that have implications for teacher education and teaching, specifically in such areas as: (1) candidate selection of students for teacher education programs and the importance of social identities as a selection criterion; (2) teacher education curriculum and scholarship and its application for equity and diversity work in both local and global socio-economic and political context (Kincheloe et al., 2000); (3) the exploration of intellectual and political support for teachers, and building alliances with other progressive teachers, including community activists, parents, and students, among others. Furthermore, we examine UD teachers' understanding of their own identity and how these identities mediate their teaching for equity in very diverse classrooms and schools. Markedly, their nuanced relationships with students, parents, and teacher colleagues are examined from the participants' perspectives and their own lived experiences working in various school settings.

How Conceptions of Social Identity Mediate Teaching

UD teachers expressed tensions that resulted from the apparent disconnect between popular conceptualizing of social identity and their actual lived experience. There is tension between how one experiences marginalization through living in opposition to dominant society, and how one's race is *read* (Van Dijk, 2002). For example, Perron's responses point to how discourses of social identity, regularly framed in racial terms, are often set in a binary of "Black"/"White" that excludes the experience of people who are read as neither "Black" nor "White" or in any singular or dichotomous sense:

I don't know if I see myself as part of the dominant group. People question where I'm from because I'm not White and I'm not a visible, visible minority. So they kind of look at me questioningly and I know that they don't want to ask because they don't want to appear rude. Sometimes I'll tell them that my parents are from Morocco and I tell them little stories about my parents and where they grew up. (Perron)

While she is unsure how to categorize herself along the "dominant"/"minority" binary provided by popular discourse, Perron draws upon her family heritage as her identifying characteristics by providing an example that does not fit the dominant narrative. Although significant to her sense of self, her response questions what qualifies as a "minority" or "dominant" experience, and reveals the complexities involved in how social identity can be defined and/or understood.

There was also evidence of UD graduates actively resisting popular categories of social identity and the ways in which such categorization may tend to constrain and limit how one understands oneself and others. Marcus had this to say when he was asked about his identity:

I was trying to discover my identity that is very much rooted in the kind of rigid Black male construction of myself, so I would approach teaching from that authoritative kind of critical standpoint. We need to think critically. Black people need to do this; Black people need to do that, etc. I think it was rigid in terms of my own identity politics. In the last three years I think my sense of identity is always something that's shifting and evolving. Being biracial and just understanding my personality, I see many sides of things, so I'm a lot more of an inclusive thinker than when I was in the UD program. I am a lot more open, a lot more curious about differences that go beyond Black and White.... I am more interested in the greys and the different shades of grey that exist. (Marcus)

Marcus's rejection of the way Black men are categorized led him to embrace the ambiguity and complexity inherent in issues of social identity. In turn, his evolving understanding of his own social identity has greatly influenced how he understands his students and his role as a teacher committed to equitable ideals.

> I think it's evolved identity of self. It's a lot more open; it's a lot more of the complexities of life. So whereas now if I left the school and went to another school where my students were predominantly White, I would still be able to do equity and diversity work; I wouldn't be reluctant to go there. There are too many students who are White, of dominant cultures that need exposure to diversity and social difference. (Marcus)

This kind of self-analysis and reflection on identity was common among both White teachers and teachers of colour. Both groups of teachers recognize the awareness of identity as integral to their own personal and professional philosophy and approach to teaching.

The UD program provided White teachers with the impetus to recognize their own implication in the workings of racial privilege. White teachers' awareness and understanding of their power and privilege led to a critical consciousness of their understanding of their own racial identity and that of others. For example, Amelda had this to say about the UD program's impact on her awareness of her own privilege as a White teacher:

> I think awareness of privilege was the biggest thing for me and constantly searching for that knapsack, that thing inside me that I had always taken for granted. I try still to critically look at everything that's going on around me, and the things that are coming out of me. Without vigilance you miss something or let something go by, and it is kind of a nauseating feeling, so I think the awareness is the biggest thing. (Amelda)

In addition to an awareness of her own privileges, Amelda realized the limitations of just being tolerant and accepting of minorities. Her engagement with critical and anti-racist theories helped her to confront taken-for-granted systemic, institutional, and structural racism as is evidenced by her comments in Chapter 1. She also acknowledges the diversity education aspect of the program as critical to shifting her thinking. This recognition speaks to the importance of focusing specifically on exploring issues of race and identity in teacher education programs. "For me, the program really expanded my awareness, constantly; I became very aware of every person I ran into and how they were perceiving that world." The UD program sparked Amelda's recognition of her position of privilege and revealed how her personal experience has shaped and limited her understanding of identity markers such as race and its potential impact on people of colour.

Others bypassed a critical engagement with issues of identity, looking instead to transcend notions of predetermined social categories all together. In one instance, Teresa adopts a seemingly colour-blind approach to making sense of identity:

> At the beginning of my career I was really focused on my identity as a woman of East Indian descent. But now I find that I am in a different space, I'm trying to transcend all that. I just want to look at people more spiritually now and transcend what's on the surface. I know that this goes against a lot of what we were taught, but I hope that one day people can also transcend skin colour and our gender and like just really relate to others as spiritual beings. (Teresa)

Similarly, Marcus rejects the notions of labels and categorization by race and gender:

> The real problem is seeing each other as separate; seeing that person as in a female body. I'm in a male body, she has black

skin, I have white skin, I have [a] Hindu title and she has a Jewish title. These are labels and they push us away from actually experiencing and seeing that there is a person regardless of their skin, their race, their status, their job title, their name, and their form, fat or thin. I think we would see a lot of change in the world if we resist labels. (Marcus)

Both respondents express frustration with the limits of popular categorizations of social identity and convey an ideal integral to their world views that moves beyond the constraints of categories. Their responses are quite common in teaching and teacher education, and the diversity education aspect of the UD program is geared toward self-awareness, self-analysis, and a critical engagement with issues of identity. The UD program seeks to acknowledge and actively resist the reality that categories of social identity are evoked in the school system and are experienced in various forms of discrimination.

HOW SOCIAL IDENTITIES INFLUENCE ROLES AS AGENTS OF CHANGE
Many UD teachers stated that their motivation to be agents of change seemed to be rooted in their social identities and the history of oppression and marginalization linked to these identities. Those who identified as being part of a "minority" relate how this has fuelled their commitment to challenge the status quo. Amy identified certain challenges for teachers based on identity and background:

To start off, being Jewish and female—female first and foremost— we know challenges are ahead of us and what we have to deal with as Jews. Our ethnic background has always been stigmatized; we teach the Holocaust in Grade 5 and it's actually a very powerful unit. We do novel studies and we focus on the hope that the people had.... But it shapes my social identity to the understanding that you have to work extremely hard; that you have to always deal with people who would like to oppress you. (Amy)

Josie spoke of her renewed commitment to student learning based on race and as a result of being in the UD program:

> When we graduated, I felt a bit more empowered in terms of changing things. I could do something as a Black teacher. I could go in and really make a difference for those kids, and then once you go in, even though I didn't start right away, I thought about the possibilities.

Frederick agreed with Josie's perspective and acknowledges also that race is central to self-imposed expectations as a teacher:

> I knew I was going to be doing something; I knew that primarily because of my preparation. I also felt that being a Black teacher, it was expected of me. This was something that I was going to live up to anyway in one way or another.

Indeed, those who experienced discrimination and marginalization as students felt that the experiences propelled them to identify with, and develop the desire to protect, students of colour. As the next example illustrates, Josie felt that she brought a degree of empathy for these students:

> For me, my social identity helps me because of the negative schooling experience I went through. I'm extremely sensitive to the kids who are going through that, and so for me the obvious is to affirm, affirm, affirm so that they feel like there is a safe place. So they feel like somebody has made room for all of them, for the whole person; someone has made room for their emotional self, for the self that they probably don't like because of their social situation. So having gone through it, I go out of the way to be protective—to make sure they don't go through that negative thing. Hopefully, the people I'm going to hang out with are not

negative; they are politically conscious, socially aware, and culturally in touch with what's going on with kids, so social markers of race, ethnicity, culture, and gender help. Anybody who
struggles because of their social identities has their consciousness raised and is prepared to help minority students. (Josie)

Marcus also felt that his personal experience of being a person of colour
allowed him to be more open to implementing the practices informed
by theory:

I don't think it [diversity effort of other teachers] was grounded
as much as some of the work that I was doing because I kind
of felt like the work that I was doing was really theoretically
informed by the work in the faculty, and I also had a personal
interest in it, and I think just by the way of doing academic
work I kind of found a way to weave it in more rather than just
addressing it every so often. (Marcus)

Another teacher of colour, Vera, also felt that her own identity and her
experience with "social difference" allowed her to teach for diversity more
easily than her "White" colleagues:

I've gone into other classes and I've seen other people teach and
I'm thinking, "This curriculum is so White." I guess because of
their past experiences they do things this way and they don't
realize how they are impacting the kids in the class. I look at
the students and I'm seeing all these different shades of brown
and all the characters in the books are White, or the names of
the characters are White. Even when you are reading that story,
instead of using "Sarah" or "Jane," you could substitute "Alicia"
or "Mohammed." Often when I'm doing diversity, it's natural for
me to get a book that reflects the diversity of the students. Teachers don't mean any harm, but the opportunity to diversify just

goes right by them. It is something that they don't even think about because they bring privilege; their perspectives and practices are limited by their privileged life experiences. (Vera)

The personal experience of teachers of colour also motivated them to embrace the added challenge of being positive role models to students of colour.

I just want to be a positive role model for all students, and I want them to know that I will always put them first. I would always advocate for students. With regard to diversity, I want students of colour to look at me and say, "Well, if Mr. Francis can make it, I can make it," after I tell them my background, where I'm coming from, and what I had to go through to get to this stage of my life. (Francis)

Forming a point of reference from which to view and understand the situations of new Canadians, Zora shared her personal knowledge of the trials and tribulations of her parents' immigrant experience to sensitize herself to their challenges:

I think it [social identity] does a bit of both [hinders and helps]. I've had my own challenges being European, female, Portuguese, and being from a male-dominated culture. I have had my challenges with that, but I can also see that there are a lot of groups that have many more challenges than I do. So by understanding that, little challenges that I've had, it helps me in terms of trying to give something positive to the system—to encompass and accept [that] everyone ... has something unique or special about them. Having immigrant parents who had to settle and didn't speak English, went to night school, worked and fed children, and went to parent-teacher interviews and not know what the teacher was saying to them was quite a challenge. I think it has grounded me in the sense morally. I'm trying daily to make sure that, as a person, I'm aware of racism, prejudice, and stereotypes that exist on a daily basis. (Zora)

On the other hand, Amelda's responses appear to support the idea that being from a visible majority background can hinder a teacher's ability to teach for equity and diversity. Amelda believed that because she was unaware of the negative experiences of her own ethnic community, she felt removed from her students and at times was unable to relate to them:

I think if it [being a visible majority] is going to hinder me, it's going to be those notions that I have, or those ideas that I don't even recognize that I am thinking or feeling because I come from a community in which I didn't have to think about—ever—how hard it was to get a job, or to go to school, or to walk in a store without being followed or be followed around or anything. I have free rein in this culture, and I think that still to this day, I know that would still hinder my ability to be as aware as I need to be, and that's the thing I am trying to fight continually. (Amelda)

Although she may not have believed herself to be fully "aware" of the workings of privilege within her classroom, through her ability to think critically, Amelda felt responsible for fighting against injustice. She also acknowledged that her social identity had assisted by providing her with the opportunity to become the type of teacher who does such critical work:

Being Caucasian and female is a help because it offered me the ability to meet with the people, to have the knowledge, to get the knowledge, to go to school, to talk with people. I talk with people on a very different level than I would otherwise. And it has allowed me to become aware and allowed me to want to become

critical and evaluate things that are going on around me. That's
been part of my heritage as well. (Amelda)

Peggy McIntosh's (1989) work, *White Privilege: Unpacking the Invisible Knapsack*, is particularly instructive here. She argues that Whites are
carefully taught not to recognize (or acknowledge) their privilege and,
as a result, it becomes "an invisible weightless backpack of special provisions, maps, codebooks, clothes, tools, and blank checks.... Describing white privilege makes one newly accountable" (p. 31). Amelda has
developed the critical consciousness to recognize the impact of privilege on the lived experiences of groups in society and how this may be
manifested in schools and classrooms.

Moving beyond White privilege identity becomes more nuanced
when the dynamics of religion and culture are added to the mix. Amy
found herself in a conservative, Jewish school, where although she did
not appear visibly different, she was viewed as different by the Jewish
school community. This caused a dramatic shift in her view of her role
as a teacher of diversity. Consequently, she came to understand that
she was in a minority position while in that monocultural setting, and
found that such an experience defined her role as an agent of change.

So when I was hired, I had a very different perception of what
my role was going to be because I thought I was going to be
in public school, and I was going to be working with a whole
variety of ethnic backgrounds, and us being able to work as colleagues and as teachers and students together. But when I found
myself as the minority, it [the role] changed completely and I
then saw myself as "the other" and I used my teacher education
to get through. I worked positively and I still saw my principal
role as a change agent. (Amy)

It appears that Amy had appropriated the language used to describe
the way that races and ethnicities are "othered" by a dominant discourse

and applied it to her own situation as a more secular-oriented teacher in a conservative Jewish school. Important to this discussion was that her understanding of her social identity status had a significant impact on how she approached and made sense of herself as a teacher for social justice in her career. This process of self-reflection was a critical aspect of identifying oneself in relation to those involved in the teaching and learning of social justice.

In summary, beyond supporting the generalization that minority or dominant social positioning affects a teacher's ability to teach for equity and diversity, our findings attest to the significant complexity inherent in the relationship between social identity and teaching. As Dilg (2003) notes, "Teachers reside—and conduct their classes—within a vortex of contradictory contemporary attitudes and behaviours related to race and culture" (p. 87). Throughout this study, we have seen how teachers resist and employ existing social and pedagogical categorizations in determining their social identities. Not only does this highlight the lack of alternative language available to teachers promoting equity and diversity, it also articulates the way that prevailing categorizations of races and cultures are problematic and limiting, particularly as they may constrain effective practice. As Yon (1999) states:

> While multiculturalism has been popularly critiqued for its preoccupation with presenting to students fossilized cultural traditions, its theoretical successor, anti-racism, offers little alternative to the ways that culture and domination are theorized.... A persistent tension concerns how both culture and community continue to be reduced to stable and knowable sets of identity attributes. This trope of culture haunts the field of educational research. (p. 624)

Promoting a critical reflection of teachers' social identities had proven essential to many UD teachers' abilities to critically reflect on how their identities affected their teaching. The next sections focus on the teachers' critical reflections about how their social identities are implicated in their relationships with students, parents, and colleagues.

TEACHERS' IDENTITIES AND RELATIONSHIPS WITH STUDENTS

UD teachers reveal that they experience tensions in the classroom related to their social identities. Teachers of colour, in particular, experience discrimination and often overt racism from students. Francis's comments describe how students employ the popular discourse of racial identities, employing stereotypes in order to cope with the atypical experience of having a Black teacher:

> A lot of them had never had a Black teacher. My first year of teaching was very trying because they didn't know how to react to me. They called me "Michael Jordan." "Are you related to this athlete? Are you this, are you that?" They thought I was going to be intimidating and yelling, but when I started talking to them, it came to the point where I was a pushover because I was not the mean person they had envisioned. A lot of them at first didn't know how to react to me. It was really sad to know that a lot of these kids—even students of colour, even though community demographic changed over the years—had never had a teacher of colour and didn't know how to react to a Black teacher. But eventually they started saying things like, "He is the coolest teacher on staff; he is the best teacher." (Francis)

Eventually Francis was able to persist in resisting and pushing beyond the stereotypes, but not without some disturbing experiences:

> I remember coming to school one morning and outside of my classroom window was spray-painted "I hate niggers." And I immediately went to the office and told the admin, and it was just kind of covered up. The caretaker hurried up and cleaned it off the window and nothing else was ever mentioned. Because

at that time I was new to teaching and I didn't want to push any buttons and I was scared because I thought okay, maybe this was going to be taken to the school board, but nothing happened. I never received a phone call from the superintendent; my principal never spoke to me about the racist incident ever again, and that always sticks in my mind. (Francis)

Silence around issues of race and racism is pervasive in Canadian society. This is particularly disturbing for a society that claims to be racially tolerant and multicultural. This response supports the systemic nature of racism experienced by teachers of colour. Even in "diverse" school settings, the current of racism was a reality that was continually reinforced.

My colleague and I were talking about skin colour differences, and it became very frustrating for our children too. They were still preferring white. It [the responses] came from them. They were saying that there is a teacher that they had and they didn't like him because his skin is so dark. (Mary)

On the other hand, while teachers of colour experience discrimination in classrooms, they also report that in many circumstances their racial identity allows them to connect more readily with students of colour, as Gail explains: "I do think that some of the kids identified with me, some of the 'visible minority kids,' especially Black students. I think they are identifying with me in some ways." Gail's claim was supported by other teachers of colour in the study and consistent with findings of other research on social identities and the schooling process. For example, Solomon's (1997) work on race and ethnocultural representation in teaching revealed that students tend to gravitate toward teachers on the basis of similar identities. Such gravitation was very pronounced in school environments with a high level of students of colour and a correspondingly low representation of teachers of colour. Teachers reported that positive associations were built through students' visits to their classrooms during "down time," such as breaks, lunchtime, and after-school, extracurricular activities, and specific culture-based activities (e.g., playing cricket or dominoes). To encourage and build such relationships, teachers strategically played "identity politics" because they are committed to being positive role models for students who do not often see themselves represented in positions of responsibility and power.

It is clear from our findings that "White" teachers have a different experience regarding how their social identity relates to their teaching for equity and diversity. They saw themselves as agents of equity through expressions of empathy to their students. Similar to the teachers of colour, Samantha, a "White" teacher, felt she had to prove herself to the students, but for her it was about proving that she is approachable and "on their side." In other words, while she feels that students of colour judge her by her racial identity, she deals with it on an emotional level and explains how she went about developing a positive relationship across the racial divide.

> I welcomed them into my classroom, saying, "Hello, guys. I have a planning period. Come in. It's a cold day and let's have a hot chocolate. Sit down and chat with me while I'm doing my work." They came in. One is from South America and the other is from Jamaica, and they were sitting here and both of them are immigrants within the last five years. They sat down and had hot chocolate and now they are like my best friends. They are always knocking on my door. They started getting into the fact that my classroom is different; it's warm and it looks good. If that's my role for them, then that's fine. So in a way I think that just my personality catches a lot of kids. (Samantha)

Samantha also felt that being female helps her to reach out to her students. Her role as a gym teacher facilitated strong bonding with her female students. These relationships often move beyond the classroom and the gym and into students' personal and family lives, especially in times of need. She relates: "One of my students tried to commit suicide and called me from the hospital, asking for permission to communicate with me. So obviously, I must have filled something in her life at this time of need."

Interestingly, Samantha identifies a number of interrelating factors for the relationships she develops with students: her personality, approachability, her classroom ambiance, her ethic of caring, and her gender. It is significant that although it may be difficult for teachers to separate their personalities from their social identities, upon reflection and interpretation of their teaching experiences, they are able to develop an awareness of how their social identities impact their attempts to be inclusive educators.

TEACHERS AND THEIR NUANCED RELATIONSHIPS WITH PARENTS

This section explores the complex and often ambiguous ways that UD teachers' social identities mediate their relationships with parents. Issues of cross-race relationships are evident, but so are contradictory narratives about the presumed "cultural match" between teachers and parents of the same ethnocultural group.

Similar to their experiences with students, teachers of colour experienced discrimination from parents as well, which hindered their ability to promote a specific agenda for social change and diversity in their practice. For example, starting at a new school, Francis believed he faced much resistance from parents because of his race and because he believed they felt he truly needed to prove himself professionally. Consequently, it took a long time for him to feel appreciated and accepted. Opportunities for teachers to develop and foster a constructive sense of self and positive self-esteem within their teaching practice are essential to providing the professional basis from which to enact a transformative program.

It was hard for the parents to accept me initially. "Who is this young Black male teacher who comes in here and wants to change everything, who wants people to celebrate all these different holidays?"

But as they got to know me and realized that my first objective was for the kids, and I wanted all their kids to benefit from learning about diversity, and the fact that I was actively involved in the school culture with regard to coaching and running homework clubs, they warmed up to me…. They didn't see me as this Black figure anymore; they saw me more as a human being and started warming up and sending me little gifts with their kids. Those things were like rewarding me, but it took years. (Francis)

This experience was echoed by other teachers, who related that their racial identities have placed them in situations with parents where they have had to work more diligently to prove their professionalism and worthiness of their teaching positions. Here Marcus reports negative experiences with parents: "I think initially some parents were judgmental. There was one girl in particular…. Her father told her that he is kind of suspect of Black people; he was the kind of parent that would say 'Black people are bad people.'"

Gail concurred and she felt also that her students' parents were judging her unfairly:

Well, they [parents] were mostly White at the time, and very skeptical. I've had questions at "Meet the Teacher Night." I had questions about my credentials: Am I qualified to teach? And I thought to myself, if I were a Caucasian teacher, would somebody be asking me if I was qualified to teach Grade 1? I've had parents who were blatantly racist and had racial statements made about me to my principal. She decided, "You know what? I am going to communicate with this parent from now on. You just worry about teaching the student." And I had to literally have my principal as my go-between in communication with this parent. (Gail)

However, similar to the situation with students in many other circumstances, as a teacher of colour, Gail's social identity assisted them in understanding and thereby meeting the needs of parents of colour:

> I had this parent, a West Indian woman, and her child was having some challenges throughout the years. She had come to me and she felt that she could sit and talk to me comfortably. She said other teachers tried to help, but she was really nervous when she speaks to them. But with me, she said she found a comfortable parent-teacher relationship. (Gail)

By the same token, Gail and other teachers of colour argue that their racial identity was key to the productive and trusting relationships developed with parents of colour that made a difference in students' lives. For example, students with a history of inappropriate behaviours (they were described as having "thick school records") developed more pro-social behaviours as a result of racial bonding. As Gail reports a mother's claim: "You know, you have been that teacher who changed the way my son thinks.... He is responsible now and he really identified with you. I just wanted you to know that." Teachers also observed that parents of colour who initially stayed away from the school were now more comfortable in attending parent-teachers interviews and other school-based activities. Nonetheless, it is important to note that common racial identification between teacher and parent does not guarantee good relations.

> I've had one incident where I had a Black parent who was skeptical about my qualifications to teach because she wanted her daughter in the White teacher's class. And I would say that I have had quite a few incidents throughout the years dealing with that kind of thing. I have known [how] to deal with it by just doing my job, teach effectively and be respectful, and if they want to be ignorant, I show them that I don't want to go to that level. (Gail)

It is particularly important to point out that social class conflicts can interfere with teacher-parent relationships in the schooling process. Both Sharlene and Sandra identified the difficulty of connecting with some parents of colour:

> You would think that I might be able to get along with the parents in my community from a Caribbean background. Well, I tell you they are the ones that are the most resistant to me.... There is a sense of resistance. I'm talking about my community because of who I am in my position [as a teacher] ... a rejection of that socio-economic class structure. (Sharlene)

This comment relates to the pervasive social-class hierarchies, a legacy of post-colonial societies. Such stratifications structure the relationship between teachers and parents in Caribbean societies. Teachers who are perceived as working class bear the brunt of resistance from those who see themselves to be of a higher socio-economic status. These attitudes and behaviours tend to reproduce themselves in immigrant parents in their Canadian host society.

Also similar to the situation with students, the White teachers faced very different tensions in their relations with parents from different cultural backgrounds. Although some of the evidence mentioned suggests that parents preferred White teachers, the disconnect between a teacher's experience and those of her students' families can also hinder her ability to connect on a meaningful level with parents. Despite recognizing that she could not relate on a personal level to families of a different racial background from herself, Samantha fell back on the liberal language of equality and universalism to cope with the situation:

> [Social identity] can hinder making connections in the sense that you do get parents who may look at you and say, "Oh, you have no idea what I'm talking about." And, yeah, I don't have their experience, but I have a kind heart to treat the racially different

child with the same respect that I treat every single child. I'll be fair and that to me is the most important thing. (Samantha)

Samantha was sensitive to her privileged position, but was also at a loss as to how to approach the cultural disconnect beyond valuing the student's individual situation. This situation points to a struggle that White teachers face wherein they have the theoretical understanding of social inequities, but lack the appropriate tools to implement this knowledge in their relations with students and parents. The recognition of, and reflection upon, social identities is a first step in attaining such knowledge.

TEACHERS' RELATIONSHIPS WITH COLLEAGUES

UD teachers of colour, by virtue of their racial markers, find themselves with "outsider" status on the margins of the dominant school culture. They feel that when they are hired, they are expected to fill the roles of link people and associate with ethnocultural communities served by the schools. Here a supply teacher of colour describes her experience as an outsider:

Supplying was interesting because in certain schools you felt welcomed and then in other schools, you felt like, "Well, who is she, coming into our school?" It was interesting because in some schools in which I supplied, I literally had teachers craning their necks to see who was this person of colour in their school. This response was quite evident in the students too. (Sharlene)

In this example, Sharlene believed that because supply teachers are traditionally marginalized in school cultures, supply teachers of colour are doubly outsiders.

Another important theme that emerged from the study was the "pigeonholing" of teachers of colour as one-dimensional—the diversity experts. Commonly expected to be the "expert" on the social group with which they are categorized, or on minority groups in general, UD teachers often viewed these stigmatizing experiences as problematic. Sakshi's case is particularly interesting in this regard; her Asian identity was a factor in her hiring, but the administrator was not sensitive to the various identities that fall within the category of "Asian." Consequently, Sakshi was erroneously pegged as an expert on "Asianness" and "Koreanness":

> When I graduated and went for my job interview, the principal directly asked what is it that I can do for the school, so I talked about my teacher education and she wanted to know how I could help get parents involved in the school community even though I wasn't of that particular culture—a lot of the parents are Chinese. I said I would be able to help liaise with parents who are of Korean heritage, as well as all parents, and try to get them more involved, and we were able to do that to some extent. (Sakshi)

Sakshi also points out the danger of being considered the "expert" in the school on one's own culture, particularly when she is a second-generation Canadian:

> You are always asked to be the expert, or to know all about your culture. The worst one was when we did a heritage day thing and they asked me to do a little pavilion about Korea. It totally cracks me up because I grew up here [in Canada] my whole life; I came when I was one. So I kind of went to my mom and said, "Give me a couple of games and a couple of things and I'll go to school in my costume." That's the last thing I wanted to do, but it's better than doing nothing. But at the same time, who am I to be an expert at Korean culture? (Sakshi)

Here Frederick, a Black teacher, shares his experience of racial encapsulation:

One of my colleagues asked, "So what are you going to do? Are you going to do an assembly for Black History month?" I questioned, "Why are you asking me that?" The only reason I could come up with is [that] because I'm Black, I have to do it. Why can't he do it? You don't have to be Black to be an authority and assume responsibilities for Black issues.

This grouping trend can be viewed as patronizing and discourages any real interruption of systemic racism. As a result, White teachers may frequently find themselves leaving the anti-racist and multicultural work to teachers of colour. Furthermore, it hinders any real examination of the issues by the staff as a whole. In turn, anti-racist and multicultural work is not respected for its transformative potential for all; instead, it is seen as the responsibility of teachers of colour. Marcus concludes: "I was known as the equity guy, and towards the end I resented that because it's patronizing." Chantelle reports a similar experience. Her sense of her professional identity as the "diversity expert" related strongly to her sense of having to "prove" herself professionally:

Anything that came up that was even remotely related to diversity or social justice, I was the one who was thrust forward, whether I did it on my own or people assumed that I would take that role. I guess I just didn't ask to because I just felt that was just part of who I was anyway. So if anything came up, whether it was a committee or an assembly or organizing to have [a] guest come in and do storytelling, I was the one. What happened after a couple of months is that people just assumed that you would take the role, and they come to you with questions: "Oh, I am having difficulty with a particular student concerning race. What should I do? How do I handle it?" I became the expert, particularly with African-Canadian students. I became the expert on anything to do with them. (Chantelle)

Sometimes Chantelle felt that the schools took advantage of her, and she felt overwhelmed and burdened with the full responsibility of doing equity work. Incredibly, in Gail's case, the "pigeonholing" had gone as far as having Black students placed in her class:

> I have one teacher who wants to move all the Black males to my class and really not having any justification for wanting to do that except for not wanting them. So sometimes that happens that they feel that you could be dumped on, that you are the expert, so you need to handle them. (Chantelle)

These types of tensions greatly discourage unity among the staff. Marisa touches on her experience of trying to make the equity committee at her school more diverse:

> When I came to teach at this school, there was an equity contact person who got all the mailings about Black History month and stuff like that, and had to go to equity-related meetings. The task always fell on one of the three Black people on staff. I had worked with them around different curriculum stuff and we talked about equity. We had a computer committee model that involved a good cross-section of staff, and it had some power in the school, so I proposed [that] we set up something like that for equity as opposed to a one-person contact for equity-related matters. (Marisa)

She goes on to explain how her social identity allows her to promote unity among the staff and to promote equity and diversity within the school: "I've been able to use my identity to advantage. My family is mixed-race and I'm married to a Chinese man, so every once in a while, I can use this identity to advance equity at my school." Marisa personifies the elusive nature of social identity as it relates to teaching. Her personal experience and self-identification did not equate with how others read her. She described the surprise with which her diversity initiatives were greeted when people, reading her whiteness, were not aware of her own family's mixed race:

> I found in some ways it's been helpful because people don't expect it [diversity work] from me. They expect a little bit from the ESL perspective, but they don't expect the equity push, and they don't expect taking it one level deeper and taking responsibility for the thing. (Marisa)

Social identity is thus critical to how teachers are able to integrate and promote social justice among their school staff. Having an administrator who is also a person of colour can be advantageous. Paulette gives this example: "I feel very comfortable as a Black woman working in the school. If I was in another school, I would still have the strong sense of self there, but I don't know if it would be a hindrance being a minority. Here it is not, it is a plus."

Summary

> Be prepared to have your race be called in question. Be prepared to have your identity be called into question.... Be prepared to be criticized for that background and admired for it.... I think that's the hardest part about being a teacher of color at [my school] because I went in, and I know who I am, and I formed my identity. But just because you know who you are doesn't mean the students are going to accept it. They're going to play with it. They're going to tweak it. —Alejandr (Achinstein & Aguirre, 2008)

Alejandr, the teacher of colour quoted above, sums up the nuanced ways in which race (and other social identities) plays out in the pedagogical process. This chapter demonstrates that teachers' social identities are critically implicated in their teaching for equity and diversity. However, it is not a simple case of one's social identity either helping or hindering one's ability to teach for social justice. Issues of race are prevalent in teachers' discussion of identity issues, but they are interfaced with teachers' perceptions of how multiple identities—for example, culture, ethnicity, gender, spiritual lifestyle, and immigrant status—may also affect their teaching. Teachers are working through the tensions resulting from the disconnect between how popular discourse defines them and their own lived, multi-layered, and textured experiences of identity. Teachers simultaneously resist and employ popular categorizations of social identity. This points to the need for constant critical reflection on constructions of race and culture, and promotes the need for a new language to address and conceptualize these complexities.

Although the experiences of teachers of colour were as nuanced as those of White teachers, this chapter points to strong themes that demonstrate a marked difference between the experiences of teachers of colour and those of White teachers. Paramount to this difference is the systemic racism experienced by the former and their sense of having to prove themselves professionally as evidenced through their perceptions of their relationships with students, parents, and colleagues. However, our study recognizes that no teacher's pursuit of democratic education can be made easier by the teacher's social identity alone. The study suggests that depending on the circumstances of one's teaching environment, social identities can both help and hinder teachers' experiences and motivations, as well as their relations with students, parents, and colleagues. The study is indicative of the ambiguous and complex nature of how social identity is experienced and performed. Teachers who found themselves in homogeneous school communities were forced to re-examine their concept of teaching for diversity and to re-evaluate how their social identities would play to their advantage or disadvantage. Evidently, UD teachers expected that teaching for diversity meant teaching in a diverse school. When they found themselves in a minority position without students of a similar minority background for whom to work for inclusion, their notions of their teaching identities were challenged. Consequently, these teachers were forced to critically reflect on the workings of identity in a way not consistent with what had been normalized in their teacher education. This study demonstrates that the ways in which teachers perceive their social identities in relation to their teaching practice, and how others interpret their social identities in relation to their teaching, are very much imbedded in preconceived notions of "who" a teacher is or "should be." Popular understandings of teaching normalize White females as teachers (Solomon & Rezai-Rashti, 2004) Thus, in order to examine exactly how a teacher's social identity impacts her or his ability to teach for social justice, we must be cognizant of the implications of ambivalent and complex teacher identity formation.

In a critical self-reflection of how his own social identity interfaces with his ability to teach for social justice, Goodman (2004) examines the challenges he faces as a White male trying "to identify and mitigate the negative implication of power imbalance inherent in the student/ teacher relationship coupled with the white racial issues" (p. 5). Thus, issues of a teacher's race, gender, class, culture, ethnicity, and religion are further complicated by the governing identity inherent in the cultural myths of the role of the teacher (see Britzman, 2003; Zembylas, 2003; Sumara & Luce-Kapler, 1996). Graham and Young (1998) maintain that the constant effort to theorize a concept of praxis that references the dual themes of cultural diversity and emerging teacher identities makes both problematic and personal everyday matters of curriculum development, classroom practice, and institutional structures.

CHAPTER 5

Transformative Schooling

JORDAN SINGER

Since 1992, numerous studies of pre-service teachers in both Canada and the United States have shown that many teachers believe, and continue to hold negative and often unspoken assumptions about, racialized and minoritized others (e.g., Sleeter, 1992a, 1992b; Frankenberg, 1993; Derman-Sparks & Phillips, 1997; Solomon, Levine-Rasky & Singer, 2003). The assumptions that underlie many teachers' beliefs have been directly linked to school failure for racialized students in Canada (Dei et al., 1997; Lawson et al., 2002; Brown & Sinay, 2008). In part, these beliefs may be understood by the cultural demographics of those who aspire to be and become teachers. Concurrently, their belief system must also be examined as an internalized expression of the systemic dynamics that have created and continue to support their thoughts, ideals, and actions. Changing the attitudes of teachers toward those outside of the dominant culture is not only an ethical imperative, but also is, at this moment in history, particularly urgent given the present demographic differences between many teachers and their students. To illustrate, students from minoritized backgrounds in the Toronto District School Board (O'Reilly & Yau, 2006) accounts for approximately 78 percent of the student body. In contrast, the percentage of teachers from minoritized backgrounds is 33 percent.

In response to the increasingly diverse cultural, racial and linguistic character of many urban centres and the continuing mostly static character of educators' racial, cultural and linguistic backgrounds, research is turning toward examining how the impact of inclusive teaching methods grounded in a broad-based conception of diversity and issues of equity can increase the academic success of students who are traditionally labelled "at risk." We begin with the understanding that acknowledging and working with diverse student identities is fundamental to making any changes in the schooling system and beyond. Additionally, we believe that it is vital to consider and question what precisely needs to be transformed in order to achieve social justice aims. To do this we will focus on: (1) how all stakeholders in the educational process function; (2) the dynamic interrelationships among stakeholders; (3) how the dynamics between these educational actors affect teachers' actions and students' learning in the classroom.

Transformative schooling requires all stakeholders to work together to create educational spaces that engage with difference in non-reductionistic ways, and that enable teacher candidates to critically process contradictions between their own past experiences and perceptions concerning social difference and social justice, and what they will be learning from others' diverse experiences and perceptions. The hope and logic underlying this work holds that by fleshing out and grappling with these incongruities, shifting cognitive frameworks, and often ambivalent emotional variables considering difference, prospective teachers will develop enhanced critical thinking skills, which, in turn, will lead to a more inclusive world view and a desire to create progressive and socially just classroom environments. Methodologically speaking, students first learn about the complexity of their own identities, the experiences and perceptions of others, while engaging with how these new insights transform how they view the world around them. In classroom practice, students learn about, question, participate, and experience democratic principles in action through anti-oppressive teaching and learning how to modify the curriculum in response to the contextual needs of their communities. These contextual needs are informed by key variables such as culture, language, race, socio-economic status, and geographical location.

Fundamentally, transformative schooling is a democratic project that informs educational practices for fostering open-mindedness, social responsibility, and academic success, as well as confidence in oneself and security with one's identity. Moving schooling and our thinking about teaching and learning in this progressive direction leads to the creation of opportunities in the classroom where discussions that problematize difference and diversity, culture and race, politics and social justice can occur. In an important sense, these discussions involve students in a pursuit of knowledge that is experienced as an emergent process and thereby invokes a notion of classroom dynamics (and, by extension, social dynamics) as democratically inclusive. Thinking about knowledge as a process rather than as a product can also assist educators in reconceptualizing the importance of including issues of difference and diversity in classrooms and schools, not as external considerations that disrupt learning, but as ever-present dynamics that are a necessary and beneficial aspect of learning. Furthermore, by engaging students in knowledge building through critical discussions, the relations of power/knowledge that sustain the status quo, neo-liberal/ neo-conservative discourses of accountability, standardized testing, and essentialized difference may be undermined as these discourses view education, knowledge, teaching, and learning as a prefabricated product to be built upon so-called "universal" ideals and homogeneous notions of the role of identity, whereas social justice teaching shatters the validity of these perspectives.

Educators who strive to create socially equitable learning environments utilize a number of pedagogical strategies in their day-to-day teaching. This is an absolute necessity given how the school system and student success is skewed toward the dominant culture in addition to their shared and, in our opinion, realistic perception that the recent standards-based reforms has reframed the role of teachers as technicians and transformed the role of students into passive receptacles of discrete bits of predetermined knowledge. In response to this diminution of the meaning of education, the de-professionalization of teachers in general, and the standardized curriculum, social justice educators must be both innovative and strategic in their approaches to classroom teaching and learning if they are to be successful. At this point, it is important to keep in mind that this study occurred during a time of major educational reform and restructuring by the Conservative government, as detailed in the Introduction. Presently, due to the election of a Liberal government, relations with teachers have improved. Nevertheless, while this most recent crisis period may be in partial remission, and a serious attempt to reduce the number of curricular outcomes is well underway, many of the destructive policies that were previously implemented have not been reformulated and continue to impact all levels of the education sector. Moreover, the economic and ideologically based business logic that brought about these changes also remains relatively unchanged despite changes in governments or even the 2008/2009 recession. To be sure, the neo-liberal plan to further centralize and confine power and capital to corporations and their government partners continues to gain momentum. Thus, we continue to see the educational trends and dynamics we have described in our research as exceedingly relevant for some time to come.

Most teachers who participated in this study remarked that they needed to develop meta-strategies in order to integrate culturally responsive and anti-oppressive pedagogy within their daily routines. While most acknowledged the difficulties involved in challenging the new Ontario curriculum, many still managed to integrate issues of social justice by incorporating four specific strategies concerning equity and diversity.

Under each of these headings, we explore key strategies that teachers used to integrate social justice education into their classrooms. These strategies work best in tandem rather than in a haphazard manner. Something else to keep in mind is that while teachers have used these strategies to develop ways of inclusive teaching, they are doing this despite the many ideological, structural, and interpersonal obstacles heretofore noted in this study.

Working toward a Democratic Classroom

Anti-oppressive pedagogy demands the creation of democratic spaces. To create this type of atmosphere requires fostering genuine, caring relationships among the diverse members of a given school environment. In the case of many of the participants in this study, the first place to initiate and sustain such relationships is within the classroom, between the teacher and students, and among the students themselves. To achieve this, participants focus on four key strategies:

1. Creating a safe, nurturing, and inclusive classroom environment
2. Bringing the community into the classroom
3. Fostering critical thinking and agency
4. "Stretching" the curriculum

Teachers remark that these strategies have been very successful in developing democratically progressive, pedagogical spaces. An important caveat expressed by many participants in our study is that these strategies need to be understood holistically, meaning that each strategy supports and strengthens the other strategies.

1. CREATING A SAFE, NURTURING, AND INCLUSIVE CLASSROOM ENVIRONMENT

Providing a safe environment that fosters and exemplifies care, trust, and fairness is crucial to opening democratic spaces within the classroom. These spaces allow for dialogue that makes possible the collective generation and processing of context-specific learning and knowledge. Teachers' approaches and attitudes, which should communicate an acceptance of difficult ideas, issues, and opinions, are essential in creating a mutually generated open dialogue that can flow without initial correction, judgments, and/or attempts to provide the answers. Of course, when harmful attitudes or extremely intolerant views are expressed, a teacher should intervene to preserve student safety, but the goal of building an open, critical, and trusting environment should be to increase the parameters of what can be safely explored emotionally and intellectually. The suspension of a teacher's natural propensity to intervene with the right answers and/or immediately contribute ideas creates a space, a place, and a time where students can discuss, explore, and express what they think and feel about thoughts, concerns, and experiences that are important in their lives.

> I think you need to provide an environment that is safe for them where they have trust so that they can feel free to have their own opinions even if somebody might disagree with them. (Josie)

In order to foster a safe and nurturing environment, many respondents mentioned the importance of understanding how the concept of inclusion (in its various forms) must inform this environment. One fundamental aspect of inclusion frequently mentioned is modifying the curriculum so that it represents the experiences, identities, and world views of others outside the dominant culture. To accomplish this, many teachers acknowledge that they must also foster an environment in which students learn to respect others who are different from themselves. Modifying the curriculum into a more inclusive document and fostering respect for fellow students together increase the potential of successfully creating an inclusive and safe environment for all students. Inclusion must also be extended to the overall school environment and influence how teachers speak with their students, how they speak among themselves about their students, and how they communicate with and about parents. Without this type of environment in the classroom and in the larger culture of the school, it is extremely difficult to maintain a consistently inclusive and respectful environment for students as negative teacher attitudes toward them and their parents undermine the efforts of progressive teachers. What follows is an example of one teacher's experience in trying to foster a more open-minded and inclusive mindset among her colleagues.

> I was trying to organize teachers to support me in my efforts.... Often you would hear teachers talking about parents, talking about children, talking about social workers (who would come into the schools to support the students) in negative ways. Also, in the staff room during our whole lunchtime, that's what they spent their time doing, so I wasn't very popular, to say the least, if I said we really shouldn't be saying that. And I thought, if you are feeling this way about a parent ... if there is a concern with that [parent's] child, you won't bother to call because you think that that child's mother is a "prostitute." I was trying to make them see that one attitude relates to the other, and that they were there to serve the children, but they didn't see it that way. (Donnette)

The connection between how disrespectful expressions and attitudes toward some parents can translate into unprofessional actions toward a particular student is lost on this group of teachers. Sadly, this type of counterproductive, negative talk may not only represent prejudice or ignorance, but could also be a way of laying blame and expressing their frustration at the obstacles they face in their attempts to teach the diverse students in their classrooms, students whose cultures they do not understand or are not prepared to teach. Other teachers in our study reiterated the difficulty in fostering positive teacher attitudes toward marginalized students and parents, claiming that changing the attitudes of their co-workers remains a primary goal of their mission.

The discourse of inclusion is also continuously tied to notions of accepting difference. Key in this respect, teachers report their constant striving to represent the diversity of their students in both classroom materials and among the teaching staff by ensuring that "student voices would be heard." Indeed, teachers in this study used a variety of methods to achieve inclusive classroom dynamics. Many mentioned that they made sure that their teaching and classroom reflected the children in terms of the pictures on the walls, the books that were used, and the classroom discussions.

> [I]n our classroom we have things like a student coach corner, where every week a specific child would bring in things that we can put up in a display area in the classroom where that child can expose their culture to the rest of the kids in the classroom. (Frederick)

> We ... let everybody know about different cultures because it's the best way to get an insight into people who are not from the same culture that you are. (Frederick)

Often classroom discussions about these issues allowed the students a platform to talk about and examine their culture, their religion, their preconceptions, biases, and stereotypes. In doing this, students from different parts of the world become aware of and feel pride in their cultural, social, and economic backgrounds, while also developing a sense of criticality, respect, and perspective about the origins of their beliefs as well as those of others. It is important here to note that our Urban Diversity graduates stressed that an examination of Others must include the *voices* and perspectives of those who are not physically represented in the classroom (or school) environment. Our participants stress that while their school communities may be homogeneous, they must remember that they are preparing students to live in the larger community and within a world where heterogeneous populations are increasingly common. Consequently, teachers must also provide students with opportunities to engage with ideas, cultures, and people who represent the larger community within which we all live.

While it is important to be inclusive in this general sense, it is also incumbent upon teachers to represent the actual groups that make up a schooling population. This understanding of inclusion subverts the stereotypical dichotomies that have permeated popular notions of difference. To clarify, a number of teachers mentioned that diversity teaching must move beyond a simple focus on Black and White, and that racism must be understood as something that extends beyond the dichotomy of "blackness" and "whiteness," especially if a school population is primarily composed of other groups. To illustrate:

> The school was 95 percent visible minorities. Most of them were actually Tamil or Sri Lankan, and even though we did a lot of things in Black History ... we didn't really do anything that valued where they came from. (Vera)

> I am not ... boxed into discourse on blackness.... [I]n some ways I try and reject a predominant discourse on blackness because there are a lot of Black students in my class, but there are also a lot of other students within the school culture and in my classroom who are not Black, and it is necessary for them to have a sense of place, so I have to teach and speak and use examples that include all of them as well.... (Marcus)

The preceding narratives expand the notion of inclusion to represent those whose physical, social, linguistic, and cultural realities actually make up the schooling population, while noting that "inclusion" and "diversity" are terms that ought to be understood most broadly. As the first narrative indicates, when 95 percent of the student body are visible minorities, the majority of which are Tamil or Sri Lankan, activities undertaken during Black History month may not speak to students' immediate realities, whereas discussion of the history behind the recent hostilities in Sri Lanka would. To be clear, we are not suggesting the exclusion of materials and perspectives that do not speak to students' immediate experience, but the necessity of making sure that some do. This sentiment is echoed in the second narrative. This dual understanding of inclusion—one that represents actual members of a school environment and that simultaneously honours the groups marginalized in society—figures centrally in creating a democratic classroom environment that is safe and nurturing, while at the same time attuned to the larger community and the world.

2. BRINGING THE COMMUNITY INTO THE CLASSROOM

An integral aspect of developing democratic classroom relations involves bringing the community into the classroom. Students are situated beings who are part of a historical, socio-economic, and cultural context. As such, their communities and families are important facets of their individual/social identities. Teachers' sensitivity to social difference, empathy to the needs and experiences of diverse student populations, and advocacy for social change are brought together under the banner of community-building. Earlier we discussed teachers' thoughts on the importance of respecting their students' communities and families. Here our discussion encompasses the notion of community-building as another way to foster democracy in the classroom.

Anti-oppressive educators treat students as integral members of a family, a circle of friends, a community, and, accordingly, do not treat their students as autonomous, isolated individuals. Teachers often see themselves as "liaison[s] between communities and students, between communities and parents, between parents and the administration, between communities and administration, between administration and students" (Mary). In their role as liaisons, teachers establish a connectedness with community, students, and parents. Fostering connectedness is instrumental in forging democratic spaces within the classroom.

One important strategy that teachers utilize to develop these types of democratic relationships is making their classrooms more accessible to parents and other community members. The following narrative shows how parental involvement in the classroom promotes spaces for a democratic learning environment:

> One of my achievements this year was to ... have an open house in my classroom ... and I encouraged my parents to stay as long as they wanted. It was really nice because it was like a family atmosphere in my classroom, and I let them come and go. They brought their children.... [T]he school didn't really encourage baby strollers in the classroom [and] that really disturbed me, so I really had an open house. It was really great. (Keppaithara, Cohort 2)

Other strategies for involving parents in the classroom included taking the time to talk with them about themselves and their experiences, implicitly recognizing the value and wealth of information that they have to offer. Some teachers also mentioned that discussion should be broadened beyond just talking about school work to talking about what's going on within their families. The effect of these strategies are readily apparent because when parents—especially those who have traditionally felt alienated by the educational system, intimidated, or who are suspicious of the school system—are welcomed in the classroom, a bond begins to develop among teachers and parents and students. This three-way connection fosters democratic educational partnerships by encouraging dialogue and allows for the possibility of open, honest, and respectful constructive criticism and support.

Another related strategy concerns overcoming some of the language barriers that non-native English speakers often face. Some teachers suggest attempting to pick up at least some of the language(s) their students speak, and find that when they do this, students become very excited and want to teach them more. This reciprocal language exchange, while obviously more focused on English acquisition, goes a long way toward fostering inclusion for ESL and ELL speakers, as well as reducing the anxiety that is often a part of joining a new culture, a new school, and learning a new language. This strategy can also foster a sense of comfort and trust with parents who also have difficulty with the English language.

> I found that a lot of the parents didn't know any English and I didn't want them feeling like they couldn't come into the classroom. I really made sure that they felt welcomed in my classroom even though there was a language barrier. And I know from their facial expressions and from the people who were interpreting that they felt comfortable with me. I was really happy about that because that's one of the things I wanted to achieve. I wanted them to feel like they were at home—that I was approachable. (Keppaithara, Cohort 2)

Language barriers often play a large role in alienating parents and community members from the classroom. Taking the time to identify the languages that parents and community members speak while becoming better acquainted with them can help demystify our educational system for them. Demystification occurs when we value their language and culture, make efforts to help them feel included, educate them about the specifics of our school system, and include them as equal partners in the education of their children. One teacher has gone so far as to initiate language workshops for parents and other community members. Yet, despite her efforts, some community members have continued to be suspicious of these types of programs.

> We decided to focus some of the workshops, so our literacy coordinators were doing specific workshops for new parents and newcomers ... and it wasn't very well received. So we are getting a sense that our community will come out for big events, ... and if grade teams are going to have specific things, they'll come out and support specific grade teams' initiatives.... It's just

interesting to see how certain community groups view teachers
and administration in the school. (Sharlene)

The preceding narrative illustrates how difficult it can be to bring parents and community members into the classroom. Evidently, it takes
time, patience, and perseverance to encourage further parental participation. And, as we discussed in Chapter 3, we must also keep in mind
the many possible reasons why parents may choose not to participate
in the schooling process. Despite these challenges, many of the teachers we interviewed continued to maintain that bringing parents and
community members on board remains integral to their equity work,
adding that they found this to be an extremely worthwhile endeavour,
which, when successful, proved to be transformative.

From the above narratives we can conclude that most UD program
graduates are committed to inclusive schooling, which recognizes each
student as a socially embedded individual. The meaning and importance of this recognition is described by Boyle-Baise (2005):

> [T]eachers who practice culturally responsive teaching validate
> students' life experiences. They teach to the whole child as a stu-
> dent, family, and community member. They utilize the cultures
> and histories of minority group students as teaching resources
> and they question universal versions of truth. (p. 448)

She adds that families are key sources of knowledge and learning in
life skills, moral teachings, cultural information, and historic memories (Boyle-Baise, 2005: 448). In "20 Ways to Build Community and
Empower Students," Obenchain, Abernathy, and Lock (2003) add
that having students conduct community interviews can be a way to
tap into and encourage learning partnerships between communities
and schools. Consistent with the thinking of many participants in this
study, they highlight the importance of fostering student agency and
providing students with choice and encouraging self-assessment among

their list of effective teaching strategies. Furthermore, they argue that creating an inclusive environment where there is both intellectual and emotional openness and where students influence matters are the key factors in building a classroom community: "A healthy classroom community exists when students feel included in the group, know they have influence in how the community functions, and trust they can be open with their feelings, abilities, and opinions" (Obenchain, Abernathy & Lock, 2003: 60).

Indeed, the importance of student voice and agency emerged as a key theme in our research. In another related study, Ball (2000) examined how teachable moments in a community-based organization can be used to understand learning outside the traditional classroom context in order to reflect on school-based practice. Her study also highlighted the importance of voice and agency, and she identified a continuum along which individual teachers practise critical pedagogy. Teachers' location along this "continuum of implementation" was evaluated according to how they promote students "to move from considerations of agency at an individual level to considerations of agency at a group level, and from considerations of agency within a restricted domain to consider-ations of agency within an elaborate domain on matters of choice" (Ball, 2000: 1009–1010). The responses of the participants in this study show a great concern for the individual needs of particular students and the relationship between their needs and the larger structural impediments they face. Thus, attention to the ways that student agency is fostered is intrinsically linked to teachers' commitment to equity and diversity, as well as to their ability to influence students' success.

3. FOSTERING CRITICAL THINKING AND AGENCY

Critical thinking is central to the promotion of a democratic citizenry capable of making informed and self-aware decisions concerning issues of equity, diversity, and social justice. Often the perpetuation of injus-tice occurs because people are not capable or willing to critically inter-rogate issues of power and privilege that reproduce marginalization, oppression, and discrimination. Participants in our study reveal critical ways in which democratic education facilitates "voice," which, in turn, provides students with a sense of agency in learning. We look at two key strategies that teachers use in their daily work: (a) promoting reflection and critical self-awareness in themselves and their students, and (b) initiating critical dialogue, discussion, and multiple perspectives.

A. Promoting reflection and critical self-awareness in themselves and their students

Central to social justice educators' work is the capacity to reflect on their daily practices in order to develop a deeper self-awareness. Our participants discussed why the continual re-evaluation of their teaching practice and how they and their students are implicated in this work is so important. Also, a number of participants associated the growth and development of critical thinking with anti-oppressive practices that expose positions of privilege. At the heart of this approach to critical thinking is the belief that through an exploration of self, social difference, otherness, individual responsibility, and inequity, one's abilities to think critically are awakened and honed. Moreover, in order to achieve an equitable society, we need to look at ourselves and one another with the aim of fostering those qualities that are best in us all.

> When you are talking about racism or if you talk about other people being disadvantaged, then you must say, "Well, if they are disadvantaged, then I'm advantaged, so there might be something wrong with me." And no one wants to see if there is anything wrong with them or they just don't want to give up power. So if we start advocating for other people, it means that some of us are going to have to give up our power to make things equal. So I think teachers will participate more in environmental social justice activities or the social justice they'll teach if it's in a faraway land … like raising money for a school in Bangladesh or stopping female mutilation. But when it comes to doing things

in their backyard, they think, "Well, wait a minute, it means that I'm on the wrong side, I'm wrong." So they'll help other people far away because it doesn't do anything to them immediately. And it's funny because going into a classroom, you see that they are writing letters to stop something happening in Nigeria or in another country far away, but they can do the same things right in Toronto, but they chose not to. (Vera)

This narrative is particularly interesting as it points to several common elements that are influential when choosing to engage with particular social justice work; such as a tendency to look for issues which allow one to deny any direct complicity in sustaining the social justice issue one has chosen. Also, both in tandem and in addition, this involves finding an issue which appears on its surface as completely foreign to one's personal life and/or social experience. Not surprisingly, geographical, psychological, social, cultural and linguistic differences often characterize the type of social work one chooses to do. Of course, there is great irony alluded to in this description of how one chooses a cause to become committed to, which is that by making "safe" social justice choices concerning those who are far away, one is, in actuality, helping to sustain inequity in one's own backyard, so to speak, by not bringing to light the racist, ethnocentric, and classicist ideologies that underpin much of the curriculum in our *local* schools. Also, by choosing to do social justice work that is far removed from the classroom (the distant and removed systemic application), we avoid questioning issues dealing with racism in our society. Another good example of this approach is how readily teachers take up environmental issues (as a positive contribution to society) because these issues tend to be more neutral in terms of how personal responsibility is implicated (one need only pick up garbage), whereas to examine ethnocentrism and racism in one's immediate environment not only challenges how one benefits from a privileged position of power, but demands that one does something here and now. Often this something involves questioning deeply held beliefs, in addition to becoming politically involved to contribute to rectifying injustices. To restate, a strategic and effective approach to social justice education requires a much more critical analysis and application of responsibility that requires all of us to question our intellectual, emotional, political, ideological, racial, and socio-cultural position(s) and subsequent actions concerning these issues.

It is not easy to look critically at one's practices, especially when they may negatively implicate aspects of the self and one's social identity. Such implications run deep and often prompt troubling questions concerning the foundations of one's entire belief system. Such existential questioning may force one to fundamentally reassess the accuracy and intentions of those who contributed to our sense of who we are, and how we understand ourselves and the world. The objects of our doubts and queries often concern our parents, our culture, our class positioning, our understanding of race, and our education. As a result of these intense existential pressures, and despite the desire to integrate equity and social justice into their practices, many teachers fall back on entrenched teaching approaches that inevitably perpetuate the status quo:

> … we didn't question our teachers or the way they taught us, and some of it didn't sit right with us, and we had our favourite teachers and those who influenced us. That's why it's really hard for me to really go against the grain, and that's why I keep talking about finding the little spaces and for now that's all I can do and maybe somewhere down the road, bigger opportunities will open up. (Sakshi)

Critically examining one's practices in order to find "little spaces" within which to integrate issues of equity and social justice is often the most teachers *believe* they can do to make the curriculum more just and equitable. One teacher talks about how she encourages her students to be critical of stereotypical notions of difference on a daily basis:

For example, right off at the beginning of the year, they started forming little cliques—who could be here and who could not. So one day when they came in, I said, "Everyone that has blond hair today you can go play. Everyone that has black today you have to do the blond people's work, plus your own." And they kind of just looked at me and some were angry and some were shocked, some were ready to cry. And I kind of stood and watched their reactions and the blond kids even weren't sure how to react. And then we stopped and said, "Is there something wrong"? And they said, "Well, that's not fair, and why? Well, you just can't do that! You can't make me do something because of the colour of my hair." So we talked about what is happening when you [the students] say, "You [a girl] can't come to my snow club because you are a girl." I say little things about boys and girls because it has surfaced a lot in our room that girls are not able to do things like boys, or are not as strong as boys. We talk about this a lot, especially when we are voting in the classroom. I say, "Now you know that a vote means you get to voice your opinion. Does it always mean you are going to win? No." And girls get to vote … "And did you know that it wasn't until a little while ago that women were actually allowed to vote? And girls, how does that make you feel?" Issues come up and that's how we talked about racism. That's how we talked about stereotypes and about preju-dice. It was all through real experiences that were valid for them. (Zora)

Here we can see a teacher responding to the needs of her students in ways that speak to their own concerns, guided by the class's priori-ties, all within the context of the larger curriculum. Simultaneously, she is creatively teaching her students to think critically about issues of diversity and exclusion by grounding these discussions in their own life experiences, and not simply in some abstract notion of social justice.

B. Initiating critical dialogue, discussion, and multiple perspectives

While personal, sustained reflection about one's daily practices is instrumental in facilitating a learning environment committed to issues of social justice, these reflections on their own are not sufficient. Teachers also need to promote a culture of open dialogue and discussion both in the classroom and beyond. One participant notes: "I think discussions are very important in that it gives the children a chance to make their voices heard and for them to see that as their teacher, I'm open to their differences and their background. I want to learn about it and try to find opportunity to dialogue with them. (Paulette)

And another adds:

I think [...] critical thinking is challenging kids to really come up with deep questioning thoughts. Some of the most vocal students who are visible minorities were also clearly empowered by the fact that they could cross any lines and hold their own in any situation. (Eric)

One teacher spoke about the importance of having the students express their thoughts and feelings after 9/11. On another occasion, he spoke of watching films about the history of the Israeli-Palestinian situation, followed by a discussion about this complex situation. Central to these kinds of emotional and political discussions must be a pedagogical approach that is guided by exploration, discovery, and, of course, safety as it is only within such an environment that teachers and students can respectfully experience other points of view. The ultimate goal of this type of perspective-enhancing and open dialogue is to foster students' abilities to experience, understand, and engage with multiple perspectives—to put themselves in the proverbial "other's shoe"—and/or to realize that the complexity of many situations and social problems demand a great deal of critical questioning. Finally, these explorations involve students in discovering for themselves that simple answers concerning politics, history, social justice, and diversity are often based on a lack of information or an experiential bias of some form.

4. "STRETCHING" THE CURRICULUM

Most teachers in this study critique the restrictive nature of the new Ontario curriculum, particularly because they contend that it does not pay sufficient attention to social difference and social justice. Despite this deficiency, however, many reported on the strategies they have used to continue their equity work. They refer to this work as "expanding the curriculum." One way to do this is by "stretching" the curriculum in ways that make it conducive to incorporating progressive pedagogy. For the most part, teachers describe three central strategies to "stretch" the curriculum:

A. moving beyond a culture of celebration toward anti-oppressive pedagogy and a culture of diversity integration
B. creating "teachable moments" and other entry points
C. "clustering" the curriculum

A. Moving beyond a culture of celebration toward anti-oppressive pedagogy and a culture of diversity integration

In order for social justice education to be successful, it is crucial for teachers to be attentive to how they can integrate progressive methods within the broader framework of the standards-based curriculum. Very often issues of equitable treatment, and the various ways of understanding and applying inclusion into educational environments, are treated as epiphenomena to be added on to a curriculum, which is thought to be "complete." When anti-oppressive education is approached in this manner, events that seemingly (on the surface) promote issues of inclusion, diversity, and social justice, such as Black History month, can be understood as hegemonic in nature. This is because initiatives like this one and others like it become mere celebratory events, relegated to particular times of the year, to specialized contexts, or to particular groups of people *who are always framed as outside the normative culture*. Isolating particular groups in this way has the effect of containing minority groups, and therefore re-instantiates an insider-outsider binary by labelling difference as marginal, while simultaneously defining others' social identity in comparison to stereotypical notions of the dominant culture and the other. Teachers in this study strategically resist this trend and consider that valuing diversity is not about patting ourselves on the back because we have made religious accommodations, shared ethnic foods, or surveyed other cultures. It is about moving beyond celebrations and the perceptions associated with accommodation, particularly as these perceptions reflect the intentions of assimilation.

> I want the kids ... to find their voices. And I suppose literature was a really easy way for me to do that. Exposing kids to lots of different flavours and making sure we moved from *celebration to education*—I think that was a big part of it. Achieving the objective of equity and inclusion was a daily thing. It was making sure that when you were looking for literature to teach, that you were pulling from as many different cultural groups as possible so you didn't need to highlight one [in] one month and then you leave it for the rest of the year. (Jeanine; emphasis added)

Moving beyond a culture of celebration to a culture of integration (or education), as the preceding quotation indicates, requires "stretching" the curriculum by altering its central focus. It requires integrating multicultural issues into the core curriculum rather than relegating them to celebratory events. This is not to say that initiatives such as Black History month are intrinsically flawed. Rather, it is to elucidate a point that teachers in our study have continually made, which is that instead of focusing on culture or events highlighting others in a tokenistic way, teachers committed to anti-oppressive education must take a sustained approach to these issues and thus move from a perception of accommodation to actions consistent with anti-oppressive pedagogy, integration, and inclusion.

In order to sustain an integrated and inclusive approach, our teachers mentioned that it is necessary to have an administrative culture/structure committed to implementing social justice directives. In the following quote, a teacher discusses how equity, diversity, and social justice (in one school where she taught) had become part of the teaching culture of the staff:

> It was ingrained in the staff that equity is a part of everything that we had to do. So we didn't have to have a committee to say we are going to do this, we are going to [do] that. It was just done. (Vera)

Morgan went on to suggest that the creation of an equity committee in schools should not be the goal. Rather, the goal should be that such an outlook becomes a natural part of a teacher's practices in the classroom and beyond. In order to ensure that a school becomes socially conscious, she makes it clear that support from staff is essential in continuing one's commitments to progressive education. Having a principal committed to issues of equity is instrumental in this regard:

> I think a lot of the teachers at my new school had to do diversity and equity ... because that was expected [by] the principal. It was almost like teaching math and language. You had to do it. It wasn't a question [of] I have a choice of maybe not doing it because the principal would go into classrooms and she would take books out that she didn't think were appropriate, or she would say to people, "Now look at your walls. Look at your classroom. Maybe you should have more things on your walls." (Vera)

What is interesting in the above narrative is that the principal in question had a goal that went further than merely *celebrating* diversity initiatives in her school. Her expectations were nothing less than ensuring that culturally responsive and socially just pedagogy would become the norm in her school. Consequently, as a result of her attitude and effort, it did!

B. Creating "teachable moments" and other entry points

Another key strategy involves those "teachable moments" through which teachers are able to "stretch" the curriculum. We found that respondents reflected in similar ways about how important it was to find "teachable moments" and other creative entry points in the standards-based curriculum. Some articulate this in terms of "weaving," "integrating," and "infusing" issues of equity. In the words of some participants:

> I kind of found a way to weave it in more rather than just say addressing it every so often. (Marcus)

> I am always looking for how I can integrate this. (Stavros)

> I just try to infuse everything. (Josie)

Others talked about "seizing the moment," finding "entry points," creating "pockets of space," and finding ways to "improvise" where they can bring in issues of social justice:

> It was a struggle [working toward diversity], [but] I didn't give up, and in particular it was as situations arose. So if something came into discussion, I would literally put our curriculum aside and I would seize the moment and we would talk about it, and we would have great detailed discussions. (Alykhan)

> It's easy to get sidetracked by the sheer number of expectations you are supposed to cover, so it's definitely not impossible to continue to do work of equity, diversity, and social justice, but you really have to look for those entry points because in the middle

of a very fast-paced math unit, you have to take that time to try to go and integrate a lot of these issues. (Sakshi)

Most common in these responses was the attitude that equity-based instruction was not an activity that teachers do or a unit that they teach, but rather it's more a *way* of teaching, a way of *doing*, and a way of *knowing*. It is indeed a philosophy that informs all aspects of teaching and education.

In addition to looking for "teachable moments," having the necessary resources to take advantage of these entry points is crucial. A number of teachers spoke of this need to be prepared for dealing with a diverse array of situations by having the necessary resources available. Finding these resources and discovering a realistic way of bringing them into classroom lessons necessitates both creativity and planning.

> It's really up to you to go out and find other kinds of resources to make sure that it's got a wide range, otherwise you are told, "This is what we are using." ... So you just have to use it in different and creative ways.... You have to find those spaces of entry. (Sakshi)

On the same subject, another teacher talks about how she believes her advanced preparation can work to make it more likely that other teachers will include anti-oppressive perspectives in their classrooms:

> With the new curriculum ... teachers have also recognized that it is not encompassing equity at all. So, they've tried to tie together curriculum expectations and equity with every grade level. Every month there is a theme that relates to some form of equity or racism. I have created a section in the library where we hold a lot of the books on the lesson that they've scheduled or created, and I've made it available to teachers at every grade level. I just keep encouraging the teachers to go there and use

those ready-made lesson plans that relate to the curriculum that has an equity focus. I thought at least that they are getting equity and anti-racism within their classrooms. (Gail)

A classroom environment that is rich in diverse resources invites discussion and critical thinking about issues of social justice. While some teachers are able to integrate these resources into the school environment at large, as the narrative above indicates, in important instances, there is a need to find ways to bring in issues of social justice behind classroom doors:

Unfortunately, I could not do anything upfront. I could not do any multicultural lessons in the first school I was at in the ultra-religious [school] because these children are not allowed to watch TV, they are not allowed to read newspaper by their families. Their families don't want them to know that anything exists outside of their bubble. So what ended up happening in those kinds of situations was a more subversive kind of teaching—more informal.... In my second school, even though it was also a private Jewish school, it was conservative, more open. Parents were looking for more diverse lessons, so I would specifically try to do cross-curricular integration and really include as much as possible. (Stella)

C. "Clustering" the curriculum

In addition to creating "teachable moments," teachers committed to progressive teaching approached the curriculum in non-linear, interconnected ways. This type of strategy works best within a classroom that has fostered a culture of integration rather than one of celebration. In practical terms, this outlook entails being able to perceive underlying connections between different curriculum document sections and "clustering" or integrating these various parts together in a seamless way:

I look at the curriculum and I usually expand it. For example, the medieval unit basically says you are talking about what's happening in Europe. It talks about Muslims and about China. I bring out what's happening in Africa during medieval times. I do it because first of all, I have a lot of Black kids in my classroom and [when] doing medieval study, if I only teach what's happening in Europe, it's implying that nobody else existed during medieval times—that it was only the Europeans that were … making great discoveries. But there were tons of things happening in [the] Islamic world in terms of art and medicine and mathematics; tons of things were happening in Africa. I'll say, "Well, this is what was happening with the kings and queens in Europe, but this is what was happening to the kings and queens in Africa. This is what was happening with the great civilizations in other parts of the world." It makes them feel included in the unit. (Vera)

Another teacher describes how clustering that centres social justice education can assist in meeting curriculum skills-based expectations while getting students to think critically.

The language of the curriculum says that they have to read a variety of material and support with evidence, and discuss using their own opinions and things that they've remembered. Well, any novel can do that, any picture book can do that, whether you are reading *Little Red Riding Hood* one day or you are reading [*Lorne Ho Po*, the tale from China], they still have a universal message [in] them and it can still be incorporated. You can show the difference, you can compare, you can contrast. The curriculum is supposed to be interpreted as a skills-based document. Teaching students to use particular skills in their learning and there are some specifics obviously having to learn conventions, but you can use any material to do that. (Desmond)

"Clustering" means flexibility and creativity in bringing together seemingly disparate issues. More importantly, it means approaching the curriculum as a guide that is open to interpretation, as well as having the necessary knowledge and preparation to uncover underlying connections between different themes. Many teachers mentioned that arts-based catalysts for clustering are often extremely effective because these initiatives tend to draw people in as the pieces are "meant to be performed" (Eric) and through the performance (and conversations linked to what they are doing), ideas linked to diversity of culture, ethnicity, and race are expressed as well as embodied.

One of the most commonly mentioned arts-based initiatives is music. Clustering with music is particularly empowering for both students and teachers alike because, as our UD graduates state, it effectively gives everyone "a literal voice." Choosing a variety of music from different cultures that express aspects of a particular culture and history is a wonderful starting point for further exploring the cultures in which the music originated. In addition to music-based arts initiatives, teachers also identified utilizing diverse literature and role-playing as very effective curriculum areas for clustering. Below, teachers discuss how they utilize these curriculum areas as pivot points for "clustering" the curriculum:

> ... I am a music teacher so I could always use the arts as an avenue. I came to teaching with not only a music background, but with an interest and a certain amount of knowledge in musicology. So right from day one we sang songs in different languages from different countries with different feelings and rhythms. It was a great discussion starter because especially younger children, their first kind of instinct when they heard something new is to laugh.... So there was a lot of discussion around that kind of thing in my room. I've always been a sort of facilitator than a teacher. We always talked about everything from homophobia to racism to anything that was on their mind. Usually I try to find a song to meet with the kids' work time. (Jerome)

Another catalyst for integration is the use of diverse literature, as one teacher explains:

> Reading stories that are diverse lets them see different races and things in stories that allow them to have self-respect as well as respect for others.... (Johnson, Cohort 1)

Another means by which teachers "cluster" the curriculum is through role-playing linked with persuasive writing:

> ... we do role-playing based on some of the issues that were raised to do with the Palestinian and Israeli conflict.... That's one example of doing persuasive writing—trying to get them to write a persuasive paragraph, get them to think about something that they feel very strongly about, encourage some discussion around that, and then say, "Okay, you feel passionate about it. Let's look through the stages of how to write a persuasive paragraph." ... I still show videos in the library and ... encourage discussion around different issues. (Marcus)

Clearly, arts-based approaches offer an avenue into issues of social justice. Doing this type of clustering work, as some teachers note, involves extra effort such as reading carefully through curriculum documents because "if you are too literal in the interpretation of what it says in the curriculum, you become very mechanical, you become an automaton" (Desmond). The extra work also requires viewing the art/act of teaching itself as *a dynamic and emergent process* regardless of how static the curriculum documents may seem. To do this "requires work, it requires a lot of effort and some late nights, but it's worth it if the kids are interested" (Desmond). As mentioned earlier, this careful and critical reading of the curriculum must be undertaken while thinking about how different themes can be amalgamated while simultaneously planning which resources may be needed to support such initiatives. Without question, the onus in finding ways to cluster the curriculum is on social justice educators who, almost without exception, reported that the extra effort "is worth it." In these discussions, many spoke about how it took time and experience to develop their ability to thematize the curriculum and then cluster it to meet equity objectives. They recall that in their first years of teaching, there was an overwhelming feeling that everything in the curriculum had to be covered. During this period, they expressed feelings of being consumed by this expectation, at the price of students becoming disengaged in a classroom that they admitted lacked creativity and critical engagements. Over time, opportunities to "cluster" more culturally appropriate pedagogy became apparent. One important consequence of this strategy is making learning meaningful. In the following quote, one of our participants talks about how making the curriculum meaningful through clustering can have dramatically positive effects on both their students as well as parents.

I don't teach in isolation. I teach [by] cluster[ing] everything together and I try to show that one thing is linked to another in space and time. I was trying to show them all the connections in life and that no one stands on their own, no one is isolated. So they started seeing that they were a part of this puzzle, like they had a part to play and whether they did well or not. It affected them, it affected their parents, it affected their younger brothers and sisters, it affected me, and it affected society later on. When I saw those moments of connection and them getting it, it was just totally amazing for them, and it was totally amazing for me. At those moments, I think, okay, I can do this for a while longer, or this is why I'm here. Once parents saw that their children were becoming different or asking questions or trying to find their way, most were supportive. (Donnette)

These examples clearly demonstrate that if students learn that knowledge is about making connections between different aspects of their lives, then they become involved in the knowledge they create. Becoming a part of the learning process develops a sense of agency in the students concerning their learning because when they acknowledge that they are part of a larger context that includes family, community, and a global cultural domain, they begin to realize that their thinking and actions *do* make a difference. They start to interrogate their own assumptions and ask more difficult questions. And this questioning indicates the activation of the initial stage of developing an equity-minded consciousness.

As we have seen, teachers committed to progressive and culturally responsive teaching tend to approach the curriculum as an open document that can be extended or expanded and reconceived in multiple directions. They are resourceful in preparing themselves to recognize "teachable moments" and they take the time to understand curriculum documents in holistic ways. This is consistent with Sawyer's (2000) study, which suggested that UD participants are progressive in their view of the curriculum as adaptable to a social justice agenda. His study found that many teachers' implicit notions of curriculum "function as alibis," so while they might agree rhetorically with the idea of adapting curriculum to students' cultural values, they disagree when considering particular subjects such as writing or mathematics. Sawyer also found that American teachers in his study frequently framed discussions of adapting curriculum to an individualistic, student-centred orientation, whereby adaptation is related to notions of individual student characteristics such as learning styles, individual differences, and personalities. Thus, there is a lack of willingness (or awareness) to modify the curriculum to students' cultural identifications and communally based experiences. Conversely, UD graduates appear committed to culturally responsive pedagogy.

Gaining Support from All Stakeholders: Generating Critical Mass

In our interviews and our own experiences, we found that the success and progress of equity and social justice work are directly linked to

broad bases of support. A number of respondents highlight the importance of creating a critical mass of support. Once reached, this critical mass provides sufficient momentum in the school culture for anti-
oppressive approaches to the curriculum and pedagogy. When asked
about what they perceive is involved in generating such critical mass,
teachers identified three key strategies:

1. Assessing the "lay of the land"
2. Drawing on sources of support within the school environment
3. Seeking external sources of support

STRATEGY 1: ASSESSING THE "LAY OF THE LAND"
A number of the teachers spoke about the importance of assessing the
school and community culture before attempting to initiate progressive pedagogy and social justice initiatives. Related to this, a number
of teachers discussed the futility of initially "going in [with] full guns
blazing," and perceived social change as "a subtle process that develops
over time" (Desmond). Most agreed that teachers should first observe
the school's demographic makeup, in addition to its unique social environment, before introducing progressive perspectives in their class or
communicating their intentions with other staff members. They explain
that the challenges one faces in doing this kind of work necessitates
first figuring out where one does or does not fit in the school culture.
As a new teacher, it takes time to gain acceptance among the staff and
to develop a real sense of belonging. Being a part of the school culture
is essential because if one does not belong (if one is an outsider), it is
extremely difficult to do anything progressive. This cautiousness is particularly important, given the divisive nature of anti-oppressive pedagogy and issues of diversity and social justice.

As newcomers to a school culture, some felt somewhat self-con-
scious about their own positions in the new school. Others saw their
role in political terms and began to strategize immediately after assessing the school culture by looking for opportunities to create the kinds

of democratic spaces that would allow them to make changes. Many kept in mind Michael Fullan's observation that "Deep change requires individual action to alter their own environment. As more people take action, there is a greater chance of them intersecting and 'formulating the critical mass necessary for system change'" (1991: 125–130).

STRATEGY 2: DRAWING ON SOURCES OF SUPPORT WITHIN THE SCHOOL ENVIRONMENT

It is much easier for the social justice educator to become an insider within the school culture if the climate is supportive of culturally and politically progressive teaching. Support within the school can take on multiple forms, three of which were discussed by the teachers in this study: student support, administrative support, and staff support. If teachers can draw on these support structures, then their work will be facilitated. If not, their work will be resisted. Some respondents reported on existing infrastructures of support. Others discussed the need to politically strategize about how to encourage others to support equity initiatives.

Among the different forms of support, teachers perceived administrative and staff encouragement to be most instrumental in facilitating equity initiatives, a theme that is echoed throughout this study. Notwithstanding administrative and staff support, it is also important to have student support, which is crucial. The difference is that students do not have direct institutional/administrative power, although their attitudes and actions (often as a result of transformational teaching) can affect school culture and how those in positions of power understand educational success, as we shall see below.

Central to the idea of generating a critical mass of support is the notion of constantly maintaining a group of people in the school environment who are committed to issues of social justice. Often, however, this is difficult, especially if staff members who began these initiatives move to other schools. With this in mind, our teachers suggest that these initiatives have to be undertaken with a view toward their long-term survival. An important part of achieving this long-term stability is the necessity of including other staff members in one's initiatives, as the following narrative explains:

> Build in capacity so that whatever it is that you are doing, you include other people in it so when you stop doing it, at least they've done it in the past, they've seen how it's done, they can add their own ideas to it.... When people were being hired to replace the people who were leaving, there was a real push on our part to make sure that the people who were coming in were reflective ... and held our values. So when I left, I said, "Okay, this is what I was doing. Can you take this over, and can you take that over? Here are my notes and here is this and here is that." (Donnette)

Hiring practices that represent diversity and mentoring practices that encourage an equity consciousness in new teachers are also instrumental in generating sufficient critical mass in the school environment. When ideas are simultaneously endorsed by a large number of people, the effects are often deeply transformative. As one teacher describes it:

> I'm a facilitator, but there were also other voices that spoke ... louder than myself, like the teacher ... [who] put together the Black History month for our school, which was really groundbreaking. It's an incredible organization with lots of stuff that students were able to get into. Originally there were a minority of Black students represented that were clearly expressing and experiencing racism at the school. Within a year we noticed a huge change, and I think it was because the school got down and just said we have a problem, we have a big problem. (Eric)

Other comments from teachers in this regard stressed that one has to be willing "to make waves" and experience resistance in the short term in order to bring more people together in the long term. This wisdom (and the patience and fortitude one requires to believe and follow it), according to our teachers' stories, must also inform how teachers build support from like-minded colleagues as well as those who are resistant to change.

In addition to the understanding that large bases of support can indeed make a difference, teachers mention that it is important that they are not always perceived as the ones who initiate these programs. Specifically, some were wary of how their initiatives might be perceived and received due to their racial identification. As a result, a number of participants encouraged like-minded "White" colleagues to make suggestions regarding culturally responsive pedagogy and social justice-based initiatives. As one teacher expresses:

> When the message is coming from you, there is a lot of resistance, but if you can get support from other people who may not look like you or sound like you ... people are more receptive to what's being said. (Virginia).

And another:

> The school environment was not conducive. It was a good old boys' club—people set in their ways who felt threatened, so we had to tread very carefully. And as a Black woman, it was obvious that I was going to be the mouthpiece. So I ... basically got some of my Italian friends to be the mouthpieces because I figured if they look like you, then you would more likely listen to them if the message is coming from them as opposed to coming from me, so they became my mouthpiece. (Virginia)

When colleagues become a part of the process, many teachers reported that it became much easier to integrate their progressive initiatives. However, bringing people on board is a difficult process that requires classroom evidence of "leading by example":

I think the longer I do it, the more teachers will see what I'm doing. They pass by my classroom and they see art that the kids have done or stories that they've written. And it's funny because the kids in my class don't really use the typical European names. They'll use ethnic names in their stories and that's because when I'm writing stories on the board with the class, I will use different types of names—maybe not necessarily the names of the kids in my class, but I'll use names to provide kids the opportunity to familiarize themselves with difference. (Vera)

One aspect of leading by example is by disseminating current information concerning issues of diversity and social justice:

You know the little quote, "If the world were a hundred people"? I find these little interesting quotes, which say that 36 percent of these people would have this, and that they'd be this religion. I literally photocopied it and stuck it into everyone's box, I said, "Don't forget we are erasing prejudice in the library." Every once in a while I put something like that into mailboxes or I would mention it at staff meetings, just to keep them abreast to anything current that relates to anti-racism or equity. (Gail)

Others took a negotiator's role:

One partner … was very much on board and very much into equity and diversity and, well, so even though the environment wasn't necessarily conducive, we started trying to figure out strategically how we could move people along without them feeling like we were attacking them. And that was where the community came in because people saw all the individuals who were interested. Some people just came out of interest, while others came because they wanted to stir up trouble. But we had already targeted those people, so we anticipated what they were going to be bringing into our conversations and recognized that we needed to bring them along. We actually won some of those people over to a certain point, and they became active members of the group, even if it was in a more destructive way, but we really felt we needed to validate those people and their opinions. It became a very strategic game that we played for six years. (Williams, Cohort 2)

As reflected in other narratives, teachers who perceive themselves as change agents and activists see their roles as political. As a result, a great emphasis is placed on "bringing others along." This entails "recognizing that all teachers were on different levels of a continuum" (Virginia). By "doing a little advertising," by taking the time to educate others, and by strategizing on how to move others along a continuum of becoming open to issues of social justice, participants engage in what was referred to above as a "very strategic game." This game is an extremely serious one where the goal of bringing others to a point where they support social justice education may make or break the success of these initiatives.

STRATEGY 3: SEEKING EXTERNAL SOURCES OF SUPPORT

Extending teacher networks of support beyond the school is also an essential goal in building diversity consciousness in the schooling environment. Teachers strategize on how to create this network of support through face-to-face encounters and online forums:

In my six years I was also part of the diversity network, which was established before I got into the teaching profession, and basically it was a way of connecting online and talking about diversity issues. I became a member of the committee initially in just Scarborough and then it became board-wide, where teachers of like mind could talk about some of the issues, network, and encourage each other. (Virginia)

The same teacher also reflected on the importance of soliciting parents' support in promoting issues of diversity and social justice:

> One parent in particular was in my class and she had refused to allow her daughter to go to the library. She took a very political stance because there wasn't enough diversity represented. So I kind of pulled her along without them knowing, and she came because she was the president of the parent council, and she came at another time after a coaching session, and went to the principal and basically thought she needed to address the staff. So I knew there was going to be a lot of ruckus and backlash from this, but nobody knew except for my little crew that we were the instigators of this.... But we actually strategized and had the parent come in. After her little discussion, the school was a-buzz for quite a few weeks, and diversity now became the forefront. There was some kind of discussion and dialogue that whether it was positive or negative, there was talk happening, which had never happened before. So that was part of the instigation and the strategizing to get the issue on the table, and to kind of wake people up so it didn't start off positive, but we knew it would open the door to other discussions. (Virginia)

As this participant notes, sometimes having parents become one's "mouthpiece" can generate momentum in school toward highlighting issues of diversity and social justice.

Together, along with initially assessing the school culture, these different sources of internal and external support are instrumental strategies in generating the kind of critical mass necessary for transforming schools. McKenzie and Scheurick (2004) also touch on the importance of promoting a critical mass. Their critique calls for transformative democratic education that exist merely in the abstract, theoretical realm, insisting on developing, promoting, and sustaining a critical mass through theory grounded in practice that speaks about and is accessible to all stakeholders in education:

> We are calling for a critical theory that is widely accessible to everyday people because it flows directly out of their daily struggles to survive and thrive within this society. We are calling for critical scholarship that is conducted collaboratively with schools and communities and that speaks in the languages of teachers, families, and communities of all kinds. We are calling for a critical education theory that emerges out of grounded, dialogical struggles in schools to educate all children well, to address the deep inequities embedded in schooling, and to build an equitable democracy that becomes the center of who we all are as a people together. (McKenzie & Scheurick, 2004: 443)

McKenzie and Scheurick's agenda is not only central to the theoretical and political intention of this study, but also complements and speaks to the efforts and commitments of the UD program graduates in this study. Fecho (2000) also highlights the importance of supporting new teachers and building a community to sustain a critical mass that links faculties of education, school boards, administrators, and teachers to promote and sustain a pedagogy centred in critical inquiry. Evidently, the success of any social justice-oriented pedagogy depends on the emergence, promotion, and persistence of a critical mass of support, commitment, and resources drawing on and rising from all levels of educational work and including all stakeholders.

Conclusions

This chapter has highlighted a number of key strategies that participants in this study found instrumental in helping them move beyond the standards-based curriculum in order to integrate social justice education in their teaching practice. Creating the necessary conditions for a democratic classroom includes striving toward an inclusive classroom that facilitates dialogue, critical thinking, agency, and culturally responsive curriculum and pedagogy. In addition, creating teachable moments through which teachers "stretch" and "cluster" the curriculum within a framework of integration moves equity education beyond the tokenistic celebratory focus that it had traditionally taken. Finally, teachers expressed the importance of being sufficiently informed about the school and community culture to seek and draw on different sources of support to generate critical mass for social reconstruction. Significantly, teachers committed to issues of social justice often do their work under adverse conditions. They employ some or all the strategies outlined in this chapter, while facing the difficulties of transforming the standardized curriculum, and while encountering a significant measure of multivalent resistance. The strategies they use, the approaches they rely on, and the positive attitudes they have regarding their work have been instrumental in their continuous work and success in transforming our schools.

CHAPTER 6

Progressive Curriculum and Pedagogy: Practices from the Workplace

ARLENE CAMPBELL

Teaching is a performative act. And it is that aspect of our work that offers the space for change, invention, spontaneous shifts, that can serve as a catalyst drawing out the unique elements in each classroom. (hooks, 1994: 11)

This chapter explores the exemplary practices of UD graduates who continue to ground their work in equity, diversity, and social justice. Their collective voices and perspectives reflect more than just the commitment, caring, and critical consciousness that they have invested in their work. Their insights, innovations, and idiosyncrasies also interweave their narratives to form an open vessel of triumphs and tribulations that reveals vital information to educators at various stages of their careers. In attempting to present the complex scope of their knowledge and experiences through their stories and insights, we felt it was not only important to gather first-hand experiences that parallel, contradict, and ignite new ways of knowing and doing, but to represent their practices through their own words and insights.

Their stories intervene and reverberate in areas of difficult knowledge where most teachers fear to tread; they interrogate issues of race and racism, social class, and privilege while moving education beyond the classroom walls. In addition, they share their experiences in the broader community to help identify and acknowledge multiple perspectives that diverge from the constrained, standardized, and socially controlled knowledge forms that reside in public institutions. Their stories are also meant to engage teaching as an act of resistance that undermines and subverts the structural regulations that are undemocratically imposed upon them. Throughout their narratives we ask the reader to consider: How does their advocacy for progressive teaching foster culturally responsive pedagogy beyond the classroom? And how may their narratives further shape and inform the practice for teachers?

Embedded in the practical works of the graduate teachers that follow are social justice themes that often engage communities outside schools. Clearly, embedded in these domains of schooling are a critical consciousness and an ethic of caring. The following are key points that emerge from UD graduate teachers' work:

Curriculum:

- Creating the necessary conditions for a democratic classroom includes striving toward an inclusive classroom that facilitates dialogue, choice, excellence, and critical thinking in order to encourage an equitable learning context.
- Creating teachable moments through which teachers "stretch" and "cluster" the curriculum within a framework of integration moves equity education beyond the tokenistic celebratory focus it traditionally acquires.
- Resisting the standardized, outcome-based curriculum creates room for equity education (Hyland & Meacham, 2004).
- Challenging and confronting oppressive assumptions, beliefs, and behaviours, e.g., pre-assessment and structuring for a

conducive, democratic-constructivist learning environment; structuring content to address key concepts in social justice education; and accommodating a variety of learning styles will facilitate an inclusive classroom.

Collaboration of school partners:

- Expanding beyond the classroom boundaries is essential to the survival of anti-racist/anti-oppressive education. Most participants in the study were knowledgeable about the power relations and hierarchies within schools and the school administrator's location therein.
- Teachers strategize to create a network of support that extends beyond the school to include interfacing online and social networks. These teachers also reflect on the importance of soliciting parents' support to promote issues of democratic schooling.

The Ethic of Caring

Collins (2000) identifies the characteristics that define an ethic of caring as central within communities: "The ethic of caring suggests that personal expressiveness, emotions and empathy are central to the knowledge validation process" (p. 263). These include the importance of developing individual uniqueness within a communal space in which no individual suppresses or dominates another. As we will see, teachers exhibited this ethic of caring. For example, they demonstrated how much they cared about what happened to the students, and they clearly articulated how they were able to establish rapport and engage in building trust.

Hairspray and Other Issues of Race

Name: Tafadzwa Holden
Year of graduation: 2007
Current teaching assignment: Grades 4 and 5 split French immersion, Toronto District School Board
Additional credentials: J/I teaching qualifications

I graduated from the Urban Diversity Initiative with a sense of mission. After a year of examining education through a lens of equity, diversity, and social justice, I felt motivated and enthusiastic about empowering my students to become critical thinkers. I developed a classroom ambiance that communicated that my class would welcome and embrace diversity. I planned lessons for my grades 4 and 5 students that involved discussing countries from around the world. I made attempts to integrate issues of equity and diversity as naturally as I could, but I felt like it was not enough. One day, I made another desperate attempt at diversity by teaching a polygon lesson using flags of many nations. Even after this lesson, however, I felt disappointed that I was having such difficulty moving beyond a superficial approach to inclusive education. To my surprise, later that same day, an unplanned event precipitated out of a routine "read-aloud," resulting in a rich, meaningful discussion. I saw my students thinking critically about issues of race and making connections to their own racialized, lived experiences. They began tackling issues of multiculturalism and anti-racism that adults still struggle with. It was an unexpected event that illustrated the fact that significant learning experiences do not come only from the formal curriculum. I know that learning was taking place because my students were engaged and involved in the topic. We were talking about real life. It started with the word "Negro."

I was reading the book *Holes* by Louis Sachar (2000), which had become a part of our daily routine. I was reading a part of the book that described one of the characters as a Negro. One of my students put up his hand to ask what the word "Negro" meant. I explained that the term is not used much anymore, but that it is meant to describe a Black person. There was a chorus of gasps, accompanied by covered mouths, when I said the word "Black." I was surprised by this reaction, but continued to explain the word's meaning and use. Just as I finished emphasizing the point that the word "Negro" is not used anymore, another of my students yelled out that now we use the word "nigger"! My initial thoughts were that I did not feel prepared to have this kind of discussion with my students at that moment. It was the end of the day, and I already felt overwhelmed with the upcoming report cards, field trip, and teacher evaluation. However, I could not leave this comment unanswered. I calmly explained that "nigger" is not a word that should be used to describe anyone. I explained the idea that when certain groups of people are perceived as racially different, there are often mean names created to describe these groups. This word was an example of one of these created names. One of my students, a Black boy, was upset that his classmate had used this word. I reassured him that I understood that he felt upset, but explained that I did not react negatively to his classmate's comment because the meaning of this word must not have been fully understood since it was used so freely in our class setting. When I added that perhaps some confusion came from the fact that this word is heard frequently in various settings, such as music, a few students agreed that this was indeed a place where they had heard it used. I again tried my best to explain that although this is not an appropriate word to use due to its origins, there are certain adults who choose to use it. My goal was to foster a spirit of communication, so that no student felt attacked or defensive, and so that all students would remain open to the learning process.

I quickly put my students in a community circle, and I proceeded to tell them how proud I was to be the teacher of such a diverse class. I told them that they were all very lucky to have friends and classmates who are all unique in their own way. I mentioned that classes did not always look the way ours did. There was a time when everyone in a class looked the same. One student asked if life used to be like it was in the movie *Hairspray*, where White people danced on one side of the dance floor and coloured people danced on the other. I told her that life was indeed like that in some places. I tried to explain that although *Hairspray* is a newly released movie, it is set in a time and place where not all people were seen as equal.

At this point, a flood of comments started to come in. One student shared that although she was Black, her mother said that she would not send her to the new Black-focused school that was being discussed in Toronto. Another student shared what an older cousin had told her about life in high school for Black students. She said that Black students were seen as being worse than the White students because they seemed to get into more trouble. She added that this could be due to racism and favouritism. I told her that these were two important words that we should discuss further. Another student raised his hand and shared that he just learned that people do not have to be Black to be Muslim. One of his classmates is Black and a Muslim, so he may have been excited to share his new revelation with the class. I told him that he was quite correct to recognize that we cannot look at people and make assumptions or judgments about them. A young girl next to me added that we should not judge a book by its cover. I smiled at her appropriate conclusion. Since my students were at this point late for their next class, I had to end our conversation. Even as I walked with them downstairs, the comments continued. The same girl who was sitting next to me came up to me and asked if "Negro Day" still existed once a week as it did in the movie *Hairspray*. I smiled again at her innocence and told her that every day was Negro Day! As we left the classroom, another student told me that two important words we should talk about are "integration" and "segregation." Just before I left them, one more student came up to me with a revelation. He told me that when he visits Lebanon in the summer, it's not the Black and White people who are separated, it is the men and the women. I returned to my quiet classroom feeling so proud of my students for having made connections to their personal lives and for sharing their experiences and feelings. Along with this pride came a series of realizations and questions.

I realized that these students were thirsty for a forum to discuss these topics. I realized that these children were a wealth of knowledge, opinions, and experiences. I also realized that there is confusion about the conflicting messages they see and hear around race, culture, religion, and gender. One reason for this confusion could be because so much of what we perceive and learn about race is unspoken:

> ... what is especially powerful about racial images and messages is that they are not always communicated directly. Rather, they are conveyed through meta-communications which are subtle and often unspoken messages that are learned early in life and reinforced without the aid of spoken words. (Thompson & Carter, 1997: 8)

The conversation with my students began due to confusion about certain words. Students were unclear about the meaning of the words "Negro" and "nigger," and they reacted in a dramatic way to the description "Black." They were able to state the words "racism," "favouritism," "integration," and "segregation," but I do not know how deeply they understand these terms. At one point in our class conversation, about half of the class admitted that they felt uncomfortable describing the colour of their skin when giving a description of themselves. Verbal communication needs to become a more common aspect of racial socialization. As a society, we must therefore build a consistent vocabulary in order to properly discuss these issues. In my opinion, silence around issues of race perpetuates confusion, stereotypes, and a diluted sense of identity.

One focus of critical multicultural education is "identity development and empowerment" (Ghosh, 2002: 14). Empowering students begins with showing them that they have a voice in school and in their communities. Students must also feel validated and valued. Open dialogue about stereotypes and current issues allows students to share their ideas and opinions, and it also allows them to identify the misleading non-verbal or verbal messages often transmitted by various media.

Guiding a class through such delicate topics takes sensitivity and preparation on the teacher's part. A teacher must first have a strong sense of his or her own identity. The benefit of going through a teacher education program with a diverse group of people and discussing various issues of identity is that they are able to reflect on their beliefs and perspectives, and see how these could potentially influence, positively or negatively, their interactions with people who are socially different. As the ethnic landscape of urban communities becomes more and more diverse, it is important for educators to be aware of their own prejudices. Learning how to overcome these prejudices is a useful experience to draw upon when helping students to overcome their own mis-education. This preparation is best suited at the preservice phase since classroom experiences are spontaneous, and the more prepared the teacher, the further he or she will be able to take students into the process of thinking critically about issues of diversity and social difference.

In a multicultural society it can become very easy to make assumptions about various groups of people. We should take advantage of the diversity in our classrooms and dispel these wrongful assumptions by making explicit what our society communicates silently. Words empower our students by giving them a vocabulary to discuss difficult social issues. I hope to provide other opportunities for my students to participate in this sort of discussion so that my classroom can be a vehicle for positive and healthy identity development.

"Studies and Stuff": Engaging Community

Name: Keri Peachman-Ewart
Year of graduation: 2001
Current teaching assignment: Grade 5, Peel District School Board
Additional credentials: P/J/I teaching qualifications, M.Ed., reading specialist

The Urban Diversity program ignited a fire inside me that would forever fight for social justice, equality, and equity in the classroom, my school, my school board, and the community. My first practicum placement was in a Grade 4 classroom, followed by a Grade 8 placement, where I quickly learned that many children in these inner-city schools were living in poverty. Very often they had not eaten breakfast in the morning, had no lunch with them, and didn't know if there would be dinner on the table when they got home. On top of this, they were expected to get their homework completed, pay attention all day long in class, and behave appropriately. These were the expectations; however, many times these children had difficulty attaining them. Although some of the parents of these children were supportive and available to meet the needs of their child, many were busy working two or three jobs to help support their offspring and, therefore, were not available to help or guide their children. Older brothers or sisters would be the authority figures when the parent was not. In turn, these young children would end up "hanging out" with their older siblings and getting into a lot of trouble. In reality, several of the students in my placement classes had juvenile records as a result of participating in delinquent acts at an early age.

Being from a "privileged" position as a White female from an affluent suburban community, this came as a very harsh realization for me, and one that completely affected me personally and professionally. It also set me apart from the students I was teaching. Although I felt that I understood what they were going through, I truly did not comprehend the depth to which it affected their daily lives. At first, this dramatic difference created a gap and affected my relationship-building with these youth from the inner city. I was not able to relate to them. Any advice or suggestions I gave were looked down upon, not necessarily because they were irrational or unreasonable, but because they came from "the White teacher." This caused many difficult times and hurdles for me to overcome. An example of such a hurdle occurred during my Grade 8 placement class when a young lady refused to do work for me. She said that I didn't know where she was coming from and until I understood, she would not do any work for me. The truth is, I didn't sincerely know where she was coming from until I decided to drive through the student's community and see first-hand what life was like for them. What I saw surprised me to say the least. I took a real hard look at my own life and the lives of these students, and at that moment, I had an epiphany. I realized that I came into this experience being extremely closed-minded, with an attitude that I could save the world, and not with a realistic idea of life in this Jamestown community. It dawned on me that these students need love, a teacher to care for them, accept them for who they were, motivate them to achieve all they could, teach them success, and show an interest in them. This transformed my perception of my students and myself, and from that moment, I realized there was something I could do for these children, which is what led to the initiation of the "Studies and Stuff" after-school program. This was my way to get the students into a program with a purpose.

In the Urban Diversity program, one of our requirements was to constructively engage the community in the immediate area of our practice teaching school. My dyad (teaching partner) and I were extremely excited about this as we would gain a greater insight into our students' lives outside the school setting. After doing our "community walk" to ascertain the needs and resources of the community and its residents, we decided to initiate a program at the local community centre. We called our program "Studies and Stuff," which included helping with homework and studying, as well as sports and activities.

The program supervisor at the centre was very keen on having such a program and suggested we submit a proposal to the City of Toronto and the Parks and Recreation Services. He helped us to get all of the paperwork organized. Furthermore, because it was a program of volunteers and was non-profit, we did not have to worry about funding requests. After receiving approval from the city, our "Studies and Stuff" program was up and running. We offered this program to students in grades 1 to 8 from Elmbank Junior Middle School and other elementary and middle schools in the area, including Greenhome, and ran it on Monday, Wednesday, and Thursday from 3:30 to 5:30 p.m. Through announcements in the schools and word of mouth, the program commenced with a spectacular roster of 87 students. All students had to receive written permission to attend "Studies and Stuff" and had to have a way to get home safely from the program.

When students arrived after school, they participated in a one-hour tutoring session. In this way, we were able to help the children with any difficulties they were having with their homework, projects, and assignments. Furthermore, we were able to stay on top of the homework so it was submitted daily. If the students did not have any homework for that evening, we did mini-lessons pertaining to developing and increasing reading strategies, acquiring and strengthening math skills, teaching organizational skills through the use of graphic organizers and checklists, and also taught the children how to be better students. This was the "Studies" element of the program. The second hour was the "Stuff," which included, sports, games, dance, Olympic activities, etc. The goal was to get the children active and working as a team. The entire foundation of the program focused on community involvement and the students' involvement with each other as a community. Having the students work to the best of their ability, maintain a positive attitude at all times, and work as a community were the main objectives of our program. All of these lessons—both curricular/academic and positive life skills experiences—were transferred and applied back in the mainstream classroom. As a result, teachers were seeing a remarkable difference in their students' work ethic, the breadth and depth of work that they would submit, and their overall demeanor in the classroom.

The last important element of the program was the "snack." As mentioned, many of these children did not have proper nutrition or missed many meals throughout the day. As a result, we decided that offering a healthy snack was very important in this program. Originally, we went to the local grocery store each session and financed the students' snacks out of our own budget. However, this quickly became very expensive and unaffordable for us. Consequently, as an alternative, we sought out the local Tim Hortons to see how they could help. They offered our students the "day-old doughnuts program" at no cost, which we greatly appreciated. This included perfectly edible items that were not purchased the day before, but which, according to their store policy, had to be thrown out. Items included bagels, doughnuts, biscuits, yogurt, juice, sandwiches, and, at times, pastries. It gave the students a brain boost that would energize them for an additional two hours after school.

From this experience I learned several things. First of all, all children deserve every opportunity to succeed both in the classroom and in life. The program helped set these children up for success. It gave them a purpose, namely, a place to go to finish schoolwork and feel as though they are a part of something great. In addition, it was something to look forward to. Most importantly, it got these children off the streets and into a structured learning environment. These students entered our program, some with very little self-esteem and very few opportunities in life. They left with a positive sense of self-sufficiency, a better outlook on life, strategies to make good choices about their lives, and had learned how to make the best out of every situation. We gave these students a chance to be successful in their daily lives, all while promoting equity and social justice in the community—a perpetually rewarding experience.

Initiating, executing, and managing the "Studies and Stuff" program required a great deal of teamwork and collaboration among us as project leaders. We were cross-cultural dyads who learned to work as a unit toward a common goal, resulting in the success of our program. There were ups and downs, but we resolved all issues through open communication, which fostered equity and interdependence. This, in turn, nurtured conflict-resolution skills among our students.

On a personal note, in the beginning as mentioned, I had many hurdles to overcome, namely, just in identifying with the students, but once I found my place as a teacher candidate and project leader, all that followed were triumphs. The students were motivated in school, they felt good about themselves, both parents and teachers provided feedback indicating that a positive change had been observed in school and at home, and, most importantly, these students were part of a community and all played an important role in it.

This program became a success story like many of its attendees. It sustained itself over the years as a vibrant, engaging community project. Because of its success, the government decided to fund this program, which provided meaningful employment for members of the community. The public was involved with decisions affecting this program, and it allowed for teacher candidates to be involved year after year.

After graduating from the Urban Diversity program, I took with me a passion for making a change in economically underprivileged communities. The goal here was not simply to be altruistic, to give back to the community, but to understand the reality of poverty in the inner city and help in transforming the community. I got a job as a Grade 4 teacher at an elementary school in an inner-city disadvantaged Mississauga school. Like the Jamestown/Rexdale community, no affordable after-school programs were available to the students; therefore, I took the initiative to start a "Studies and Stuff" program at the local community centre. The response to the implementation of this program was again so positive, and many children from the local schools attended and are still attending today. We are awaiting financial support, and I am confident we will get some due to the remarkable benefits for the students and involvement of the community. The outcome of this program for the children and volunteers involved is priceless.

Girls, Sports, and "Border Crossing"

Name: Veronica Castellon
Year of graduation: 2006
Current teaching assignment: Grade 2, Toronto District School Board
Additional credentials: B.Ed. (York University), B.A. (Psychology), E.C.E. Diploma
AQs: Reading Part 1, Math Part 1, Special Education Part 1

Name: Sharron Rosen
Year of graduation: 2006
Current teaching assignment: Grade 2, Toronto District School Board
Additional credentials: B.A. (Sociology), E.C.E. Diploma
AQs: Reading Part 1, and Part 2, Special Education Part 1, Physical Education Part 1, graduate student in Education (York University); Jane and Finch board of directors and advisory committee member of the community organization Women of Race Climbing It Together

My practicum experience took place in a Toronto inner-city school and also involved a community project implementing a homework club for the children living at a local women's shelter. When I graduated from Urban Diversity, my hope was that I would work within the inner city, but instead I was offered a teaching position in an affluent school with a majority of third-generation Canadian Caucasian families. As I began my teaching experience, I discovered that my passion for equity, diversity, and social justice was difficult to introduce during staff meetings or within the school environment. Challenging concepts that invited teachers to rethink traditional ideas were met with silence and rejection. My entire first year of teaching was a lonely journey during which I found comfort by staying in my classroom and sharing my ideas with only my students and their families. I often wondered in my first year of teaching if there would ever be a time when I could share my passion for teaching, learning, diversity, and social justice outside my classroom and engage in equity-based teaching initiatives. Then, at the beginning of my second teaching year, I met Veronica Castellon, new to the school and on a similar quest for equity, diversity, and social justice for all students and their families.

Veronica Castellon strongly believes in fostering racial equity and cross-cultural understanding. She strongly believes in the African idiom that asserts, "It takes a village to raise a child." Teaching at these inner-city schools taught her the reality of this idiom as it demonstrated the power of having staff, parents, and the community foster an inclusive and equitable environment. This is what I lived by and learned from throughout her early teaching experience.

NAVIGATING THE CULTURE OF COMPETITION AND HOMOPHILY

The school has a reputation for winning in most sporting events that students participate in. There is a lot of pressure for students and staff to bring home the banner that symbolizes winning. At this school, staff has always been committed to coaching teams. During a September staff meeting, sports teams at our school were discussed. It was mentioned that a girls' hockey team would most likely replace the Grade 5 girls' basketball team, since the basketball team would have to compete with "those Jane and Finch kids." One of the staff members said that playing the Jane and Finch basketball team would be "devastating" for our girls, that it would leave them crying, so it wasn't worth it. At that moment, I looked around the room, stunned by what was just said. I wish I had stopped the meeting and questioned the staff member. "Those Jane and Finch kids" is loaded with meaning. It implies Black, inner-city students who are stereotyped as "naturally talented" basketball players who would demoralize their competitors from White, middle-class schools. Still searching for my voice long after the meeting, I discussed this experience with Veronica Castellon.

We both agreed that our Grade 5 girls would benefit from interacting with "those Jane and Finch kids." Coming from diverse teaching backgrounds, we both knew how meaningful it could be for two communities that rarely interact with each other to cross socio-economic and ethno-racial boundaries and, hopefully, learn from each other. We agreed to coach the girls' basketball team against the requests of our colleagues. We also agreed that this was a terrifying as well as empowering experience for us as new educators.

Eager and excited about our new venture, we approached our principal, who was equally thrilled with the idea and provided us with her support. The decision that there would be a Grade 5 girls' basketball team was not taken well by the rest of the staff. We felt instant disapproval from a few staff members, especially those involved in coaching, and our school's physical education department. We were then informed that it had always been a tradition in our school to choose the top eight outstanding athletes to represent our school. This practice accounted for a very small number of students, most of whom participated in team sports at the elementary level. This means that the same eight "elite" are always chosen for every team, marginalizing others. Once the formal announcement was made declaring an official Grade 5 girls' basketball team, the response was overwhelming. A total of 36 girls signed up for tryouts, signalling that our students really wanted to be part of this team. This gave both of us a strong feeling of accomplishment right at the beginning of our coaching careers.

Our coaching philosophy and vision was clearly communicated to our students—we were going to choose a team of girls who showed not only skill but spirit. The purpose of competing would not be focused on winning a banner but on learning to be mutually supportive team members, and meeting other students from different communities. We wanted to help our team understand that what counts in sports is not "victory" but the "magnificence" of the struggle. When staff became aware of this approach to competition, they were very disappointed. We were questioned about our view of competition and reminded of the "backfire" that our philosophy would provoke in students, staff, and parents. Sticking to our democratic, egalitarian approach to sports, we launched our program. For the first time in the history of our school's team selection process, we proudly announced that 16 girls had made it onto our team.

BRING IT ON!

When the list of our 16 team members was posted, there was a huge frenzy among fellow staff members and parents. For the first time in my role as an educator, I felt fear and, above all, confusion. We were trying to level the playing field for all those girls who wanted to be part of this team, and we wondered why so many people were upset at our efforts to provide equal opportunities for all. After all, this egalitarian philosophy is strongly embedded in our school board policy. Why, then, would anyone respond negatively to our initiative?

We had taken an initiative to work across race and social class boundaries. We knew that there was a lot of work to be done in taking our basketball team to compete against Jane and Finch schools against the staff's judgment. However, our focus was on developing relationships across borders rather than on winning games. We both felt we succeeded at this initiative because our girls expressed unanimous pleasure at the experience of playing on our basketball team. Over the course of the season, we shared our vision with our team and encouraged them to introduce themselves to players on the other teams when they met at games. We discussed the importance of not defining a group of individuals based on barriers of religion, culture, colour, or socio-economic status. Team practices combined the development of basketball skills with meaningful engagement with issues of diversity, community, and authenticity. We worked at developing connections with other schools and colleagues to arrange basketball games to give our students a safe and welcoming environment, and to provide the members of all teams with an opportunity to meet each other. We achieved this goal despite the many obstacles from our colleagues. We finished the season as a success story that was not based on winning but on the enrichment of students' lives through competing against and meeting the members of other teams. Our goal of working across race and social class barriers was achieved as we welcomed students from diverse communities into our school and, in turn, were welcomed into their schools. We took pride in watching our students sitting together with other students from different schools during a tournament, cheering on teams, and getting to know one another. Unfortunately, we still feel alienated from our colleagues because of our selection and coaching philosophy. However, we also feel a sense of worth and pride not only because the girls loved playing on our team, but also because other coaches, apparently inspired by our example, have now begun to use a similar approach to team sports at the elementary level.

We know that continued work across social difference borders (race, class, gender) is needed within our classrooms, schools, and communities. Furthermore, we realize that we were fortunate to build a collaborative relationship with each other to navigate the institutional barriers we confronted. It was difficult to implement new ideas and an equity-based approach into a competitive team environment, but during the next season, the coaches for the grades 5 and 6 boys' basketball teams also chose 16 players to represent our school. Although much cross-border work remains to be done, we feel that we have opened a window of opportunity that will enable many more young students to benefit from the philosophy and practice of collaboration and team-building within a competitive school culture.

Making Literacy Work for Everyone

Name: Velma Morgan
Year of graduation: 1997
Current teaching assignment: Senior policy adviser, Province of Ontario
Additional credentials: ESL specialist, reading specialist, intermediate physical education

Publications: "Successful Teaching in a Cultural Mosaic Classroom," Toronto District School Board, and "Blurred Vision," Elementary Teachers' Federation of Ontario

BACKGROUND

The Toronto District School Board launched an Early Years Literacy Project (EYLP) in 1999 to promote literacy development of all students. The intent of the project was to ensure that all students in the primary years will read and write at grade level. The 93 schools that participated had the lowest literacy scores based on the Grade 3 provincial testing results. These schools were given a literacy coordinator and a reading recovery teacher. The literacy coordinator provided support to teachers and managed the literacy resources. The school was given a number of resources for class use, professional development, and assessment. The reading recovery teacher provided a one-on-one intervention program for students in Grade 1 who were at risk for not being able to read by the age of seven.

In the second year of the program, my school received an additional allotment for a literacy coordinator, and my principal asked me to fill that position. I was asked because I had shown interest in the position and was one of the few teachers who fully participated during the first year of the program. The position was challenging for that very same reason because in the previous year, the coordinator was not able to get full participation from the primary teachers. My task was to fulfill the mandate of the project to create a school-wide focus on literacy to improve reading and writing skills for all students in Kindergarten to Grade 3.

The school's student population and teaching staff were very diverse. We had a high population of immigrants and for many, English was their second language. In addition, the socio-economic status was also diverse due to the French immersion stream—they tended to have more affluent students bused in from different areas. Half the teaching staff were visible minorities, with the majority being of African-Canadian and Caribbean descent. There was a good mix of new and experienced teachers and male and female staff, a mix that was intentionally created by my principal. She felt that the teaching population should represent the students and the community within which they worked.

In order to fulfill this mandate, the team (including administration) not only had to establish a two-hour literacy block in the morning for all primary classes, but also had to ensure that all primary teachers were using this time for literacy-based activities. In addition, our responsibilities included ensuring that all primary teachers were delivering a balanced literacy program with effective modifications for those students who needed it. I also had to ensure that they assessed the students with the appropriate assessment tools provided to us by the project, the Direct Reading Assessment (DRA). Finally, and most importantly, we had to get teachers to "buy into" the changes taking place in the school and the system as a whole.

My job was to create a community of learners by engaging all our school partners (administration, teachers, assistants, parents, and the community). The key to doing this was having the *visible* support from my principal and superintendent. Without their support, I don't think it would have been as successful. I believe that in any environment you are in, attitudes originate from the top. Their attitudes sent a signal to all involved (teachers, students, parents, and the community) that this project was needed in our school and they were on board to ensure its success.

TEACHERS

We had to create an environment where the primary teachers would feel comfortable in having me in their classrooms and trust me enough to try some of the teaching strategies we wanted to implement. The previous literacy coordinator had created a literacy lounge with books for children that correspond with various reading levels and literacy resources for teachers (video, journals, and material that could be reproduced). However, the room seemed to be in a very difficult location for some teachers, so I changed the location of the lounge to the main hallway, next door to the photocopying and supply room. This made it easier for teachers to obtain resources. I had charts and sample bulletin boards to show what a balanced literacy program should consist of in the classroom. I also put couches and a TV in the lounge. This made the lounge and the new resources more inviting and practical for teachers.

Next, I scheduled time throughout the morning to go into classes to demonstrate strategies such as Readers' Theatre and story-mapping with each class. During this time I teamed up with the classroom teacher to deliver the program in the class. I also released each primary teacher to do the DRA with the students because many complained that it was hard to do while trying to deal with classroom management issues.

As part of their professional development, I provided teachers with reproducible language material and journal articles about literacy. It also helped that I was the primary curriculum chair so I was able to use our primary division meetings to talk about and brainstorm ideas to make literacy more effective in the classrooms. We also watched videos of best practices during our meetings and discussed ways we could make them work for our school and classroom settings. In addition, I also withdrew kids who needed remedial help or needed to have their language program extended. I did this in the hope that the primary teachers would see how beneficial this project was to them and the students. Teachers started to see improvements in their students and their growing enthusiasm toward literacy. They had an input into what was happening, which caused them to take ownership and they soon wanted to see the program succeed as much as I did.

STUDENTS

To engage the students I had themes for months and special days, such as poetry month, and Reach for the Stars. We had an information wall that showed the favourite books of the adults in the school, including the secretaries and custodians. (This demonstrated to them that reading is a lifelong activity that everyone does.) We had a Get Caught Reading month, which will be explained later. I was also able to get funding for the homework literacy bags. The homework literacy bag was my idea for our school to implement, but not my invention. I heard about it from a teacher who worked at Parkdale, where they had the literacy bag and it worked well. After doing some research and talking to my principal, we decided to implement the program, but it would cost us money that was not in the budget. I wrote a proposal to our superintendent and she approved and funded the project. The homework bags consisted of books with translations in a variety of different languages that reflected the multilingualism of the school community. This especially benefited the ESL learners and their parents. Finally, ESL parents were able assist their children with homework and get more involved in their education. The literacy-based activities and their extensions addressed the expectations in the Ontario Ministry document, specifically in the areas of language and math connections to social studies, science, and the arts. The bags were designed for parents to use with their children. The project was to be implemented in two phases over two years. The first phase was for grades 1 and 2, and the second phase was for junior kindergarten/senior kindergarten and Grade 3. I was on leave when the first phase started, but I was told that the feedback from teachers, students, and parents was very positive.

SCHOOL
It didn't take long for the junior division to get involved in some of our activities. The French immersion teachers also wanted to be a part of what we were doing. They started to collect and create levelled books and professional materials in French. I also created a play adapted from a book called *Mufaro's Beautiful Daughters* and invited grades 3 to 6 to be a part of it. Then I sought the help of the drama and dance teacher. Together we were able to create a magnificent play, which the students performed for the entire school. What was so wonderful about this play was the process. We were able to create everything from scratch with the help of our dedicated and enthusiastic students. We wanted all students who wanted to participate to be involved even if they could not

be actors in the play. We gave them roles, such as stagehands, props people, and music directors, to name a few. We were able to show all students participating the many tasks involved in putting together a production whether it is on stage, on TV, or at school. We taught them that every role was important for the success of the final product. This really boosted our school morale.

PARENTS

Since our school was an early years literacy school and our focus was on literacy, I thought it was crucial that we got the parents involved. As a result, we included literacy news and strategies in every issue of the school newsletter. I also wanted to ensure that parents were also given the necessary skills and strategies needed so that what teachers were teaching their children was also being demonstrated at home. My principal and the primary teachers agreed. I planned the parents' literacy night. I asked teachers to volunteer to do workshops on one aspect of the balance literacy program, which parents could use at home (my administration also made presentations). Parents were treated to a potluck dinner and they were able to rotate among three different workshops. We ended the evening with a storyteller and raffles. We also had book displays by vendors in the halls. Parents went away empowered with information to assist their children at home.

COMMUNITY

I was able to engage the community by coordinating the Get Caught Reading month during which I asked people from diverse backgrounds (race, socio-economic, and gender) in the community to come in and read their favourite book to classes. I arranged for the principal from a neighbouring high school, the city councillor for the area, firefighters, police, news anchors, our principal, and parents to come in and demonstrate their love of reading to almost all classes in the school, including some of the junior classes.

RESULTS

At the end of the day, it is all about the students and doing all that we could to ensure that every one of them lived up to his or her potential. That meant providing them with the opportunity and tools to be successful. I also truly believe that the teachers I worked with really enjoyed watching their students engage in the literacy activities and excelling at reading, writing, and oral communication. Attitudes changed and so did the school environment.

Our school truly became a literacy-based school and our focus was clear. Every child was going to be literate! When you walked through the school halls and classrooms, you saw literacy-based activities, signs, and posters. We didn't have interruptions on the public announcements during the two-hour literacy block. We had plenty of diverse books and literacy-based materials, primary assemblies were always in the afternoon, and primary prep was usually in the afternoon or literacy-based.

After two years, the end results were astounding. In reflecting, I know that this was a result of allowing all partners to participate at the level at which they were comfortable during the period of change and restructuring. Some were able to accept it faster than others. But, in the end, all partners were on board because they realized that they had an integral stake in the Early Years Literacy Project and they saw the results and the improvement in their students, the enthusiasm of the parents, and the collaboration with colleagues.

As a teacher I never accepted the words "I can't" from my students, and as literacy coordinator, I never accept those same words from teachers. Therefore, at times I had to be persistent and patient. I realized that teachers, like everyone else, are afraid of change and/or getting out of their comfort zone. I learned that a clearly communicated plan of action and expected results were key to having full participation. People also needed the opportunity to express their opinions and suggestions. I had to think of creative ways to implement these suggestions and acknowledge those teachers.

I was nominated for an ETFO (Elementary Teachers' Federation of

Ontario) teacher literacy award by one of the teachers for the job I did as literacy coordinator. I thought that was great, especially since I was just doing my job—making literacy work for everyone!

Africentricity and other Best Practices

Name: Nekesha Holdipp
Year of graduation: 2006
Current teaching assignment: Grade 5, [Urban] Public School
Additional credentials: M.A. (Environmental Studies)

I have been asked to present a best practice model that fosters equity, diversity, and social justice (EDSJ). My approach to EDSJ is about going beyond present efforts that append people to an exclusive curriculum. In writing this piece, I critically reflected on my UD and present classroom practice, academic career, and life experiences.

As a parent with a school-age child, I found a regional disparity in education quality, which suggested to me that the disparity in educational opportunities fuels social inequity. Moreover, the confines of socioeconomic and other environmental challenges have demonstrated that, although parents will do what they can to ensure a sound future, the ability to parent under pressure and navigate social systems (education) will become increasingly difficult as social conditions intensify.

As an academic, I am trained to read between social lines. Critical analyses have revealed the vital importance of educators acknowledging that public educational curricula contain hidden agendas, social *-isms*, or outright neglect. In fact, there is an overwhelming amount of research that points to curricula as one of the main mechanisms used to subjugate those who sit on the social margins. My graduate research on environmental racism and the school-prison pipeline has allowed me to hone in on the role that a deficient educational system and its agents have in impeding healthy self-development.

As a teacher, I have found a number of helps and hindrances to creating a nurturing learning environment. Teaching under challenging conditions and trying to make a positive impact is like working in a pressure cooker. That said, supportive staff, community members, and parents have balanced the bitter with the sweet. Altogether, my journey has demonstrated the significance and (moral) responsibility of the teaching profession; suffice it to say that society has entrusted its most prized possessions to you.

BEST PRACTICE STEP 1: GET TO KNOW YOUR DESIRED POPULATION—CONFERENCES

After attending the conference "Challenging the Genius" (Philadelphia), hosted by African-American educators, my eyes were opened to a whole new world of what education really means (Woodson, 1990) and can mean to those on the social fringes. After this, I attended an experiential education conference at York University, which solidified my understanding that one's environment (in which one has experiences) has an immense impact on the learning process, as well as its outcomes.

BEST PRACTICE STEP 2: CURRICULUM TRANSFORMATION— RESEARCH-RELEVANT IDEOLOGIES

With my sights set on working in urban centres, I not only researched urban education, but because these corridors are usually occupied by people of colour, I concentrated on Black-focused, Africentric learning environments.[1] I also did my alternative placement at such a location, later sent my child to this school, and volunteered there. Accordingly, I was able to compare and contrast this pedagogical approach to public education environments from a number of angles.

BEST PRACTICE STEP 3: FIND LOCAL EXAMPLES/MODEL SCHOOLS—UMOJA LEARNING CIRCLE (ULC)

Located in Etobicoke, Ontario, this Africentric independent, non-profit elementary school is registered with the Ministry of Schools and

Training Private Schools Division. With its surroundings prominently displaying culturally relevant materials from Africa and the diaspora, the curriculum integrates the rudiments of African life in order to connect children with the historical and cultural legacies of African peoples. The pedagogical approach promotes spiritual, mental, emotional, and physical development. Starting every morning with activities that improve one's sense of self sets the moral tone of the day and reinforces the philosophy of the school, as well as its expected behaviours. Using traditional African values,[2] education is taught as a tool of self-determination.

Students from ULC are prepared for dealing with Canada's issues of equity and diversity through teaching from the perspective of "oneness." By starting with knowing the self first, children learn to take pride in who they are as Africans, so they can truly appreciate differences.[3] Likewise, resources available at the school refer to cultures of the world and the Aboriginal peoples of the West. Moreover, the teaching staff represents varied racial and cultural groups.[4] Benefits of this pedagogy lie in teaching about "differences" in a non-judgmental fashion, encouraging children to think outside the box and to question stereotypes. This is achieved by using a multiple intelligence, student-centred, practical, hands-on approach to learning; lessons in social and environmental responsibility; and the cultivation of interdependence and independence.

ULC reaches the spirit of the child in order to develop the child's character. Classroom pedagogy is reflective of starting with every child where he or she is. Each child is accepted for who he or she is, and his or her strengths are acknowledged rather than overlooked. Curriculum is delivered in a way that appeals to the child's learning style and pace. In this way ULC has unquestionably set a best practice standard for schools and educators alike.

What Did I Learn? Process and Outcome—Grade 5 and Grade 1

My experiences to date, but especially those from the time at ULC, have been integral in formulating my teaching practice and efforts in environmental change, community development, and curriculum intervention/transformation. Having taken stock of who I am and who I am teaching, I have made every effort to bring my students into the class, from using reading texts that reflect my student demographic to giving assignments that require students to explore and present on various aspects of their cultures.

CONCRETE EXAMPLES

At the Grade 5 level, when making world connections or discussing technologies, I ensured that the unit either explored or focused on the students' country of origin (social studies/science). Most projects required students to explore the concept from the reference point of their country of origin, comparing and contrasting it to their host country (Canada). At the Grade 1 level, I used music and art forms from the students' cultures to fulfill the expectations. Not only did I solicit staff to assist me, but the Internet was also an invaluable resource. The tasks were a resounding success, and the students and staff appreciated being reflected in the learning environment.

From this, you can see that grade level was not a barrier, nor were the experiences superficial; rather, they were integral to the students' learning. Introducing learning materials that children can connect with doesn't mean compromising expectations. If anything, I found that it raises the standard as students not only learn more about themselves but also study mainstream material. I am not suggesting that this task is straightforward as it does involve tedious research, limitless creativity, and continuous outreach to community or staff members.

I will warn against the equating of oppressions, although they are all "bad." Although I am a woman of colour (African) raised in impoverished conditions, the majority of my students were recent Southeast

Asian immigrants. Hence, my work required me to connect from their reference point, have them see the value in being Southeast Asian, Asian, Black, mixed ancestry, all while meeting expectations and addressing learning as well as language difficulties. Some days I felt more successful than others, but no one is perfect. Sometimes all I had was the thought that any positive impact, no matter how large or small, can play a role in community development for those plagued by social challenges.

I will say unapologetically that teaching is not for everyone. We are charged with creating our future, a task that requires more than the transmission of information. One has to remember that it is easier to teach happy students, communicate with happy parents, and work within happy communities. If we truly care about society and embrace diversity and social equity, then we should make the same efforts as when there are world crises, for not only do these children deserve to be taught to ensure success, but this is an opportunity to correct historical crises and injustices by delivering a liberating, enlightening, and empowering education.

Notes

1. See *Model Schools for Inner City Taskforce Report* for more details, http://www. tdsb.on.ca/newsroom/latebreaknews/pdf/InnerCityReportMay2005.pdf
2. An African-centred (Black-focused) school is a learning environment that exudes a Pan-African philosophy. Ministry-approved African-centred schools use Ministry expectations within an environment that validates the African (Black) identity, and highlights community contributions to both Western and Eastern civilizations. This is unarguably the same methodology used in other Ministry-approved ideologically centred schools, i.e., religious, gender, and sexual orientation. However, unlike these schools, they are not segregated and therefore society is grossly misinformed by the suggestion that only African (Black) children attend these schools. In fact, heads of these schools support the admittance of children from other cultures, and it has been noted that Southeast Asian,

as well as European, students have attended these schools, both in Canada and the U.S.

3. Virtues such as truth, justice, peace, harmony, and balance; a strong focus on natural science studies and connection to the Earth.

4. With the head teacher being of mixed African and East Indian heritage, the children are exposed to African, Afro-Caribbean, and East Indian culture; the dance teacher is of European descent.

CHAPTER 7

Advocacy and Activism:
Progressive Curriculum and Pedagogy beyond K–12

Until Difference Makes No Difference

Name: Jeffrey Wilkinson
Year of graduation: 1998
Current teaching assignment: Equity resource teacher, Peel District School Board

In the very first Diversity Initiative program, we created a class sweatshirt to help us remember the challenges we faced and recognize the growth that we had undergone during our year together. We chose to inscribe the shirts with the quote "…Until difference makes no difference." Indeed, all of my email communications are still appended with these simple, but powerful words. It captures what equity work really is—a relentless advocacy for those whose issues and voices have been muted and/or silenced. Surely, I have now come to believe that this is a continual and dynamic process that demands long-term commitment, abiding passion for building partnerships, as well as vision and an innovative and determined spirit.

After many years as an itinerant string teacher, in the spring of 1995, I graduated from the first Diversity Initiative teacher training program at York University. As a former music consultant for many years in Scarborough, Ontario, with the good fortune of obtaining a music position for the fall in Peel, I was brimming with confidence. I believed I could change the world (or at least my school) into a beacon for equity and social justice. However, I soon realized that this work is more of a gradual climb, a never-ending cascade of peaks of various shapes and sizes, rather than one giant leap over a seeming Mount Everest. I also learned that a key aspect of this climb included a personal journey that necessitated dealing with my own personal outrage at all injustice, both blatant and covert, which tested my willingness even to stay on the mountain, let alone climb it.

My next 10 years as a classroom music teacher was an evolutionary process that was, at times, shaped by gradual erosions and, at other times, by inner seismic disturbances that challenged my sense of identity, specifically where I placed myself in terms of my position and power in a systemic sense, and how I had formulated a self-imposed place on the margins. From this position, I could speak out against systemic oppression while remaining in my comfortable place as the radical music teacher.

While growing in my ability and willingness to interrupt and push boundaries around equity education at school, I also began to present workshops on inclusive education at many pre-service faculties of education, community groups, and teacher conferences. This move toward the centre of systemic power in education became formalized in the fall of 2005, when I accepted the position of equity resource teacher at the Peel District School Board.

Despite my position, however, what remained unanswered is how and where I experienced marginality and, perhaps more germane, where were the places where my privilege allowed me to choose when to be visible in my advocacy. Even in this writing, I wonder, are my "whiteness" or my "straightness" apparent? My deck is stacked also by being male, middle-class, and English-speaking. In addition, there are the hidden segments of my identity to consider—my stuttering (which appears usually only in public speaking), my Judaism, and my family's direct connection to the Holocaust. Again, these are usually voluntary revelations that allow me to position my marginality or my privilege as I choose. All these identities together are intrinsically connected to my work as an equity officer. I relate to the stories, questions, and concerns that are brought to me through these lenses. I am also viewed through these identities, most specifically my whiteness, an identity that I ignored as even significant for many years.

I began my role with a cursory "knowing" of what I was getting into. Praxis was a theoretical concept of great import for me going into the job. My sense of praxis is that theory and practice must always be interrelated. This became my reality. Equity at the board was about having documents and policies rather than living them. Praxis is where an equity worker lives. I was swimming in the ocean between theory and practice.

I will now examine my role as the equity resource teacher. Specifically, I will explore whether site-based equity training sessions promote any tangible change. And, what is the effect of working with student leaders? Lastly, I will think about how to continue to deconstruct power in myself and within the structures I work in order to advocate for systemic change.

Often equity education seems to default to a multicultural celebration of difference approach. George Dei reminds us that such a default position often lead to "the mere acknowledging of difference without responding to difference" (Dei, 2003: 2). He also implores us to maintain a critical perspective which avoids simplistic displays of diversity. Ira Shor refers to this paradigm as the "zone of transformation where students and teachers meet" (Shor, 1992: 203). While my school board has developed equity documents that are wholly directed at creating this "zone of transformation," my work boils down to provoking, cajoling, and supporting a space where difference is responded to rather than simply acknowledged.

Invitations to present to a school staff often comes with the tacit assumption that I will present and leave, and long-term change will be left up to those who choose it. The issues range from fostering an inclusive literature program to responding to incidents of homophobic and/or racist harassment, to developing a restorative approach to school discipline. While the topics vary, it is imperative that I promote an anti-oppression position, always posing that real change comes not from the workshop delivery, but from the participants' willingness to challenge their own values, assumptions, and beliefs and use this learning to alter their teaching space.

The role has provided me with many opportunities to work with groups of students, both in classrooms and at student leadership conferences. Before a keynote address I was giving to the Student Trustees Association of Ontario in Ottawa, I witnessed a student-led board meeting during which the current chair of the board was impeached for disagreeing with a past directive. In my presentation, I reminded them that the way they used positional power to advance a particular view was an example of how well we had taught them. They had learned how to maintain power rather than using power to create systemic change.

Though teacher training is an essential part of promoting social justice in schools, I have realized more gain in challenging students to question the status quo. This mirrored my experience as a music teacher when I had a greater impact on my colleagues by working with students in the music room and energizing them to the point that they encouraged change in their classroom teachers than by speaking directly with the teachers.

I have also had to recognize that messages of submissiveness to oppressive authorities live within me. At times, I resist and remain clear, though I have also pulled back after I was chastised for making waves. I rail at their attempts to silence my voice, and then I chose silence as a response. These juxtapositions speak to the complexity of anti-oppression work. The grand question is always: Did I make a difference? Though we are never the best judge of ourselves, my answer is that I have provided spaces where educators can challenge their assumptions. I provided language for those who want to further the work with their students and parent communities. I have challenged my own journey, which has created an authenticity to the challenge I provide for others. In the end, I'm unclear if my work has created any long-lasting change in my three years in the role.

Advocacy for me is a living, breathing expression of equity work. It is a gradual and, at times, circuitous climb up a mountain that may have a more inclusive society abiding on the summit. We carve out spaces, or we chisel away at the mountain as we continue our ascent "…Until difference makes no difference." We all must "advocate" until this dream becomes our reality.

The World of TV Learning

Name: Stacie Goldin
Year of graduation: 1994–1995 (First year of UD Initiative)
Current assignment: Educator/research adviser, TVO Kids (since 2002)
Publications and programs: A number of her articles can be accessed at www.tvokids.com

It's 9:00 a.m. I make my way to the coffee shop to pick up my single-shot Americano, and head through the shiny metallic double doors to the land of the underground. It is here that I feel the intensity of the diversity of our city, Toronto. In one glimpse I see a Hasidic man wearing a yarmulke proudly; a woman wearing a cream-coloured hijab, tatted at the bottom; two ethnically ambiguous teen girls in their trendy outfits; and a multitude of people, in various styles of dress, reflecting the many colours of our society. This is the subway, the TTC, the epitome of the multicultural "mosaic." Where do I fit in?

The answer to that question is a simple one. I am a member of this society, one who cares about my *fellow* members of society, regardless of class or culture. I am a human being, striving for social justice. The fact that I am a Jewish woman, married to a Jewish man, brought up in a Jewish community, attended private Hebrew school, and taught in a private Hebrew school has been relevant at different points of my life. Throughout my 38 years, the scale has been balanced at times and unbalanced at others, depending on my priorities at the time, which have morphed as I have morphed. This growth continues with every new experience and change that comes my way. I, too, like Canada's culturally diverse society, am a work in progress.

Little did I know that the decision to attend the Urban Diversity Teacher Education program would have such a profound effect on my life. Having attended a private Hebrew school from kindergarten to Grade 12, I had very little knowledge about diversity and multiculturalism. What I did know was that there had been something pulling me toward learning about other cultures and advocating for social justice.

I taught for a few years after getting my degree, ironically, at private Hebrew schools. My first two years as a teacher found me at a boys-only school, where I was instructed to literally tear pages out of textbooks so that the students would be saved from reading information that could be deemed religiously controversial. For example, in one of the math texts, there was a word problem about cheeseburgers that I had to remove as it went against the laws of Kashruth. (Mixing milk with meat is not kosher, and goes against the strict dietary laws that are followed by many religious Jewish people.) My years at this school were enlightening in many ways. I then found myself teaching at yet another private Hebrew school, more secular than the first, and co-ed, yet still very ethnocentric, and superficially touched on diversity and multiculturalism. After teaching for a few years, and working as a behaviour therapist for autistic kids for a couple of years, I found myself in the world of online learning. While on maternity leave with my eldest daughter, I ended up researching healthy eating, body image, and substance abuse in middle-school children, and writing online lessons that would go hand-in-hand with some interactive activities. I fell in love all over again with research and writing. Knowing that I was using my teaching knowledge to ensure that the lessons were educational, age-appropriate, engaging, and fun was a great marriage of skills for me.

I became part of the TVO Kids team in 2002 as their in-house educator. The hiring committee liked the fact that I was a parent with a toddler who watched their morning programs and a teacher by trade who had actually taught in the classroom, as well as having worked in the online education sector. The fact that I had training in diversity and multicultural education was also a great plus, considering TVO's mandate as the public educational media organization for Ontario. TVO provides high-quality educational programming and online resources that enhance and extend learning at home, preparing kids for success in the classroom. In doing so, TVO aims to reflect and promote the rich cultural diversity of the province.

TVO Kids comprises three main departments: "Gisele's Big Backyard," the all-day programming block for early learners aged two to six; "The Space," the after-school block geared to children aged six to 12; and the award-winning educational website, www.tvokids.com. Two years ago I was also asked to support two other teams at TVO: www.tvoparents.com (a website to help parents play an active role in their kids' education); and "Your Voice," the first and only live online program focused on parenting and education issues. Both of these areas are dedicated to helping parents help their children succeed in school and in life.

I have had the opportunity to incorporate my diversity and multicultural education into each of these areas at TVO. A great example is the TVO Kids project, "Time Trackers," which was developed as a response to a need for fun educational activities relating to social studies and history. After meeting with our Internet Council (a body of educators and parents who come together to discuss our projects and help us brainstorm ideas for new projects), we came up with "Time Trackers," a TV series and interactive online game that gives kids the opportunity to learn about a famous Canadian, or an event that affected Canadian history. The "Time Trackers" stories include Harriet Tubman, (which runs every year during Black History month), Tom Longboat, Laura Secord, and First Nations innovations, just to name a few. I also wrote a complete learning guide to accompany each story. (Please follow the link to check out the learning guides: http://www.tvokids.com/grownups/learning_guides/timetrackers/default.html) The guide provides teachers and parents with extra activities and ideas that integrate areas of the Ontario curriculum, while focusing on the main story. The activity ideas found in the guides can be used by parents and teachers alike and feature wonderful printable worksheets for home or school uses, as well as a slew of activities that help extend the learning beyond the TV and the computer.

Another example relates to the new www.tvoparents.com site. After a series of user-testing sessions, we found that many of the site's visitors are newcomers to Ontario. The content manager compiled a portfolio of articles about the Ontario education system that would be relevant to newcomers. However, we realized that many of those who would benefit most from the articles may not be able to read them in English. At a meeting with my colleagues of the Race Relations Advisory Committee of York Region, I asked them how to go about translating these documents economically. It was suggested that I contact the Settlement Worker's Organization, as well as People for Education. I took their advice, and found that many of these documents already existed, translated into many different languages and available as PDFs. I also learned that there was a small library of videos relating to education in Ontario that were designed as useful tools for new Ontarians. These videos and PDFs have now all been incorporated into the tvoparents.com site. Our new *Newcomers Guide to the Ontario Elementary School System* is now downloadable in 19 languages, with full credit going to the organizations that helped us enrich our site.

TVO is also proud to announce their new partnership with HIPPY (Home Instruction for Parents of Preschool Youngsters). This dynamic organization helps low-income new immigrant parents to prepare their children between the ages of three and five for school. TVO is supporting HIPPY through two large initiatives for children: the Get Ready for School resource found online and on TV and accompanied by a comprehensive workbook and materials for parents, and Gisele's Big Backyard Book Club. The Book Club features some book selections that will be used in the HIPPY curriculum. These episodes model to parents how to get the most out of reading with your child, and are available both online and on TV.

To support HIPPY further, we are in the midst of designing a microsite that will be found through the tvoparents.com site, featuring multilanguage best practices videos, other related videos, research and articles about culture and identity, and a community area where new immigrants can share stories and anecdotes with others. Thus, not only does our relationship with HIPPY support their needs, it also has enabled TVO to help meet the needs of an audience that is hard to reach—the new immigrant family.

Being involved in the HIPPY partnership has been a very moving experience for me on a personal level. This project is the epitome of cumulative effort, and the results have been remarkable. At TVO we are constantly challenging ourselves to bring richness and depth to our sites and programming by creating content that appeals to as many people as possible. We strive to collapse stereotypes through our various characters online and on TV. We believe that stereotypes are learned, and figure that we have a wonderful vehicle through which we can deconstruct old stereotypes, and build characters based on personality traits and unique attributes instead of physical characteristics.

EDSJ Has to Be the Way!

Name: Charmain M. Brown
Year of graduation: 1995 (first year of the program)
Current teaching assignment: Coordinator/instructor, elementary pre-service
Additional credentials: M.Ed., principal qualifications Parts 1 and 2: Special Education

I was elated when I was offered the position of coordinator and instructor within the elementary pre-service program at the University of Toronto. I would be responsible for several administrative and coordination aspects, as well as teaching curriculum and instructional courses. The "School and Society" course would give me the opportunity to challenge teacher candidates to examine themselves and therefore be more open to encouraging the students in their classroom to do the same. I also had an overriding goal of ensuring that they could meet the needs of their students around issues of equity, diversity, and social justice (EDSJ) in ways that would be accessible, meaningful, and valuable.

Being new to the role and having little background information as to what the 65 teacher candidates knew or understood about issues of EDSJ, I knew the first step was to give them an understanding of the goal of this type of work and the impact that it could have on the learners in their classrooms. Because they had already gone through the basic Tribes training, they had already experienced the power of making connections with one another in very basic ways and how it supports the creation of an inclusive classroom. In the course, I wanted them to experience a closer examination of how to build an inclusive classroom, especially for those students who may be marginalized for various reasons. I wanted to encourage them to meet students where they are and allow them to see themselves, their family, and what is important to them reflected in what they read, what is read to them, what they are expected to learn—that is, to see themselves and what they know and understand in the curriculum.

After some initial diagnostic exercises with the group, I noticed that the majority of the teacher candidates had little experience with others who were not like themselves culturally, religiously, or ethnically. Those who had were cautious about sharing their experiences. Many also had misconceptions as to what was appropriate to discuss in an elementary classroom or infuse within the curriculum when it came to issues of EDSJ. I knew we had to break down misconceptions, and candidates would need to do some self-examination in order to inform their teaching for student learning.

I planned several classes that provided the opportunity for the teacher candidates to consider who they were on various levels and how others may perceive them and, more importantly, how these activities will inform how they plan lessons, facilitate their classroom environment, speak to their students, and allow the students to speak to each other. I wanted to ensure that all of the classes were organized like experiential workshops where the activities the teacher candidates were participating in would allow them to experience what their students may experience when they did these activities in their classroom, thus removing the mystery and anxiety of approaching issues of EDSJ.

I read several books that explicitly or implicitly dealt with EDSJ issues, such as *Lights for Gita* by Rachna Gilmore, *Mr. Lincoln's Way* by Patricia Polacco, and *Fly Away Home* by Eve Bunting. We identified the issues presented. Then, in groups, they brainstormed how they could use these books in their language programming and create learner-focused, curriculum-based activities that would give students the opportunity to reflect and share their connections to the issues. We also critically viewed a teacher using picture books to discuss issues of EDSJ and how it was integrated within the language curriculum. This allowed the teacher candidates to see exemplary practice in action and how the students identified, empathized, and connected with the characters and content. The idea of using picture books, especially in intermediate grades, to examine these issues was an eye-opener for these teacher candidates. They really began seeing the power of literature in connecting with their students.

We also spent several classes on self-reflective activities. We started with the activity "What Do You Know? What Have You Heard?" Several large charts were placed around the room with a label identifying various groups within society (i.e., Those Who Are Overweight, Black Males, Muslims, Homosexuals, Uneducated, etc.). As a group, but working independently, they added comments of what they know or have heard about a particular group. After over an hour of writing their ideas and thoughts, we took time to debrief it individually and collectively. This activity really opened their eyes to the stereotypes they have about various groups, including those groups they identify with. It also allowed them to see what misconceptions others may have of them. We discussed where these stereotypes come from, why we have them, and how they can impact our teaching, even the positive stereotypes.

The second self-reflective activity was the Social Identity Flower from *Letters to Marcia: A Teacher's Guide to Anti-racist Education* by Enid Lee. The teacher candidates completed a flower, which asks them to identify themselves on various social levels (i.e., age, race, ethnic background, religious background, cultural influences, etc.) and share their flower within small groups. Then they were asked to code each category as either an "advantage" or a "disadvantage." Debriefing included small and large group discussions about what this exercise means about self-identification, how this could impact our teaching, and how to adapt this exercise for use with students across various grade levels.

To encourage the teacher candidates to implement what they had been examining and practising in class, one of their first assignments was to create a "diversity doll," a representation of who they are to be used as a mental set or starting point in an introductory lesson during their first practicum teaching block. The doll was not to be a contrived way of acknowledging your religion, culture, or interests, but a way to show various aspects of themselves in order to identify with the learners they would be teaching. I modelled with my own diversity doll and connected it with a picture book (*Amazing Grace* by Mary Hoffman) so they would have a clear understanding of how they could present their dolls, as well as how to tie them into curriculum expectations. After creating their dolls, writing a lesson plan, and presenting the lesson with meaningful and relevant follow-up activities to their practicum classroom, they were asked to reflect on the process in small groups and on paper. The feedback was phenomenal. They experienced how eager and excited the students were (across the grade levels) to learn about them through their doll and make personal connections to some aspect of their doll. The follow-up activities included creating mini-diversity dolls, writing letters to the teacher, reflective journals, murals, and poetry. Many teacher candidates shared that the reactions from the students were very positive. They quickly made connections with the students and the students with them. They learned about the students on a level that a reading assessment, OSR, or a standard getting-to-know-you worksheet never would. It definitely gave many of the teacher candidates the confidence to examine their lessons around issues of EDSJ.

This was only the beginning of a journey for the teacher candidates and for me as a Faculty of Education instructor. I knew that the work that was done throughout the year would be the starting point of further examination of EDSJ issues for some, and for others, it may get overshadowed by all the other initiatives and expectations placed on new teachers. At the very least, I knew that these experiences would make them think about how they plan their lessons, what books they place in the classroom, how they speak to their students' families, and how they valued the learners in their classrooms. It informed my teaching in exactly the same way. I continue to see the need to infuse EDSJ issues in all aspects of teacher education, not just in a theoretical, research-based way, but in an experiential way that will allow the next generation of teachers to see the power of allowing students to have a voice and be valued for the unique human beings they are.

Becoming an Agent of Social Change

Name: Karen Murray
Year of graduation: 1998
Current teaching assignment: Student Achievement Officer, Literacy and Numeracy Secretariat, Ministry of Education
Additional qualifications: Primary specialist, reading specialist, special education, Part 1 and 2; math, Part 1

I remember when I was accepted into the Urban Diversity program. I had no idea what awaited me. I was unaware of how this experience would transform my life. I had always believed that as a Black woman who grew up in Jane and Finch, a neighbourhood commonly referred to as inner city, my understanding of diversity and equity issues was sound. I can recall a number of times when childhood friends and peers experienced discrimination in the school environment or the community and usually I felt that I understood why these situations occurred. However, I did not have a deeper understanding of discrimination, which only the Urban Diversity program would later provide.

As I reflect on my experience in the Urban Diversity program, I can emphatically state that although I had a strong understanding of the lived experiences of racism, my ability to critically analyze these situations was limited. I was unaware of the dynamics of power and how those *without power* tend to be much more aware of the machinations of power and how those *with power* are often unaware that they have power (Delpit, 1995). I was untutored on the power that teachers and educators have in ensuring that students were represented in the curriculum in which they were taught. I may have yearned for a lived curriculum in which I could have seen myself reflected in the lessons and materials, but I was unaware of the full impact that the lack of this experience had on students. The Urban Diversity program empowered me with the knowledge and skills to challenge racism, but, more important, it made me aware of the power I would have as a teacher to effect change in the educational system.

THE LENS OF A TEACHER

I had a unique journey in becoming a classroom teacher. In pre-teacher education, my first equity challenge was to integrate visually impaired students into regular classroom settings. This provided me with an enduring insight into special education and the important role the classroom teacher plays in supporting special needs students. I held this role prior to attending the Urban Diversity program, but upon graduation after a year of being immersed in the pedagogy of equity education, I made a conscious decision to take a role as a regular classroom teacher as I felt I would be able to implement the pedagogical praxis learned in Urban Diversity and provide a greater impact that would effect the most change.

With theory in hand, I began my first year in teaching in a school where *I was the only one*—that is, the only one who looked like me, the only one who seemed to believe in incorporating equity into the curriculum, and the only one who seemed willing to try. I recall the first week of school when I met the parents of my kindergarten students and personally asked each one to help me create a welcome display. I explained to them that I wanted the word "Welcome" written in the languages that represented the students in the classroom and any other languages they could think of. I can still remember the stunned, then elated, faces of those parents who spoke a second language, and their pride in returning my blank poster sheet with the words "Welcome" written boldly and the word in the language of origin written clearly beneath. This was my first venture with these parents, so it provided them with some insight into what the year would be about. I taught only 56 kindergarten students that year, 28 in each class, but to my amazement, I received 60 posters—one from every child, some in English, others in German, French, Russian, Chinese, and many more. This simple invitation conveyed a message to the parents, and as the year progressed, they willingly accepted my invitations to become involved in my class units—everything from investigating the people in the community, to displaying pictures of community workers from diverse racial and cultural groups, to creating a unit on the festival of lights, which included the celebrations of Hanukkah, Diwali, Christmas, and Kwanzaa. In addition, some of the students and family members came in as experts to share their traditions with the class. My colleagues were somewhat baffled and questioned me about *what I was doing, why I was doing it,* and *whether it was part of the curriculum.*

These questions forced me to move from modelling within my classroom to trying to instill change and build understanding in the school. My attempts started slowly with creating displays for all cultural celebrations, setting up Black History month contests for the entire school, inviting artists and storytellers to perform for or work with the students, and sharing lessons with grade and division teams. This process took three years of consistent modelling, displaying my class work and sharing with others, but it paid off as by my third year in the school, I had all the primary and junior teachers team-planning and incorporating lessons that focused on diversity in their classrooms. Each classroom had posters that reflected diversity, and teachers were buying books that highlighted themes of diversity as they noticed the engagement of their students had changed.

CURRICULUM DEVELOPMENT

One of the most important lessons I learned from this experience was that there was a need for resources for teachers if the goal was to get them to reflect on their teaching practice and ensure that they were providing students with a lived curriculum. I found that I had spent a lot of time with my colleagues in developing and creating ideas on how to utilize units in social studies and science so they would focus on more than one perspective. This is why when I was approached to contribute to a TDSB curriculum unit, I became part of the team. My involvement was to ensure that the development of the unit would align not only with the Ministry expectations and content-specific tasks, but that the ideas and resources that focus on developing critical thinking skills in children were incorporated through the use of equity resources and perspectives. As a result, I have written several TDSB curriculum documents, including an Africentric Inclusive Curriculum—Grade 1,

My Family and I (2006), *Visual Arts Resource Guide—Kindergarten to Grade 8* (2004), and *Visual Arts in Kindergarten* (2002).

My focus for these documents was to provide resources for teachers that would empower and engage students in the curriculum content being taught, while combining the focus of equity education in students' learning on a daily basis. I found that by developing these documents, coaching and mentoring teachers, and collaborating with teachers either through professional learning teams or through in-services, I have been able to take all the lessons I have learned from the Urban Diversity program and instill them into my work as a classroom teacher, literacy lead teacher, family of schools literacy coordinator, or currently as a student achievement officer with the Literacy and Numeracy Secretariat.

COMMUNITY LITERACY INITIATIVES

For the last six years, I have co-coordinated an award-winning reading program on Saturday mornings at Oakdale Community Centre in the Jane and Finch area. This community initiative, developed in conjunction with the City of Toronto, Parks and Recreation, and Frontier College, has supported over 500 participants, ages six to 12, and youth, ages 13 to 19. The program runs from 9:30 a.m. to 12:30 p.m. and supports two groups of at-risk readers with 90 minutes of small group or individual reading intervention and literacy support. Each Saturday morning the program leaders (adult and student volunteers) are enthusiastically greeted by 40 participants eager to be a part of this literacy experience. Literacy workshops are provided for the volunteers so that they can develop effective literacy strategies to work with the participants. Volunteers not only model high-yield reading strategies, but also provide a form of mentorship. Many of the adult volunteers are professionals who once grew up in the Jane and Finch community, a small percentage being male. Students attending colleges or university are also involved. This variation in volunteers has proven successful as many of the young males in the program are elated when they are given a male volunteer as their reading partner. I have found that the involvement of male volunteers, either as adult or student volunteers, has made a significant impact as it has transformed the perception of many of the young male students in the program. As one participant stated, "I only thought women read." I recall when one of my volunteers was a member of the Toronto police force and how the participants were surprised that as a Black male, he enjoyed reading and was a part of the program. The other aspect of the program is to facilitate youth development as the high school students involved can obtain their volunteer hours as they learn to become leaders and mentors to younger children. Over the years, the reading program has generated numerous success stories, but one that stands out is a young Black male reader who came to us as a 10-year-old who had difficulty reading simple pattern books. He was reluctant to show us that he had difficulty reading, and would often leave the reading program, hiding his reading folder in his clothes as he didn't want others, especially his peers, to notice that he was a member of the group. Each week he worked with two of our male volunteers, who would openly encourage him and also share with him their interests in reading. Slowly a transformation occurred. He began to bring things to share with his reading buddies—picture of cars he found in a magazine or a manual from his video game. After each occasion, we noticed that he was no longer hiding his reading folder— he would walk in holding it in his hand. He would also be the first face to greet us each Saturday and the last to leave as he often would stay the whole morning to be a part of the group. His transformation made me realize the power I now hold in effecting change in others.

Looking for Charlie Brown in the Classroom

Name: Aamer Shujah
Year of graduation: 2000
Formerly: Elementary classroom teacher and elementary science education resource teacher, Toronto District School Board

Current teaching assignment: Assistant professor, Faculty of Education, University of Windsor; acting director of Urban Education Partnership, University of Windsor
Additional qualifications: ESL, Part 1 AQ, M.A. (Curriculum Studies), Ph.D.

I don't remember my elementary school physical education teacher's name, but I won't ever forget his face or the sound of his voice, which are indelibly imprinted into my memory. Almost 35 years ago, I was seated on the cold gym floor with the other Grade 1 boys from two classes, along with two Grade 2 classes. He bellowed out the names for attendance as he checked them off on his clipboard list, "Jimmy!" A quick response came: "Here." "Alex!" "Here." "Tony!" "Here." "Charlie Brown!" with a pause, and everyone looked around, wondering who Charlie Brown was. He called out again, "Charlie Brown!" And then again, he impatiently yelled out, "Charlie Brown! Are you here?!" This time he was looking right at the student he was calling Charlie Brown—he was looking right at me. He pointed his clipboard at me, sternly asking, "Charlie Brown, are you here?" The other boys laughed. "Sir, my name isn't Charlie Brown. It's Aamer," I offered back. He looked away dismissively and resumed checking off names. "All right, Charlie Brown, you're here!" More laughs. I didn't want to be called Charlie Brown. He was a cartoon character that everyone watched on TV after school. He was a stooge. I didn't want to be known as a stooge. It didn't make sense to me. Why was this teacher insisting on calling me Charlie Brown? I was beginning to dislike gym.

This episode repeated itself for several weeks, much to many frustrated protests that my name wasn't Charlie Brown. It became a running gag on the playground at recess and after school, which resulted in more than a few fights. After a couple of months, a new family moved into our Ossington-Bloor West neighbourhood in Toronto, just around the block from me. The family was biracial—the father was Jamaican, and the mother had an Irish background. They had two children; one was my age and was placed in my Grade 1 class. His name was Damian.

And when he joined us for the very first gym class, something interesting happened. The gym teacher called out the names for attendance in his typical fashion until he made his way to Charlie Brown. Except this time, I wasn't Charlie Brown. He looked at Damian, asking annoyingly, "Charlie Brown, are you here?" I looked at Damian with his darker complexion. I looked at the gym teacher with his pale white skin. I looked around at the rest of the boys, almost all of whom had white European faces. I looked at my hands, which were not far off from Damian's skin. Then the light bulb went off. I felt sick to my stomach. I felt sicker when the gym teacher referred to Damian's older brother, in Grade 2, as Charlie Brown, just a few moments later. And when he called me Charlie Brown, I felt like throwing up. I was outraged. I was filled with anger. I wanted to cry. I wanted to shout. I wanted to kick and punch the racist bastard. I didn't do any of that. Instead, I endured the rest of that year in silence.

I was helpless. I didn't feel that there was anyone I could turn to. Certainly not any of the teachers, some of whom witnessed this mistreatment on several occasions. I didn't want my parents to know. Some of my close friends felt bad for me and defended me from the taunts on the playground. I was powerless. Damian and I grew close to each other, but never spoke about gym class. I dreaded gym class for the rest of that year. I returned the following September only for a few weeks before my family moved. I missed my friends, but I was ecstatic that I no longer had to attend gym class with that horrible man.

Years later, while I was enrolled in the Urban Diversity Teacher Education program, engaged in exercises to reflect on personal schooling experiences, I was compelled to recall my Charlie Brown story. Professor Patrick Solomon encouraged teacher candidates to reflect on our own schooling experiences, both positive and negative, and to frame it within a context of effective student engagement and effective disengagement. I could think of no better example than my Grade 1 gym teacher. Here was an obvious example of silencing students. My gym teacher had demonstrated a complete disregard for students' identities.

In doing so, not only would some students become disengaged, disenfranchised, and further marginalized from this particular teacher, but the impact of his treatment on the student may have acted as a catalyst, affecting one's interactions with others. Often the consequence would be a lowered self-esteem and a tenuous sense of self-worth. It was a classic example of outright racism and ugly prejudice that perfectly exemplified the denigration and exclusion of some students, but my understanding of this incident wasn't thorough enough yet.

I was challenged by Professor Solomon to think beyond the visceral level of analysis. What happened here was obvious, with little attempt made to mask or conceal what was intended. What about the less obvious ways in which a student might be marginalized and/or diminished? What about the subtle conditions within the classroom that occur with little to no notice, that silence or contain voices and personalities? What about the insidious ways in which students are disregarded from the curriculum or classroom discourse unless they acquiesce to being systemically co-opted to assimilated roles or subservience to the dominant, mainstream culture and narrative? What about the insipid manner in which token inclusion serves more to exclude than empower students? What about the unspoken indoctrinating inculcation of the dominant cultural beliefs, values, and ideas that pervade Ontario classrooms to ensure a continued recapitulation of the way teaching and learning play out in our schools? And what role might I be playing to reproduce the same social strictures of schooling, despite ostensibly appearing as a role model and a reflection of the increasingly diverse student population? After all, was I not steeped in dominant White, middle-class, (neo)liberal values and social mores that reign over the Ontario school landscape?

It is this critically reflective confrontation of my own self that was at once both exciting and upsetting in my journey toward becoming an Urban Diversity teacher graduate. I had been challenged to take stock of my personal perceptions, ideas, beliefs, values, and experiences, and how they shape who I am and what I bring into the classroom to impact on my teaching and how I perceive and interact with my students. I was not the teacher in the red cape that I thought I was, one who would save students from being subjected to being called Charlie Brown. I had to rethink my notions of effective and meaningful teaching practice. I had to continually reflect on who I was and how that might influence the type of lessons I teach and the type of lessons I would avoid. I had to pause to assess which issues and ideas were emphasized in my classroom discourse and which were absent. I had to carefully take stock of the messages I was delivering to my students, knowingly and unknowingly, regarding what and who has value in this world and how that might shape my students' notions of, and interactions with, their world. I had to rethink what constituted Charlie Brown in the classroom.

It is this ongoing meta-cognitive, critically reflective dialectic exercise that has impacted how I would bring up this same story in my own elementary classroom during my years in Toronto schools. I would wait for the right time every year—following a prominent expression of a serious pejorative, racial/cultural epithet or put-down, I would tell my Charlie Brown story. Every year, I would join the students in a community circle to recount that painful experience. Every year, my students would express their sorrow and solidarity. Every year, they would understand the power of words and the messages they project. And every year, we wouldn't stop there.

This would become the catalyst to begin looking for Charlie Brown in our classroom by critically surveying the stories and texts we might be reading, by scrutinizing the subtle messages imbedded in math and science lessons and the issues that emerge, by questioning the voices and views absent in social studies lessons, by wondering about what we weren't hearing in music, by thinking about what perspectives we weren't considering in language texts and lessons. It meant expanding the skills set emphasized in media literacy and extrapolating it to other curricular contexts. It meant guiding children by asking tough questions and making their brains hurt through rigorous reflections. It meant revisiting themes and ideas throughout the school year. It meant rethinking the curriculum in my classroom. It meant practising a culturally relevant and responsive pedagogy that begins with becoming intimately aware of my students' ideas and experiences. It meant raising consciousness to many issues, asking probing and sometimes provocative questions, inciting critical thinking, and igniting enthusiasm to learn about what surrounds and affects them. It meant starting them on a journey so that they would never see themselves and the world in the same way, hoping that they would continue to ask questions and seek answers, long after they leave my classroom.

It is this same critically reflective dialectic that I offer to teacher candidates today through my class instruction in the Urban Education program in the Faculty of Education at the University of Windsor. I retell the tale of Charlie Brown to expressions ranging from appalling shock and utter disgust, to empathy and sorrow, to outrage and a desire to redress injustice. The reality is that everyone has a story to share about feeling excluded or denigrated at some point in life. I challenge all educators in the same way that Professor Solomon challenged me—to think beyond the obvious ways in which Charlie Brown rears his ugly head in the classroom to the more subtle and insidious ways he creeps in.

I deliberately ensure that they are confronted with reconsidering and rethinking their personal schooling experiences. This happens easily when, within a diverse group of individuals, there is a sharing of experiences of exclusion and marginalization in schools. Teacher candidates more readily realize that different people will be accorded different treatment based on visible markers of identity: gender, race, culture, religion, and socio-economic class/status. They are provoked to reflect on the more subtle, less obvious ways in which students can find themselves disenfranchised and marginalized: through the curriculum; through pedagogy; through classroom materials and texts; through the images that surround them on the walls of the classroom and in the school; through lesson themes; through the discourse that is permitted and that which is silenced in the classroom; through the values, ideas, and experiences given credence and those that are either ignored, denigrated, or condescendingly dismissed. So, who is the curriculum for? Who are we teaching for? What are we teaching for? What texts, images, and materials are we using to teach kids? What issues are we raising in class? What issues or discussions are we not allowing? Why?

If we espouse laudable ideals of education for equity and social justice, if we claim a genuine commitment to affording children meaningful learning experiences that engage and empower them, if we are seeking to effect positive change in schools, if we are sincere about our concern for all children, if we are serious about redressing existing grievances and inequities, then we need to be more cognizant of the daily travails of students in our schools and what can impact positively or adversely on learning in class.

It is my job to ensure that teacher candidates are made aware of the many issues that impact on teaching and learning. They need to be acutely aware of what they should be concerned about in their students' lives. When a child comes to school hungry, that is a concern. When a child is crossing unsafe terrain to get to school, that is a concern. When every day is potentially a child's last day at school because he or she might suddenly be uprooted, that is a concern. When a child is battling emotional, social, and/or domestic turbulence, that is a concern. When a child is battling learning difficulties, that is a concern. When a child is disengaged because the teacher isn't a role model that resonates with him or her, that is a concern. When a child is disengaged because his or her voice is not valued in the classroom, that is a concern. When a child is disengaged because his or her experiences are not accounted for or reflected in the curriculum, that is a concern. When a child is disengaged because the lesson has no relevance to his or her ideas and experiences, that is a concern. When a child's identity, beliefs, values, and experiences are not honoured in the classroom, that is a concern. When a child is unable to gain access to additional learning supports, that is a concern. When a child is not succeeding in school, that is a concern. These concerns, while common in so many classrooms, are especially pronounced in our urban areas, where many issues conflate the challenges of teaching children from across different socio-economic and cultural experiences, backgrounds, and communities.

The increasingly diverse and complex student population of urban classrooms demands a critically reflective and aware practitioner who is prepared to engage and empower children in emancipatory educational experiences, while at the same time rallying against a curricular environment that is moving toward greater standardization and hyper-accountability, that almost micro-manages what should be done in the classroom. We need to be interrogating ourselves: Am I truly an agent of change or am I really an agent of the state?

It is through such exercise that I continue to reflect and rethink about my own pedagogy and carefully consider the messages I propagate. I speak about the UD program, informing my classroom teaching with strategies and approaches toward confronting such personal experiences and using them to guide my own efforts to ensure meaningful student engagement, culturally relevant and responsive pedagogy, and a critical rethinking of the curriculum.

A parting message at the end of the year for teacher candidates is to make certain that when they enter schools and their own classrooms, they need to keep their critical vision constantly in examination mode and their wits about them because there are many students and teachers who continue to see anyone embodying otherness and/or racial and social difference as just another Charlie Brown in their classroom.

Course Themes

Foundations of Education Course

WEEKLY TOPIC/SEMINARS	THOUGHT QUESTIONS
Community Involvement and Culturally Relevant Pedagogy	What does it mean for you to be a culturally relevant teacher? In what school environments are you restricted in providing culturally relevant teaching? What will you do about this? How may teacher candidates' involvement in the community served by their practicum school lead to more culturally relevant pedagogy?
Urban Diversity and the Challenges of Schooling	What are some of the challenges of teaching in urban schools and communities? What awareness, knowledge, and skills do you need to develop to meet the challenges of urban diversity?

WEEKLY TOPIC/SEMINARS	THOUGHT QUESTIONS
Teacher Identity Formation	What are some of the challenges of teaching in urban schools and communities? What awareness, knowledge, and skills do you need to develop to meet the challenges of urban diversity?
School, Social Class, and Poverty	What do class and economic differences look like in your school? How are schools organized around such principles? Who benefits from schools organized around such principles? How are differences maintained? Who benefits? How do they benefit? What's the cost? What are you going to do about it in your class and in your school?
Schooling and Gender Socialization	What does gender bias look like in your school? What elements of a school's infrastructure reinforce gender differentiation? Who benefits from schools being organized around gender bias? How does your own gender identity impact the work you will do vis-à-vis cultural relevancy? What are you going to do about it in your class and in your school, especially in the overt areas that are human rights issues of emotional and psychic well-being?
Schooling in a Multiracial/ Multiethnic Society	As a teacher, your identity may or may not preclude you from the benefits of race privilege and ethnocentricity. How will you put whatever "cultural dominance" you have as a topic that is open for discussion? How will you rethink multiculturalism and anti-racism to make these pedagogies more effective in bringing about equitable schooling for race and ethnocultural minority students?

WEEKLY TOPIC/SEMINARS	THOUGHT QUESTIONS
Human Sexuality and the Schooling Process	How may you start to address the issue of human sexuality in elementary classrooms? How do you deal with the notion that human sexuality is complex and evolves over time? What are the key stereotypic myths about sexual orientation you will focus on dispelling? How will you let children know that sexual orientation is important as a human rights issue?
Learning Communities and Professional Development	What professional learning models may prove most beneficial for: (1) pre-service (2) in-service teachers? As a new professional, what should your role be in these models?
Praxis Paper	Provide a critical reflective analysis of a dimension of the topic you presented in your group seminar based on: (1) the perspectives in the relevant research literature, (2) current news reported in the print and electronic media, and (3) your experience with the issue in your practicum school and the community it serves. What are some of the potential challenges (e.g., socio-cultural, political, pedagogical, logistical) you may encounter in working with this issue in your school and/or the community it serves? What strategies may you develop to overcome these challenges?

"The Models of Education" course focuses specifically on student awareness of divergent educational philosophies and the development of a philosophical orientation to teaching. The objectives of this course are twofold: (1) to explore a range of schooling possibilities and to provide the framework and opportunity for teacher candidates to appreciate and critique alternative models of schooling as they formulate their own philosophy and practice of education, and (2) to raise and consider key philosophical and pedagogical questions for educators put forward by leading international commentators who "collectively provide a general overview of a wide area of contemporary educational theory" (Hare & Portelli, 2005: viii). Candidates also learn field research skills as a part of their professional development.

Several other core courses make up the program: (1) "Human Development and Socialization" wherein a "critical" approach to existing theories of human development and their attendant practices of learning and teaching are explored. This means that in addition to the traditional Eurocentric grand narrative of human development, other perspectives are explored, suggesting that these traditional theories tell only a part of the story of how "we" develop because these theories are framed by particular historical, religious, social, and generational contexts, and by passionately held-onto familial assumptions, beliefs, and narratives about what it means to be human. More open, complex, and emergent approaches to theories of human development can compel us to be mindful of the (ethnocentric and metaphysical) assumptions underlying our often taken-for-granted approaches to teaching children, and can also help us resist imposing our rigid ideas of human development (having been subjected to these theories in our own education). The course's main aims are:

- To consider the meanings of human and of development
- To encounter diverse theories of development and socialization of humans
- To engage in debates about the status of human(s) in relation to these theories
- To bring these theories and debates to our own examinations of development as experienced in childhood (or that of our children) and as depicted by film and literary texts
- to reflect and analyze one's own experience of "growing up" as influencing, shaping, and determining how we think about the development of (un)like others

284

- to consider how normative and humanistic theories of development impact (violently, devastatingly) upon the lives of others

Another core UD course is "Communication and Community Development in Education." This course focuses on the nature of communication and community development in pluralistic societies—that is, in societal contexts characterized by linguistic and cultural multiplicity. Emphasis is on the social uses of speaking and writing and interpreting what is being communicated in community, school, and classroom settings. Course content and organization are premised on a developmental and socio-linguistic viewpoint toward communication and community that recognizes the interdependence of language with cultural and social structures. The course aims to develop an awareness of social and cultural influences that impact on communication and is designed to help students learn, think, and contribute knowledge to:

- a discussion of theories of community development that have shaped Western thinking
- approaches to communication and community development from other cultural traditions
- how classrooms are part of the community and how communities and classrooms can be mutually supportive
- a discussion of how to create inclusive, dynamic classrooms within communities in which each child or youth is challenged and supported in his or her development

The theoretical information contained in these courses inform the practicum and, specifically, teacher candidates are expected to utilize, synthesize, and integrate the theoretical tools learned in all of their classes, combined with their community service work (see "A Service Learning Approach to Teacher Education" below) in their practicum course work and school placement. This means that within their lesson and unit plans, as well as their instructional interactions with students, they must take account of the many disparate, yet inter-related individual, cultural, social, environmental, ecological, and political factors that influence the teaching and learning process both inside and outside of the classroom. This may include the modification of instructional practices and making untraditional choices in terms of activities, altering the classroom environment, and strategically planning the formation of, and monitoring the dynamics within, classroom groups. Other manifestations of their preparation include: envisioning a variety of culturally appropriate student-teacher and teacher-parent interactions; providing and modifying instructional and assessment materials for EFL students; accounting for multiple intelligences in all aspects of lesson design; implementing, providing, and tracking services (such as interpreters) to ensure good communication with parents; making realistic and context-specific accommodations for students when necessary and appropriate; and inviting members of the community into the classroom. In addition, teachers are to remain cognizant of how they conceptualize the academic performance (and interpersonal reactions) of their students to a variety of classroom activities, experiences, and situations. In practice, this means avoiding the racist, ethnocentric, or reductionist traps of judging students with particular social class, racial, linguistic, learning, physical, and/or cultural differences as intellectually deficient, behaviourally troubled, or unable to succeed and excel in school and in life.

References

Achinstein, B. & Aguirre, J. (2008). Cultural match or culturally suspect: How new teachers of color negotiate sociocultural challenges in the classroom. *Teachers College Record*, 110(8). Retrieved from http://www.tcrecord.org, ID number: 15156

Agee, J. (2004). Negotiating a teaching identity: An African American teacher's struggle to teach in test-driven contexts. *Teachers College Record*, 106(4), 747.

Albers, P. (2002). Praxis II and African American teacher candidates (or, "Is everything Black bad?") *English Education*, 34(2), 105–126.

Allington, R.L. (2005). Ignoring the policy makers to improve teacher preparation. *Journal of Teacher Education*, 56(3), 199–204.

Altbach, P.G. (2001). Higher education and the WTO: Globalization run amok. *International Higher Education*, 23, 65–83.

Anderson, G.L. (2001). Promoting education equity in a period of growing social inequity: The silent contradictions. *Education and Urban Society*, 33(3), 320–332.

Annett, Kevin (2005). Hidden from History: The Canadian Holocaust. *The Untold Story of the Genocide of Aboriginal Peoples by Church and State in Canada.* The Truth Commission into Genocide in Canada, Second Edition.

Anrig, G. R. (1987). Teacher testing in American education: Useful but no shortcut to excellence. What is the appropriate role of testing in the teaching profession? Proceedings of a cooperative conference. Washington, DC: National Education Association.

Apple, M.W., Wayne Au and Luis Armando Gandin. (2009). *The Routledge International Handbook of Critical Education*. New York and London: Routledge.

Apple, M.W. "Can schooling contribute to a more just society?" (2008). In *Education, Citizenship and Social Justice*. November 2008 vol. 3 no. 3 239-261.

Apple, M.W. 2001. Markets, standards, teaching, and teacher education. *Journal of Teacher Education*, 52(3), 182–196.

Apple, M.W. (2001b). Comparing neo-liberal projects and inequality in education. *Comparative Education Review*, 37(4), 409–203.

Apple, M. & Weiss, L. (1983). *Ideology and practice in schooling*. Philadelphia: Temple University Press.

Appleman, D. & Thompson, M.J. (2002). Fighting the toxic status quo: Alfie Kohn on standardized tests and teacher education. *English Education*, 34(2), 95–103.

Association of Universities and Colleges Canada (AUCC). (2001). Declaration signed by AUCC, the American Council on Education, the European University Association, and the Council for Higher Education Accreditation. Retrieved from http://www.aucc.ca/_pdf/english/statements/2001/gats_10_25_e.pdf

Au, K.H. & Blake, K.M. (2003) Cultural identity and learning to teach in a diverse community: Findings from a collective case study. *Journal of Teacher Education*, 54(3), 192–205.

Au, W.W. (2008) Devising inequality: a Bernsteinian analysis of high stakes testing and social reproduction in education. British Journal of Sociology of Education. 29(6), pp.639-651.

Baez, B. (2007). *Neo-liberalism in higher education*. Paper presented at the annual meeting of the Association for the Study of Higher Education, Louisville.

Ball, A.F. (2000). Empowering pedagogies that enhance the learning of multicultural students. *Teachers College Record*, 102(6), 1006–1034.

Ball, S., Bowe, R., & Gewirtz, S. (1994). Market forces and parental choice. In S. Tomlinson (Ed.), Educational reform and its consequences (pp. 13-25). London: IPPR/Rivers Oram Press (cited in M. Apple (2001) Markets,

Standards, Teaching, and Teacher Education. *Journal of Teacher Education*, Vol. 52, No. 3 pp. 182-196).

Ball, S. & Goodson, I. (1985). *Teachers' lives and careers*. London: The Falmer Press.

Ball, S., Bowe, R., and Gewirtz, S. (1994). "Market forces and parental choice." In S. Tomlinson (ed.) Educational reform and its consequences. London: IPPR/Rivers Oram Press.

Banks, J. & Banks, C. (1995). *Handbook of research on multicultural education*. New York: Macmillan.

Banks, J.A. & Banks, C.A.M. (1995). Equity pedagogy: An essential component of multicultural education. *Theory into Practice*, 34(3), 152–158.

Bell, L.A. (1997). Theoretical foundations for social justice education. In M. Adams, L.A. Bell & P. Griffin (Eds.), *Teaching for diversity and social justice: A sourcebook* (pp. 2–15). New York: Routledge.

Bennett, C. (2001, Summer). Genres of research in multicultural education. *Review of Educational Research*, 71(2), 171–217.

Berliner, D.C. (2005, May/June). The near impossibility of testing for teacher quality. *Journal of Teacher Education*, 56(3), 205–213.

Bill 74: The Education Accountability Act, Government of Ontario. (1997).

Bill 160: The Education Improvement Act, Government of Ontario. (1997).

Boyle-Baise, M. (2005). Preparing community-oriented teachers: Reflections from a multicultural service-learning project. *Journal of Teacher Education*, 56 (5), 446–448.

Brayboy, B.M.J., Castagno, A.E. & Maughan, E. (2007). Equality and justice for all? Examining race in educational scholarship. *Review of Research in Education*, 31, 159–195.

Britzman, D. (1991). *Practice makes practice: A critical study of learning to teach*. Albany: State University of New York Press.

Britzman, D. (1998). *Lost subjects, contested objects: Toward a psychoanalytic inquiry of learning*. Albany: State University of New York Press.

Britzman, D. (2003). *Practice makes practice*. Albany: State University of New York Press.

Brown, R.S. & Sinay, E. (2008). *2006 Student census: Linking demographic data with student achievement*. Toronto: Toronto District School Board.

Canadian Heritage. Multiculturalism website. (2004, January). Retrieved from http://www.pch.gc.ca/progs/multi/respect_e.cfm.

Canadian Collaborative Mental Health Initiative. (2006). Chapter 2. "Challenges to Wellness" *Pathways to Healing: A Mental Health Guide for First Nations People*. Mississauga, ON: Author.

Capper, C.A. & Jamison, M.T. (1993). Outcomes-based education re-examined: From structural functionalism to post structuralism. *Educational Policy*, 7(4), 427–446.

Carr, P.R. (1999). Transforming the institution, or institutionalizing the transformation? Anti-racism and equity in education in Toronto. *McGill Journal of Education*, 34(1), 49–77.

Carr, P.R. & Klassen, T.R. (1997). Different perceptions of race in education: Racial minority and White teachers. *Canadian Journal of Education*, 22(1), 67–81.

Carter, D.S.G. (1994). *The policy context of recent curriculum reforms in Australia*. Paper presented at the Annual Meeting of the American Educational Research Association, New Orleans, April 4–8.

Carter, R. & Goodwin, L. (1994). Racial identity and education. In L. Darling-Hammond (Ed.), *Review of research in education*, vol. 20 (pp. 291–336). Washington: American Educational Research Association.

Chubbuck, S.M. (2004, Summer). Whiteness enacted, whiteness disrupted: The complexity of personal congruence. *American Educational Research Journal*, 41(2), 301–333.

Cochran-Smith, M. (2001). The outcomes question in teacher education. *Teaching and Teacher Education*, 17(5), 527–546.

Cochran-Smith, M. (2004, November/December). Stayers, leavers, lovers, and dreamers: Insights about teacher retention. *Journal of Teacher Education*, 55(5), 387–392.

Cochran-Smith, M. (2005). Teacher education and the outcomes trap. *Journal of Teacher Education*, 56(5), 411–417.

Collins, P. Hill. (2000). *Black feminist thought: Knowledge, consciousness, and the politics of empowerment*. New York: Routledge.

Connell, R.W. (1985). *Teachers' work*. Sydney: George Allen and Unwin.

Cooper, R. & Jordan, W.J. (2003). Cultural issues in comprehensive school reform. *Urban Education*, 38(4), 380–397.

Cross, B. Mediating Curriculum: Problems of Non-Engagement and Practices of Engagement. (1998). In R.Chávez Chávez & J. O'Donnell (Eds.), *Speaking the unpleasant: The politics of (non) engagement in the multicultural education terrain* (pp. 69-86). Albany, NY: State University of New York Press.

Coulter, D. & Orme, L. (2000). Teacher professionalism: The wrong conversation. *Education Canada*, 40(1), 4–7.

Daly, N.F. (1987). The appropriate role of testing in the teaching profession. *What is the appropriate role of testing in the teaching profession?* Washington: National Education Association.

Danielson, C. (2001). New trends in teacher evaluation. *Educational Leadership*, 58(5), 12–15.

Darder, A., Baltodano, M.P. & Torres, R.D. (Eds.). (2009). *The critical pedagogy reader*, 2nd ed. London: Routledge.

Darling-Hammond, L. (2002). Educating a profession for equitable practice. In L. Darling-Hammond, J. French & S. Paloma Garcia-Lopez (Eds.), *Learning to teach for social justice* (pp. 201–215). New York: Teachers College Press.

Davis, B. (2000). *Skills mania: Snake oil in our schools*. Toronto: Between the Lines.

Dearman, C.C. & Alber, S.R. (2005). The changing face of education: Teachers cope with challenges through collaboration and reflective study. *Reading Teacher*, 58(7), 634–640.

Dei, George J. (2000). *Removing the margins: The challenges and possibilities of inclusive schooling*. Toronto: Canadian Scholars' Press Inc.

Dei, G.J.S. (2000). Recasting antiracism and the axis of difference: Beyond the question of theory. *Race, Gender, and Class Issues in Canada, Malaysia, and United States*, 7(2), 39–56.

Dei, G.J.S. (2003). Research Forum on Race Relations: Alberta Experiences and Prospects for Change, Keynote Address: "The Perils and Desires of Anti-Oppression Work." June 13-14, Grant MacEwan College, Edmonton.

Dei, G.J.S., James-Wilson, S.V. & Zine, J. (2002). *Inclusive schooling: A teachers' companion to removing the margins*. Toronto: Canadian Scholars' Press Inc.

Dei, G.J.S., Mazzuca, J., McIsaac, E. & Zine, J. (1997). *Reconstructing dropouts: A critical ethnography of the dynamics of Black students disengagement from school*. Toronto: University of Toronto Press.

Dei, G.J.S., James, I.M., Karumanchery, L.L., James-Wilson, S. & Zine, J. (2000). *Removing the margins: The challenges and possibilities of inclusive schooling*. Toronto: Canadian Scholars' Press Inc.

Delpit, L. (1988). The silenced dialogue: Power and pedagogy in educating other people's children. Harvard Educational Review.

Delpit, L. (1995). *Other people's children*. New York: New Press.

Department of Citizenship and Immigration Canada. (2008). Canadian Heritage: Multiculturalism website. Retrieved from http://www.pch.gc.ca/progs/multi/respect_e.cfm

Department of Indian and Northern Affairs Canada. (2003). *Backgrounder: The Residential School System*. Ottawa, ON: Indian and Northern Affairs Canada. Available at http://www.ainc-inac.gc.ca/gs/schl_e.html.

Derman-Sparks, L. & Phillips, C. (1997). *Teaching/learning anti-racism: A developmental approach*. New York: Teachers College Press.

DeStigter, T. (2002). Cutting the future down to the size of the present: Three perspectives on standardized testing. *English Education*, 34(2), 157–164.

Diamond, J.B. & Gomez, K. (2004). African American parents' education orientations: The importance of social class and parents' perceptions of schools. *Education and Urban Society*, 36(4), 383–427.

Diamond, J.B. & Spillane, J.P. (2004, June). High-stakes accountability in urban elementary schools: Challenging or reproducing inequality? *Teachers College Record*, 106(6), 1145–1176.

Dilg, M. (2003). *Thriving in the multicultural classroom: Principles and practices for effective teaching*. New York: Teachers College Press.

Dunlap, L. (2004). *What all children need, theory and application* (2nd ed.). Lanham. MD: University Press of America Inc.

Education Act. England & Wales. (1993). Retrieved from http://www.legislation.gov.uk/ukpga/1993/35/contents/enacted

Education Reform Act, United Kingdom. (1988). Retrieved from http://www.legislation.gov.uk/ukpga/1988/40/contents

Edwards, A. (2000) Research and Practice: Is there a dialogue? In H. Penn (Ed.) *Early Childhood Services: Theory, policy and practice* (pp. 184-199). Buckingham: Open University Press.

Edwards, A. (2000). Research and practice: Is there a dialogue? In H. Penn (Ed.), *Early childhood services: Theory, policy, and practice*. Philadelphia: Open University Press.

Elliot, B. & Hughes, C. (1998, September). *Outcomes-driven curriculum reform-reconstructing teacher work and professionalism*. Paper presented at European Conference for Educational Research, Ljubljana, Slovenia. September.

Fecho, B. (2000). Developing critical mass: Teacher education and critical inquiry pedagogy. *Journal of Teacher Education*, 51(3), 194–199.

Fenlon, B. (2008, April 2). *Globe and Mail*. Retrieved from http://www.theglobeand-mail.com/servlet/story/RTGAM.20080402.wcensusmain0402/BNStory/census2006/home

Finn, P.J. & Finn, M.E. (2007). (Eds). *Teacher education with an attitude: Preparing teachers to educate working-class students in their collective self-interest*. Albany: SUNY Press.

Flippo, R.F. & Riccards, M.P. (2000). Initial teacher certification testing in Massachusetts: A case of the tail wagging the dog. *Phi Delta Kappan*, 82(1), 34–37.

Fordham, S. & Ogbu, J.U. (1986). Black students' school success: Coping with the burden of "acting White." *Journal of Urban Review*, 18(3), 176–206.

Fowler, R.C. (2001). What did the Massachusetts teacher test say about American education? *Phi Delta Kappan*, 82(10), 773–780.

Frank, B. (2006, November). *Equity audit: Building the foundations of equity*. Toronto: The Elementary Teachers' Federation of Ontario.

Frankenberg, R. (1993). *White women, race matters: The social construction of whiteness*. London: Routledge.

Freire, P. (1970). *Pedagogy of the oppressed*. San Francisco: Seabury.

Fullan, M. & Stiegelbauer, S. (1991). *The new meaning of educational change*, 2nd ed. New York: Teachers College Press.

Gay, G. (2002). Preparing for culturally responsive teaching. *Journal of Teacher Education*, 53(2), 106–116.

Ghosh, R. (2002). *Redefining multicultural education*, 2nd ed. Toronto: Nelson Thomson Learning.

Giroux, H. (1983). *Theory and resistance in education: A pedagogy for the opposition*. Boston: Bergin & Garvey.

Giroux, H.A. (1992). *Border crossings: Cultural workers and the politics of education*. New York: Routledge.

Giroux, H.A. (2004). Public pedagogy and the politics of neo-liberalism: Making the political more pedagogical. *Policy Futures in Education*, 2(3 & 4), 494–503.

Giroux, H.A. & McLaren, P. (1986). Teacher education and the politics of engagement: The case for democratic schooling. *Harvard Educational Review*, 56(3), 213–238.

Giroux, H.A. & McLaren, P. (Eds.). (1994). *Between borders: Pedagogy and the politics of cultural studies*. New York: Routledge.

Gluck, S.B. & Patai, D. (Eds.). (1991). *Women's words: The feminist practice of oral history*. New York: Routledge.

Gomez, M.L. (1996). Prospective teachers' perspectives on teaching "other people's children." In M. Gomez, S. Melnick & K. Zeichner (Eds.), *Current reforms in pre-service teacher education* (pp. 109–132). New York: Teachers College Press.

Goode, J., Quartz, K.H., Barraza-Lyons, K. & Thomas, A. (2003). *Supporting urban education leaders: An analysis of the multiple roles of social justice educators*. Paper presented at the 84th meeting of the American Educational Research Association, Chicago, IL. (April 21 - 25).Goodman, G.S. (2004). Introduction. In K. Carey & G.S. Goodman (Eds.), *Critical multicultural conversations* (pp. 1–7). Cresskill: Hampton Press Inc.

Gould Lundy, K. (2004) *What do I do about the kid who ... ?* Markham: Pembroke Publishers.

Government of Ontario. Office of Economic Policy: Labour and Demographic Analysis Branch. (2007, November). *Factsheet 6*. Retrieved from http://www.fin.gov.on.ca/english/economy/demographics/census/cenhi06-6.html

Graham, R. & Young, J. (1998). Curriculum, identity, and experience in multicultural teacher education. *Alberta Journal of Educational Research*, 44(4), 397–407.

Grant, C. & Sleeter, C. (2007). *Doing multicultural education for achievement and equity*. New York: Routledge.

Grant, C.A. & Zozakiewicz, C.A. (1995). Student teachers, cooperating teachers, and supervisors: Interrupting the multicultural silences of student teaching. In J.M. Larkin & C.E. Sleeter (Eds.), *Developing multicultural teacher education curricula* (pp. 259–278). Albany: State University of New York Press.

Greenman, N.P. & Dieckmann, J. (2004). Considering criticality and culture as pivotal in transformative teacher education. *Journal of Teacher Education*, 55, 240.

Haberman, M. & Post, L. (1998). Teachers for multicultural schools: The power of selection. *Theory into Practice*, 37(2), 96–104.

Haig-Brown, Celia. (1988). *Resistance and renewal: First Nations people's experiences of the residential school.* Vancouver: UBC Press.

Hallinan, M. (2001). Sociological perspectives on Black-White inequalities in American schools. *Sociology of Education,* 74(Extra Issue), 50–70.

Hare, W. & Portelli, J. (2005). *Key questions for educators.* Halifax: Edphil Books.

Hargreaves, A. (1991). Contrived collegiality: The micropolitics of teacher collaboration. In J. Blasé (Ed.), *The politics of life in schools: Power, conflict, and cooperation* (pp. 46–72). London: Sage Publications.

Harris, N. (1994). The Education Act 1993 and Local Administration of Education. *The Modern Law Review.* Vol. 57, No. 2. pp. 251-263.

Hartnett, A. & Carr, W. (1995). Education, teacher development, and the struggle for democracy. In J. Smyth (Ed.), *Critical discourses on teacher development* (pp. 39–53). Toronto: OISE Press.

Hedges, L.V. & Nowell, A. (1998). Black-White Test Score Convergence Since 1965. In C. Jencks & M. Philip (Eds.)., *The Black-White test score gap* (pp. 149–181). Washington: Brookings Institution Press.

Hextall, I., Mahony, P. & Menter, I. (2001). Just testing? An analysis of the implementation of "skills tests" for entry into the teaching profession in England. *Journal of Education for Teaching,* 27(3), 221–239.

Hill, D. (1996). Taking on the test. *Teacher Magazine,* 7(8), 36–43.

Hood, S. & Parker, L. (1991). Minorities, teacher testing, and recent U.S. Supreme Court rulings: A regressive step. *Teachers' College Record,* 92(4), 603–616.

hooks, b. (1994). *Teaching to transgress: Education as the practice of freedom.* New York: Routledge.

Howard, G.R. (1999). *We can't teach what we don't know: White teachers, multiracial schools.* New York: Teacher's College Press.

Howard, T.C. (2003, Summer). Culturally relevant pedagogy: Ingredients for critical teacher reflection. *Theory into Practice,* 42(13), 195–199.

Hyland, N. E. and S. Meacham (2004). Community knowledge-centered teacher education: A paradigm for Socially just educational transformation. *TeachingTeachers: Building a Quality School of Urban Education.*

James, C.E. (2003). *Seeing ourselves: Exploring race, ethnicity, and culture,* 3rd ed. Toronto: Thompson Educational Publishing Inc.

Jennings, L.B. & Smith, C.P. (2002, April). Examining the role of critical inquiry for transformative practices: Two joint case studies of multicultural teacher education. *Teachers College Record,* 104(3), 456–481.

Kailin, J. (1998). Preparing urban teachers for schools and communities: An anti-racist perspective. *High School Journal*, 82(2), 80.

Kincheloe, J., Slattery, P. & Steinberg, S. (2000). *Contextualizing teaching: Introduction to education and educational foundations.* New York: Longman.

King, J.E. (1991). Dysconscious racism: Ideology, identity, and the miseducation of teachers. *Journal of Negro Education*, 60(2), 133–146.

Kohn, A. (2003). Professors who profess: Making a difference as scholar activists. *Kappa Delta Pi Record*, 39(3), 108–113.

Ladson-Billings, G. (1995). Toward a theory of culturally relevant pedagogy. *American Educational Research Journal*, 32(3), 465–491.

Ladson-Billings, G. (1998). *The dreamkeepers.* San Francisco: Jossey Bass Publishers.

Lauder, H. & Hughes, D. (1999). *Trading places.* Buckingham: Open University Press.

Lawson, E., Smith, C., Chen, M., Parsons, M. & Sheena, S. (2002). *Anti-Black racism in Canada: A report on the Canadian government's compliance with the International Convention on the Elimination of All Forms of Racial Discrimination.* Toronto. African Canadian Legal Clinic.

Lea, V. & Griggs, T. (2005, Winter). Behind the mask and beneath the story: Enabling student-teachers to reflect critically on the socially-constructed nature of their "normal" practice. *Teacher Education Quarterly*, 32(1), 93–114.

Leary, M.R. & Tagney, J.P. (2003). *Handbook of self and identity.* New York: Guilford Press.

Leithwood, K., Fullan, M. & Watson, N. (2003). *The schools we need: A new blueprint for Ontario—final report.* Toronto: Ontario Institute for Studies in Education/University of Toronto.

Lightfoot, D. (2004). Some parents just don't care: Decoding the meaning of parental involvement in urban schools. *Urban Education*, 39(1), 91–107.

Lipman, P. (1998). *Race, class, and power in school restructuring.* Albany: SUNY Press.

Liston, D. & Zeichner, K. (1990). Reflective teaching and action research in preservice teacher education. *Journal of Education for Teaching*, 16(3), 235–254.

Louis Harris & Associates & Westin, A.F. New York: Louis Harris & Associates.

Lupart, J. & Webber, C. (2002). Canadian schools in transition: Moving from dual education systems to inclusive schools. *Exceptionality Education Canada*, 12(2–3), 7–52.

McAllister, G. & Irvine, J.J. (2000). Cross cultural competency and multicultural teacher education. *Review of Educational Research*, 70, 3–24.

McAllister, G. & Irvine, J.J. (2002). The role of empathy in teaching culturally diverse students: A qualitative study of teachers' beliefs. *Journal of Teacher Education*, 53(5), 433–443.

McCall, A. (1995). We were cheated! Students' responses to a multicultural, social re-constructionist teacher education course. *Equity and Excellence in Education*, 28(1), 15–24.

McIntosh, P. (1989). White privilege: Unpacking the invisible knapsack. *Independent School*, 49(2), 31–36.

McIntyre, A. (1997a). Constructing an image of a White teacher. *Teachers College Record*, 98(4), 653–677.

McIntyre, A. (1997b). *Making meaning of whiteness: Exploring racial identity with White teachers.* Albany: State University of New York Press.

McKenzie, K. & Scheurich, J.J. (2004). Equity traps: A construct for departments of educational administration. *Educational Administration Quarterly*, 40(5), 601–632.

McLaren, P. (1998). *Life in schools: An introduction to critical pedagogy in the foundations of education*, 3rd ed. New York: Longman.

McLaren. P. (2003). Revolutionary pedagogy in post-revolutionary times: Rethinking the political economy of critical education. In A. Darder, M.P. Baltodano & R.D. Torres (Eds.), *The critical pedagogy reader* (pp. 151–184). New York: Routledge.

McLaren, P. & Baltodano, M.P. (2000). The future of teacher education and the politics of resistance. *Teaching Education*, 11(1), 47–60.

McLaren, P., Fischman, G., Sunker, H. & Lankshear, C. (2005). *Critical theories, radical pedagogies, and global conflicts.* NY: Rowan & Littlefield Publishers.

McNeil, L.M. (2000). *Contradictions of school reform: Educational costs of standardized testing.* New York: Routledge.

Meier, D. (2002). *The power of their ideas: Lessons for America from a small school in Harlem.* Education Online. Retrieved from http://www.leeds.ac.uk/educol/documents/000000860.htm

Menter, I. (1989). Teaching practice stasis: Racism, sexism, and school experience in initial teacher education. *British Journal of Sociology of Education*, 10(4), 459–473.

Miles, C.A. & Lee, C. (2002). *In search of soundness in teacher testing: Beyond political validity.* Paper presented at the American Educational Research Association, New Orleans, April 4–8.

Milloy, J. (1999). *A National Crime: The Canadian Government and the Residential School System, 1879 to 1986.* Winnipeg, Manitoba: University of Manitoba Press.

Nezavdal, F. (2003). The standards testing movement: Equitable or excessive? *McGill Journal of Education*, 38(1), 65–78.

Nieto, S. (2000). Placing equity front and center: Some thoughts on transforming teacher education for a new century. *Journal of Teacher Education*, 51(3), 180–187.

Norquay, N. (1999). Who rebels? Gender and class in stories of irrelevance and resistance. *International Journal of Qualitative Studies in Education*, 12(4), 417–431.

Obenchain, K., Abernathy, T. & Lock, R. (2003). 20 ways to build community and empower students. *Intervention in School and Clinic*, 39(1), 55–60.

Office of Economic Policy. (2008). Office of Economic Policy: Labour and Demographic Analysis Branch Government of Ontario. Factsheet 6. Retrieved from http://www.fin.gov.on.ca/english/economy/demographics/census/cenhi06-6.html

Omi, M. & Winant, H. (1993). On the theoretical status of the concept race. In C. McCarthy & W. Crichlow (Eds.), *Race, identity, and representation in education* (pp. 3–10). New York: Routledge.

Parker, L. (2001, May). Statewide assessment triggers urban school reform: But how high the stakes for urban minorities? *Education and Urban Society*, 33(3), 313–319.

Portelli, J.P. & Vibert, A.B. (1997, Winter). Dare we criticize common educational standards? *McGill Journal of Education*, 32(1), 69–79.

Portelli, J. P., & Vibert, A. B. (2001). Beyond common educational standards: Toward a curriculum of life. In J. P. Portelli & R. P. Solomon (Eds.), *The erosion of democracy in education: From critique to possibilities* (pp. 63–82). Calgary, Canada: Detselig.

Portelli, J.P., Shields, C. & Vibert, A.B. (2007). National Report on "Toward an

Equitable Education: Poverty and Students 'at risk.'" Toronto, ON: OISE, August, 2007.

Portelli, J., Solomon, R.P., Barrett, S., Mujawamariya, D., Pinto, L & Jordan Singer. (2011). Stakeholders' Perspectives on Induction for New Teachers: A Critical Analysis of Teacher Testing and Mentorship. University of Toronto (OISE). Center for Learning and Diversity.

Power, S., Halpin, D. & Fitz, J. (1994). Underpinning choice and diversity? In S. Tomlinson (Ed.), *Educational reform and its consequences* (pp. 26–40). London: IPPR/Rivers Oram Press.

Progressive Conservative Party of Ontario. 1994. *The common sense revolution*. Toronto: Progressive Conservative Party of Ontario.

Reagan, T. (2000). *Non-Western educational traditions: Alternative approaches to educational thought and practice*, 2nd ed. Mahwah: Lawrence Erlbaum Associates.

Rutledge, D. (1993). *Benchmarks: A framework for judging student performance.* Canberra: Australian Curriculum Studies Association.

Sachar, L. (2000). *Holes.* New York: Yearling Books.

Sawyer, R. D. (2000). Adapting curriculum to student diversity: Patterns and perceptions among alternate-route and college-based teachers. *Urban Review, 32*(4), 343-363.

Schecter, S.R., Solomon, R.P. & Kittler, L. (2003). Integrating teacher education in a community-situated school agenda. In S.R. Schecter & C. Cummins (Eds.), *Multilingual education in practice: Using diversity as a resource* (pp. 81–96). Portsmouth: Heinemann Books.

Schick, C. & St. Denis, V. (2003). What makes anti-racist pedagogy in teacher education difficult? Three popular ideological assumptions. *The Alberta Journal of Educational Research, 49*(1), 55-69.

Sheldon, K.M. & Biddle, B.J. (1998). Standards, accountability, and school reform: Perils and pitfalls. *Teachers College Record, 100*(1), 164–180.

Shor, I. (1992). *Empowering education: Critical thinking for social change.* Chicago: University of Chicago Press.

Simon, R. (1992). *Teaching against the grain: Texts for a pedagogy of possibility.* New York: Bergin & Garvey.

Sleeter, C.E. (1992a). *Keepers of the American dream: A study of staff development and multicultural education.* London: Farmer.

Sleeter, C.E. (1992b). Resisting racial awareness: How teachers understand the social order from their racial, gender, and social class locations. *Educational Foundations*, 6, 7–32.

Snape, R. (1998). Reaching effective agreements covering services. In A. Kruger (Ed.), *The WTO as an international organization*. Chicago: University of Chicago Press.

Sobel, D.M. & Taylor, S.V. (2003, Spring). Teacher evaluation standards in practice: A standards-based assessment tool for diversity-responsive teaching. *The Teacher Educator*, 28(4), 285–302.

Solomon, R.P. (1992). *Black resistance in high school: Forging a separatist culture*. Albany: State University of New York Press.

Solomon, R.P. (1997). Race, role modeling, and representation in teacher education and teaching. *Canadian Journal of Education*, 22(4), 395–410.

Solomon, R.P., Allen, A.A. & Campbell, A. (2007). The politics of advocacy, strategies for change: Diversity and social justice pedagogy in urban schools. In R.P. Solomon & D.R. Sekayi (Eds.), *Urban teacher education and teaching: Innovative practices for diversity and social justice* (pp. 207–225). Mahwah: Lawrence Erlbaum Associates.

Solomon, R.P., Levine-Rasky, C. & Singer, J. (2003). *Teaching for equity and diversity: Research to practice*. Toronto: Canadian Scholars' Press Inc.

Solomon, R.P. & Rezai-Rashti, G. (2004). Teacher candidates' racial identity formation and the possibilities of antiracism in teacher education. *Education and Society*, 22(3), 65–89.

Suleiman, Mahmoud F. (2004). Multicultural education: A blueprint for educators. In K. Carey & G.S. Goodman (Eds.), *Critical multicultural conversations* (pp. 9–21). Cresskill: Hampton Press Inc.

Sumara, D.J. & Luce-Kapler, R. (1996). (Un)Becoming a teacher: Negotiating identities while learning to teach. *Canadian Journal of Education*, 21(1), 65–83.

Supovitz, J.A., & Brennan, R.T. (1997). Mirror, mirror on the wall, Which is the fairest test of all? An examination of the equitability of portfolio assessment relative to   standardized tests. *Harvard Educational Review*, 67(3), 472- 506.

Thompson, C.E. & Carter, R.T. (1997). *Racial identity theory: Applications to individual, group, and organizational interventions*. Mahwah: Lawrence Erlbaum Associates.

Toronto District School Board. (2007, December). TDSB Equity Foundation statement & commitments to equity policy implementation. Retrieved from http://www.tdsb.on.ca/_site/viewitem.asp?siteid=15&menuid=682 &pageid=546

Van Dijk, T.A. (2002). Discourse and racism. In D. Goldberg & J. Solomos (Eds.), *The Blackwell companion to racial & ethnic studies* (pp. 145–159). Oxford: Blackwell.

Verloop, N.J., Van Driel, J. & Meijer, P. (2001). Teacher knowledge and the knowledge base of teaching. *International Journal of Educational Research*, 35(5), 441–461.

Villegas, A.M. & Lucas, T. (2002). Preparing culturally responsive teachers: Rethinking the curriculum. *Journal of Teacher Education*, 53(1), 20–32.

Weiss, J.G. (1987). Testing teachers: Strategies for damage control: *What is the appropriate role of testing in the teaching profession?* Washington: National Education Association.

Solomon, R.P. & Allen, A. (2001). The Struggle for Equity, Diversity and Social Justice in Teacher Education. In J. Portelli & P. Solomon (Eds.) *The Erosion of Democracy in Education: From Critique to Possibilities*. Toronto: Detselig/ Temeron Books.

Wenger, E. (1998). *Communities of practice: Learning, meaning, and identity.* New York: Cambridge University Press.

Working Group. (1992). *Towards a new beginning: The report and action plan of the four level government/African Canadian community working group.* Toronto: The Working Group, funded by the Department of the Secretary of State.

O'Reilly J., & Yau, M. (2009). *2008 parent census kindergarten-grade 6 : System overview and detailed findings.* Toronto, Ontario, Canada: Toronto District School Board. Retrieved from http://www.tdsb.on.ca/wwwdocuments/about_us/media_room/docs/2008ParentCensusK-6SystemOverviewAndDetailedFindings.pdf

Woodson, C. (1990). *The Mis-education of the Negro.* Nashville: Winston-Derek Publishers, Inc.

Yon, D.A. (1999). Pedagogy and the "problem" of difference: On reading community in *The darker side of Black. Qualitative Studies in Education,* 12(6), 623–641.

Zeichner, K. (1996). Designing educative practicum experiences for prospective teachers. In K. Zeichner, S. Melnick & M. Gomez (Eds.), *Currents of reform in preservice teacher education* (pp. 215–234). New York: Teachers College Press.

Zeichner, K.M. (2003, April). The adequacies and inadequacies of three current strategies to recruit, prepare, and retain the best teachers for all students. *Teachers College Record*, 105(3), 490–519.

Zeichner, K. & Flessner, R. (2009). Educating teachers for critical education. In M. Apple, W. Au & L. Armando Gandin (Eds.), *International handbook of critical education* (pp. 296-311). New York: Erlbaum/Routledge.

Zembylas, M. (2003). Interrogating "teacher identity": Emotion, resistance, and self-formation. *Educational Theory*, 53(1), 107–127.

Ziguras, C. (2005). International trade in education services: Governing the liberalization and regulation of private enterprise. In M. Apple, J. Kenway & M. Singh (Eds.), *Globalizing education: Policies, pedagogies & politics*. New York: Peter Lang.

Index

Delpit, Lisa, 21, 268
democracy:
in classroom relations, 42, 189;
critical democratic framework, 20;
critical thinking, 62-63, 198-204, 251, 276-277;
experiential learning, 202, 230, 252;
preparing for a democratic society, 61;
questioning assumptions, 62-63, 201-202, 230-232, 276-277;
respecting community, 63-65;
as teaching pedagogy, 18-19, 61, 63, 187, 198, 202-204;
as upholding diversity, 62-65, 217, 232, 269
Department of Citizenship and Immigration Canada, 32
Department of Indian and Northern Affairs, 3
Derman-Sparks, Louise, 185
DeStigter, Todd, 96
Dewey, John, viii
Diamond, John, 139
Dilg, Mary, 157, 169
Direct Reading Assessment (DRA), 244-245
diversity:
barriers to, 78, 92, 99-109, 134;
in Canadian policies, 33;
defined as, 19-20;
demographics in Canada, 32-33;
as fragmented cultural groups, 137-138;

new immigrants, 32-33;
in Ontario's urban communities, 159;
population in Canada, 32;
representation of teachers 119-120, 171, 217, 243-244;
student resistance, 140-141, 143;
student support, 141-142

Early Years Literacy Project (EYLP), 243, 248
education and politics:
education as political, 39, 76-77, 188, 260;
de-professionalization of teachers, 89-90, 100, 117, 149-150, 153
education reform:
educational assistants, 8-9;
history of, 69-71, 73;
impact of standardization, 1, 70-74, 21-22, 96-97, 99, 101-104, 279;
pressure of raising standards, 69;
restructuring pressures, 1, 69, 70-71, 103;
standards based reform rationale, 70, 73, 99-100
education and social justice:
barriers of, 78, 83-88, 111-112, 179, 201, 238;
contextualizing the school, 215-216, 233-234, 245, 249, 278-279;
curriculum, 226-227;
poverty, 233, 237;
in practice, 225-253;

195-197;
student-teacher relationship, 172-173, 267, 273-275
research methodology, 24-26
resistance:
impact on teachers, 143-144;
administrative, 149-152
Rutledge, Donald, 11

Sachar, Louis, 228
Sawyer, Richard, 214
Schecter, Sandra, 39
Sheldon, Kennon, 116-117, 133-134
school funding, 7-8
service learning, 41-42;
community involvement & collaboration, 41-43, 220-222, 227, 235-237, 247, 262-263, 271-272
Settlement Worker's Organization, 262
Shor, Ira, 257
Simon, Roger, 2, 20
Sleeter, Christine, 21, 185
Snape, Richard, 10
Sobel, Donna, 153
Social Sciences and Humanities Research Council of Canada, x
Solomon, Patrick, ix, x, 22, 23, 31, 35, 42, 93, 153, 158, 171, 183, 185, 274, 275, 277
standardized education:
benefits of, 74-75;
common practices, 69-70-74;
curriculum, 70-74, 77-93;
limitations of, 76-83, 91-93, 114-119;

Ontario's policies, 70-73, 97, 111-112
standardized testing, 70-71, 83-86;
cultural bias, 84-86;
effects of, 72-76, 83-84;
limitations of, 84-86;
Ontario Secondary School Literacy Test, 71
strategies for change, 53-54;
beyond racial dichotomies, 193;
building community, 194-198;
clustering the curriculum, 209-214;
critical mass of support, 214-222;
dedicated social justice oriented teachers, 123-128, 156, 219-220, 248;
democratic classrooms, 189-214;
developing alliances , 53-54, 132-133;
diversity of perspectives, 203-204, 205, 211-212, 248, 250, 251, 269-270;
examination of "the Other", 168, 192, 203, 219, 241-242, 265-266;
fostering critical thinking, 198-204, 203-204, 214, 228;
interpersonal relations, 56-57, 172, 227;
moral & ethical commitment, 17, 227; 250;
parental support, 136, 138-139, 195, 221, 247;
safe, nurturing & inclusive classrooms, 189-194;
self-awareness, 54-56, 199-201, 232,

About the Authors

The late R. Patrick Solomon was Professor of Education, and the founder of the Urban Diversity Program, Faculty of Education, York University.

Jordan Singer, who has worked as an elementary and high school teacher in addition to working in a variety of clinical and educational contexts as a counselor and Director of ESL programs, is currently completing his doctorate in education at York University.

Arlene Campbell, an experienced equity educator who has taught and served as an administrator within the public school system in Quebec and Ontario, is currently completing her doctorate in education at York University.

Andrew Allen, a former elementary classroom teacher, is currently Associate Professor in the Faculty of Education, University of Windsor.

John P. Portelli is Academic Director of Graduate Programs and Co-director of the Centre for Leadership and Diversity at the Ontario Institute for Studies in Education, University of Toronto.